ROUTLEDGE LIBRARY EDITIONS: AUTOBIOGRAPHY

Volume 9

AUTOBIOGRAPHICS IN FREUD AND DERRIDA

AUTOBIOGRAPHICS IN FREUD AND DERRIDA

JANE MARIE TODD

LONDON AND NEW YORK

First published in 1990

This edition first published in 2016
by Routledge
2 Park Square, Milton Park, Abingdon, Oxon OX14 4RN

and by Routledge
711 Third Avenue, New York, NY 10017

Routledge is an imprint of the Taylor & Francis Group, an informa business

© 1990 Jane Marie Todd

All rights reserved. No part of this book may be reprinted or reproduced or utilised in any form or by any electronic, mechanical, or other means, now known or hereafter invented, including photocopying and recording, or in any information storage or retrieval system, without permission in writing from the publishers.

Trademark notice: Product or corporate names may be trademarks or registered trademarks, and are used only for identification and explanation without intent to infringe.

British Library Cataloguing in Publication Data
A catalogue record for this book is available from the British Library

ISBN: 978-1-138-93641-6 (Set)
ISBN: 978-1-315-67463-6 (Set) (ebk)
ISBN: 978-1-138-93989-9 (Volume 9) (hbk)
ISBN: 978-1-138-94197-7 (Volume 9) (pbk)
ISBN: 978-1-315-67456-8 (Volume 9) (ebk)

Publisher's Note
The publisher has gone to great lengths to ensure the quality of this reprint but points out that some imperfections in the original copies may be apparent.

Disclaimer
The publisher has made every effort to trace copyright holders and would welcome correspondence from those they have been unable to trace.

AUTOBIOGRAPHICS IN FREUD AND DERRIDA

Jane Marie Todd

GARLAND PUBLISHING
New York & London
1990

Copyright © 1990 by Jane Marie Todd
All Rights Reserved

Library of Congress Cataloging-in-Publication Data

Todd, Jane Marie.
Autobiographics in Freud and Derrida/ Jane Marie Todd.
p. cm.—(Garland studies in comparative literature)
Includes bibliographical references.
ISBN 0-8240-0001-3 (alk. paper)
1. Autobiography. 2. Biography (as a literary form) 3. Freud, Sigmund, 1856–1939—
Influence. 4. Derrida, Jacques. 5. Psychoanalysis and literature. I. Title. II. Series.
CT25.T63   1990
809'.93592—dc20   90-34444

Printed on acid-free, 250-year-life paper.
Manufactured in the United States of America

FOR STEVE
weil du das vom Pferd gewußt hast.

TABLE OF CONTENTS

INTRODUCTION   1

PART ONE
Autobiographics as Cure

The Scene of Analysis   5
Chapter   I   Obsession and Narrative Line   8
Chapter   II   Fragments of Dora/Fragments of Freud   23

PART TWO
The Genealogy of Psychoanalysis

Foundations   42
Chapter   III   Screened Memories   43
Chapter   IV   The Interpretation of Dreams as
                 Work of Mourning   55

PART THREE
The Self and the Sign

Chapter   V   The Self and the Sign   87

PART FOUR
Autobiographics as Reste: Derrida's Glas

Glas and the Logic of the Unconscious   107
Chapter   VI   Thanatopraxis   111
Chapter   VII   Signatures   131

PART FIVE
The Fort/Da of Autobiography

Psychoanalysis and the Postal Service   152
Chapter VIII   The Legacy of Beyond the
                Pleasure Principle   156
Chapter   IX   The Literary Framework   182

CONCLUSION   200

NOTES   202

BIBLIOGRAPHY   210

ABBREVIATIONS OF DERRIDA'S WORKS CITED IN THE TEXT

CP   <u>La Carte Postale</u>

DIS <u>La Dissémination</u>

EC   "Entre Crochets"

ED   <u>L'Ecriture et la Différence</u>

EP   <u>Eperons</u>

FH   <u>Les Fins de l'Homme</u>

GL   <u>Glas</u> (The letters "L" and "R" following the page reference
 designate the left and right columns respectively.)

GR   <u>De la Grammatologie</u>

JA   "Ja ou le faux-bond"

LI   "Limited Inc a b c..."

MP   <u>Marges de la Philosophie</u>

VP   <u>La Voix et le Phénomène</u>

INTRODUCTION

Autobiographics in Freud and Derrida approaches the problem
of autobiography from two directions: first, it assesses the impact
of the theories of self, consciousness, and language developed by
Freud and Derrida on the assumptions of autobiography criticism;
second, through the reading of the autobiographical aspects of
their writings, it introduces a problematic that links
autobiography to academic institutions and intellectual movements.

My aim is not to define autobiography, to distinguish it from
related genres nor to place it within a particular discipline or
domain (literature, for example); rather, I wish to articulate the
general problem of autobiography --making sense of a life by means
of representation or repetition-- with a field of psychic phenomena
that Freud discovered in his treatment of neurotics: screen
memories, the work of mourning, obsessions, hysterical symptoms,
the repetition compulsion, transference. Each of these diverse
phenomena is the repetition of a life experience (generally a
trauma or a loss) with the intent (not necessarily, or even
usually, conscious) of mastering that experience and of assigning
it a meaning. The writing of an autobiography, I shall argue, not
only fulfills the same purpose, but may often be a manifestation
of these phenomena. Thus, Freud's Interpretation of Dreams is not
simply like a work of mourning, but is actually part of the work
of mourning undertaken after his father's death. I call this
general field "autobiographics," both to insist upon its relation
to autobiography as we know it, and to stress that these psychic
phenomena comprise a "language," a semiotic system that can be
translated and interpreted.
Avrom Fleishman has raised an objection to a similar project
that views persistent themes and metaphors within an author's
corpus as "obsessions," arguing that

> the autobiographer's act of repetition... differs in kind
> from obsession. An obsessive is bound to repeat, often
> reenacting as well as returning to the past in language
> and thought. An autobiographer may be an obsessive but
> insofar as he turns to autobiographical writing, he has
> shifted from direct reenactment (including acts of
> speech) to the language of review, revision, and
> representation. Such repetition is never simply the same
> again but will inevitably generate novel features: the
> same anew.[1]

The textual analyses that follow may be taken as a response to this objection, which attempts to distinguish between two kinds of repetition, a good, controlled repetition and a bad, compulsively driven one.[2] I take as my premise Derrida's claim that writing is not an activity undertaken by an entirely self-conscious subject and guided by his intentions, but the repetition of an already constituted language within which the subject must take his place. Writing is a "reenactment" or an acting out because the subject must assume a role over which he has limited control. Autobiography cannot entail the absolute self-consciousness that would make it "differ in kind" from obsession; it is, at best, a difference in degree and, at times, no difference at all.

Part One, focusing on two of Freud's case histories, addresses this very question. For the purpose of psychoanalysis, "the talking cure," is precisely to convert obsessional or hysterical behavior into language; that is, it is an effort to make the patient aware of the meaning of his symptoms, to make him capable of initiating a discourse about them, in order to be freed of them. The first two chapters trace this task of translation, but also point to its limits, finding in the form of Freud's text the traces and remnants of the symptoms he analyzes.

Part Two turns to consider Freud's own autobiographical project in "Screen Memories" and The Interpretation of Dreams. The impact of Freud's life and personality on the birth and development of psychoanalysis has in fact long been a matter of interest and investigation. The first volume of Ernest Jones' massive biography is only the best-known of a number of studies that find in Freud's childhood experiences the seeds of his later greatness, and locate the origin of psychoanalysis in the self-analysis that Freud undertook following the death of his father.[3] Such studies stress the courage and heroism with which Freud was endowed, raising the father of psychoanalysis to the stature of a legendary figure. More recent studies have focused not on the elements that made Freud a willing researcher, the new Oedipus who did not flinch at uncovering the secrets of the unconscious, but on the limits that Freud's psyche placed on this enterprise. Thus, Marie Balmary's provocative L'Homme aux Statues: Freud et la faute cachée du père speculates that Freud's unconscious knowledge of his father's sexual "sins" led him to repress his discovery concerning the etiology of hysteria.[4]

A number of important contributions have come from feminists, who recognize that a science founded on the self-analysis of a man can only represent women as the mirror or speculum by means of which men constitute themselves, and can reveal little about the particular area of female subjectivity and sexuality.[5] The fact that much of the material about Freud's childhood is drawn from his ground-breaking scientific text, The Interpretation of Dreams, deserves consideration. Do the many autobiographical anecdotes and confessions found there qualify that text as an autobiography? It is a commonplace of literary criticism that an autobiography is not simply the record of empirical "facts" about the author but the

2

shaping of a fictional self.[6]   If this is true of <u>The Interpretation of Dreams</u> as well, how does the image of himself that Freud projects affect the science he founds and the myths and legends that have arisen about him?

Part Three attempts to span the generations that separate Freud and Derrida. It focuses on several intellectual movements that have influenced Derrida's thinking on the questions of the self and the sign: Edmund Husserl's phenomenology, J. L. Austin's speech act theory, and the structuralism of Ferdinand de Saussure and Claude Lévi-Strauss.   From this discussion, a notion of autobiography emerges as the repetition, not only of an individual unconscious, but of a philosophical heritage transmitted through language.

This, of course, raises the question of Derrida's own position within that heritage and of the function of the autobiographical features of his writings. Part Four explores the double role that autobiography plays in Derrida, both as the expression of a desire (inherited from philosophy) and as an attempt at self-criticism. At the same time, it traces Derrida's debt to Freud and places him within the genealogy of psychoanalysis.

Part Five assesses Derrida's attempt to come to terms with his debt to Freud (and to philosophy in general). "Spéculer--sur 'Freud'" is a theoretical discussion of the problem of autobiography in relation to Freud and the psychoanalytical movement: it is not only written from "within" that movement, but is also supplemented by Derrida's autobiographical "Envois." As Derrida repeats Freud even as he criticizes him, he reveals his own position in an institutional structure and suggests an analogy between the psychoanalytic movement and the increasingly influential philosophy of deconstruction. In what have been called his "seemingly self-indulgent autobiographical ruminations,"[7] Derrida presents autobiography as a social and institutional concern.

3

PART ONE

AUTOBIOGRAPHICS AS CURE

THE SCENE OF ANALYSIS

The hysterical body is a text and, in fact, an autobiographical text. Every symptom tells a story about the patient's life, or rather several stories, since it is in the nature of the hysterical symptom to be overdetermined. That is, the hysterical symptom represents a repressed thought or thoughts relating to traumatic events in the hysteric's life. And although the body's language is entirely secret, it nevertheless complies with the rules of this particular form of expression, finding expression in a small number of somatic signifiers. Freud notes that his hysterical patient Dora exhibits "the commonest of all somatic and mental symptoms" and he chooses this patient for a case history because "what is wanted is precisely an elucidation of the commonest cases and of their most frequent and typical symptoms" (VII, 23-24).[1]

This is not to say, however, that these typical symptoms always point to the _same_ thoughts in every case of hysteria. On the contrary, "the determination of Dora's symptoms is far too specific for it to be possible to expect a frequent recurrence of the same accidental aetiology" (VII, 40). Rather,

> the hysterical symptom does not carry [its] meaning with it, but the meaning is lent to it, soldered to it, as it were; and in every instance the meaning can be a different one, according to the nature of the suppressed thoughts which are struggling for expression (VII, 40-41).

Thus, the body-text remains unreadable, even to the patient, who cannot interpret the symptom but only _suffer_ it. The other, properly linguistic text, the verbal account that the hysteric gives of her life, is characteristically fragmented, incoherent. She comes to the psychoanalyst unable to make sense of her life. It is the task of the psychoanalyst to work with the patient, to collaborate on a translation of this secret and motivated language of the body into the conventional language of words. Freud writes that the somatic symptom can only occur more than once if "it has a psychical significance, a _meaning_." This capacity for repeating itself, Freud adds, "is one of the characteristics of a hysterical symptom" (VII, 40). The hysterical body is, then, an iterable, signifying text and "the clearing-up of the symptoms is achieved by looking for their psychical significance" (VII, 41), by converting the symptoms into language.

In the same way, an obsession is also an autobiographical

text, "only a dialect of the language of hysteria" (X, 157), though one that is not expressed in the form of "hysterical conversion," the conversion of body into a text of signifying symptoms. The verbal form of an obsession is also marked with "a peculiar indeterminateness," as Freud puts it. It is only in the course of the collaboration with the analyst that an explicit formulation of the compulsion can be made.

When the sense of an obsession or of a hysterical symptom is brought out, the symptom disappears. Freud calls this collaboration, this task of translation, "analysis." "Analysis" is the name given to an autobiographical practice whose principal purpose is not to testify (to bear witness to injustice or to record the thinking of an age), nor to confess (one's sins or one's devotion), though both modes may be part of an analysis. The work of analysis is autobiographics as cure.

Freud himself remarks on this fact in one of his earliest texts, Studies in Hysteria:

> I have not always been a psychotherapist. Like other neuropathologists, I was trained to employ local diagnoses and electro-prognosis, and it still strikes me myself as strange that the case histories I write should read like short stories and that, as one might say, they lack the serious stamp of science. I must console myself with the reflection that the nature of the subject is evidently responsible for this, rather than any preference of my own. The fact is that local diagnosis and electrical reactions lead nowhere in the study of hysteria, whereas a detailed description of mental processes such as we are accustomed to find in the works of imaginative writers enables me, with the use of a few psychological formulas, to obtain at least some kind of insight into the course of that affection. Case histories of this kind are intended to be judged like psychiatric ones ; they have, however, one advantage over the latter, namely an intimate connection between the story of the patient's sufferings and the symptoms of his illness --a connection for which we still search in vain in the biographies of other psychoses (II, 160-61, emphasis added).

The remark comes in the form of a protest: I am a scientist by training. As one who is not a writer (Dichter), I can only be surprised, indeed, dismayed (for I must "console myself") that my case histories read like short stories. This is not my own doing, and I am not "responsible": it is in the nature of hysteria that the cure comes, not through "local diagnosis" nor through "electro-prognosis," but by bringing the patient to an understanding of her life, of her life as short story. Aesthetics, and more exactly, the aesthetics of autobiography, comes to serve the interest of medicine.[2]

In the pages that follow, I shall examine the scene of

analysis, this operation of making sense, of translating symptom or compulsion into sign. I call this operation "autobiographics," though autobiographics is not limited to the scene of analysis. It is the act of forming a self with language, the production rather than the representation of a self (<u>Arbeit</u> as well as <u>Werk</u>), the writing of a self that is <u>constituted by writing</u>.

My task does not end there. For Freud's case histories are not merely the faithful representation of an analysis. They are themselves texts, and texts that repeat, in a curious way, the very problems of the analysis. They raise again, but in reference to Freud this time, the questions of aesthetics, of narrative, of audience, of memory, and of identity. This notion, which Derrida calls "l'autobiographie de l'écriture,"[3] suggests that the writing of a case history is also an analysis, or rather, that both case history and analysis form a part of the larger domain of autobiographics.

CHAPTER I

OBSESSION AND NARRATIVE LINE

Journey, Analysis, Narrative

"In quite a number of cases," writes Freud in "The Psycho-genesis of a Case of Homosexuality in a Woman,"

> an analysis falls into two clearly distinguishable phases .... When this is so, one may bring up as an analogy the two stages of a journey. The first comprises all the necessary preparations, to-day so complicated and hard to effect, before, ticket in hand, one can at last go on to the platform and secure a seat in the train. One then has the right, and the possibility, of travelling into a distant country; but after all these preliminary exertions one is not yet there --indeed, one is not a single mile nearer to one's goal. For this to happen one has to make the journey itself from one station to the other, and this part of the performance may well be compared with the second phase of the analysis (XVIII, 152).

In the first phase, the "preliminary exertions," the analyst

> procures from the patient the necessary information, makes him familiar with the premises and postulates of psychoanalysis, and unfolds to him the reconstruction of the genesis of his disorder as deduced from the material brought up in the analysis (XVIII, 152).

In the second stage, the journey proper, it is the patient himself who

> gets hold of the material put before him... works on it, recollects what he can of the apparently repressed memories, and tries to repeat the rest as if he were in some way living it over again. It is only during this work that he... acquires for himself the convictions that make him independent of the physician's authority (XVIII, 152).

It is only in this second phase that the patient takes on an active role, becomes, in effect, the author of his own life and so escapes the authority or authorship of the analyst. But this second stage, the journey from one station to another, is not as direct as Freud's metaphor would suggest. As we shall see, the journey contains a number of detours, so many, in fact, that they threaten to obscure the progress of the journey itself. "Notes upon a Case of Obsessional Neurosis," the case of the Rat Man, is the record of such an analysis, one that falls into two distinct parts. Freud's case history is the plotting (in more ways than one) of this journey. But it is also the analysis of another journey, the obsessional journey that the Rat Man feels obliged to take despite its apparent senselessness, and a journey that eventually leads to Vienna and the analytic session. We have, then, both the analysis of a journey (for Freud's goal is to discover the significance of the compulsion) and the journey of analysis.

The analytic journey is then replicated in the writing of the case history. This narrative journey leads the reader through the stages of analysis, to the untangling of the obsession. The narrative of the Rat Man's compulsion is undertaken, first by the patient (whom Freud quotes at length), then by the analyst, and then once more by James Strachey, Freud's translator and editor (translator of a translator, since we characterized Freud's role as the translator of a secret language). The Rat Man's obsessional journey, senseless and complex, gives Freud and Strachey no little difficulty in their effort to decipher and communicate it. What can the Rat Man's compulsive journey tell us about the others, the journey-analysis and the journey-narrative? About the metaphor or allegory of "journey" in general, especially as it touches the question of autobiographics, of autobiography as narrative text?

The Rat Man's Narrative

In his second analytic session with Freud, the patient relates "the experience which was the immediate occasion of my coming to you" (X, 165). The patient is in the army, on manoeuvres. He has lost his pince-nez, has wired his optician for a replacement. During a halt (for the compulsive journey begins at a halt), a cruel captain tells him of a certain torture that consists in compelling rats to burrow into the anus of the victim. The story terrifies the patient and he imagines that the torture is being carried out on his father (already deceased as it happens) and a lady he loves.

> That evening, he continued [writes Freud], the same captain had handed him a packet that had arrived by the post and had said: 'Lieutenant A. has paid the charges for you. You must pay him back.' The packet contained the pince-nez that he had wired for. At that instant, a 'sanction' had taken shape in his mind, namely, <u>that he was not to pay back the money</u> or it would happen --(that is, the phantasy about the rats would come true as regards his father and the lady). And immediately,

in accordance with a type of procedure with which he was familiar, to combat this sanction there had arisen a command in the shape of a vow: '<u>You must pay back the 3.80 kronen to Lieutenant A.</u>' He had said these words to himself half aloud (X, 167-68).

Thus, the compulsion begins with <u>the contracting of a debt</u>, a debt that will eventually lead the patient on his long and senseless journey.

There follows a period when the patient finds various obstacles to prevent him from repaying the debt. Finally, he offers Lieutenant A. the money, but the latter

refused to accept [itl, declaring that he had not paid anything for him and had nothing whatever to do with the post, which was the business of Lieutenant B. This had thrown my patient into great perplexity, for it meant that he was unable to keep his vow, since it had been based upon false premises. He had excogitated a very curious means of getting out of his difficulty, namely, that he should go to the post office with both the men, A. and B., that A. should give the young lady there the 3.80 <u>kronen</u>, that the young lady should give them to B., and that then he himself should pay back the 3.80 <u>kronen</u> to A. according to the wording of his vow (X, 168).

The second session of the analysis ends soon after this communication, which Freud asks the patient to repeat three times. It ends, then, with the narration of a <u>compulsion to take a journey</u>, the preliminary conditions for undertaking the journey, but without revealing the outcome of the compulsion, that is, the journey itself. This corresponds exactly to the first phase of the journey that Freud used as a metaphor for analysis.

At the end of the session, the patient is "dazed and bewildered." And, Freud interjects,

it would not surprise me to hear that at this point the reader had ceased to be able to follow. For even the detailed account which the patient gave me of the external events of these days and of his reactions to them was full of self-contradictions and sounded hopelessly confused (X, 169).

The narrative, then, does not make sense: not to the narrator, nor to the analyst, nor to the eventual reader. As long as this narrative remains confused, the compulsion, the journey itself, is also indecipherable. Freud has already noted the "peculiar indeterminateness" of the patient's remarks, the vagueness of the wording of his obsessions, and has called it "characteristic" of the neurosis. The analyst's role, in fact, is to clear up the distortions, to make explicit the wording of the compulsions, to restore the integrity of the narrative.

At this point in the case history, Freud adds :

It was only when [the patient] told the story for the
third time that I could get him to realize its
obscurities and could lay bare the errors of memory and
the displacements in which he had become involved.   I
shall spare myself the trouble of reproducing these
details, the essentials of which we shall easily be able
to pick up later on (X, 169).

This is a crucial decision on Freud's part. By failing to clear
up the obscurities when they arise, the writer of the case history
obliges the reader to enter the analysis, to go through the same
process of discovery, of reconstruction or rewriting that is the
work of analysis, to take the journey herself. The case history,
in fact, is arranged as a chronicle, and can easily be read as so
many stops on a journey toward meaning. The journey, however, is
not without its difficulties.

The Detour

At the third session, as we may expect, the Rat Man proceeds
to finish his narrative of the journey. But this journey takes a
surprising turn:

He had spent a terrible night. Arguments and counter-
arguments had struggled with one another. The chief
argument, of course, had been that the premise upon which
his vow had been based --that Lieutenant A. had paid the
money for him-- had proved to be false. However, he had
consoled himself with the thought that the business was
not yet finished, as A. would be riding with him next
morning part of the way to the railway station at P---,
so that he would still have time to ask him the necessary
favour.* As a matter of fact he had not done this, and
had allowed A. to go off without him; but he had given
instructions to his orderly to let A. know that he
intended to pay him a visit that afternoon. He himself
had reached the station at half-past nine in the morning.
He had deposited his luggage there and had seen to
various things he had to do in the small town, with the
intention of afterwards paying his visit to A.   The
village in which A. was stationed was about an hour's
drive from the town of P---. The railway journey to the
place where the post office was [Z---] would take three
hours. He had calculated, therefore, that the execution
of his complicated plan would just leave him time to
catch the evening train from P--- to Vienna. The ideas
that were struggling within him had been, on the one
hand, that he was simply being cowardly and was obviously
only trying to save himself the unpleasantness of asking
A. to make the sacrifice in question and of cutting a

foolish figure before him, and that that was why he was disregarding his vow; and, on the other hand, that it would, on the contrary, be cowardly of him to _fulfil_ his vow, since he only wanted to do so in order to be left in peace by his obsessions. When in the course of his deliberations, the patient added, he found the arguments so evenly balanced as these, it was his custom to allow his actions to be decided by chance events as though by the hand of God. When, therefore, a porter at the station had addressed him with the words, 'Ten o'clock train, sir?' he had answered 'Yes,' and in fact had gone off by the ten o' clock train. In this way he had produced a _fait accompli_ and felt greatly relieved. He had proceeded to book a seat for luncheon in the restaurant car. At the first station they had stopped at it had suddenly struck him that he still had time to get out, wait for the next down train, travel back in it to P---, drive to the place where Lieutenant A. was quartered, from there make the three hours' train journey with him to the post office, and so forth. It had only been the consideration that he had booked his seat for luncheon with the steward of the restaurant car that had prevented him carrying out this design. He had not abandoned it, however; he had only put off getting out until a later stop. In this way he had struggled through from station to station, till he had reached one at which it had seemed to him impossible to get out because he had relatives living there. He had then determined to travel through to Vienna, to look up his friend there and lay the whole matter before him, and then, after his friend had made his decision, to catch the night train back to P---. When I expressed a doubt whether this would have been feasible, he assured me that he would have had half an hour to spare between the arrival of the one train and the departure of the other. When he had arrived in Vienna, however, he had failed to find his friend at the restaurant at which he had counted on meeting him, and had not reached his friend's house till eleven o'clock at night.... His friend had held up his hands in amazement to think he could still be in doubt whether he was suffering from an obsession, and had calmed him down for the night, so that he slept excellently. Next morning they had gone together to the post office, to dispatch the 3.80 _kronen_ to the post office [Z---] at which the packet containing the pince-nez had arrived (X, 170-2, Strachey's brackets).

At the point I have marked with an asterisk, James Strachey appends a note. I shall return to it in a moment. We notice first that the sequel of the narrative reveals that the Rat Man never arrives at Z---, at his destination (for what could a place called "Z" be but a destination?). In fact, he never gets beyond the preliminaries of this journey ("so complicated and hard to effect," as Freud puts it), beyond the numerous obstacles that seem to arise.

When the journey finally begins, it leads in the opposite direction, away from Z---. At the porter's arbitrary cue ("Ten o'clock train, sir?"), the Rat Man begins a journey that is in fact a detour. The patient boards the train and begins a different journey, no less senseless, and, as Freud will make clear, no less obsessional than the first. In contrast to the first compulsive journey, however, this train ride is undertaken with no clear destination in mind, with no plan of arrival. The patient arrives, as if by accident, in Vienna. He finds his friend and with him, he sends a sum of money, the repayment of the debt, to the post office at Z---. But before attempting to interpret this detour, to establish its relation to the question of narrative line, let us return to Strachey's footnote.

The Translator Intervenes

In the middle of the Rat Man's narrative, James Strachey interrupts with the following footnote: "[Reference to the sketch-map on p. 212 may make this paragraph easier to follow.]" Freud is relating a journey, but the narrative, Strachey believes, is difficult to "follow." He prescribes a map and directs us to another footnote. When we turn to page 212, however, we find more complications. Freud explains in the footnote that

> my patient did his very best to throw confusion over the little episode of the repayment of the charges for his pince-nez, so that perhaps my own account of it may also have failed to clear it up entirely. I therefore reproduce here a little map... by means of which Mr. and Mrs. Strachey have endeavoured to make the situation at the end of the manoeuvres plainer.

Freud wants to "clear up" the confusion that the Rat Man has caused, to restore the meaning that the Rat Man held back, in short, to pay back the debt of meaning that the Rat Man contracted when he kept secret part of the episode. [1] In this interest, and with the help of the Stracheys, who feel that Freud still owes his reader something, Freud decides to reproduce a little map.

The map that Freud refers to in the note, however, does not appear in the Standard Edition. In its place is a second map, accompanied by a translator's note, appended, in brackets, to the end of Freud's note:

> Unfortunately the original map, printed in the German editions of 1924 and later, as well as in the English translation in Volume III of Freud's Collected Papers (p. 349), was itself totally inconsistent with some of the peculiar data presented in the case history. An entirely new one has therefore been constructed for the

present edition (X, 212).

At this point, the reader who is paying attention to this matter of journey and narrative cannot fail to be curious about this first map, the map that was not good enough to clarify the narrative that, in turn, was not good enough to clarify the Rat Man's confused narrative of a senseless journey. So we turn to an earlier edition,[2] to another footnote and another map. What we find is a map in the form of a cross, as if it were parodying itself by crossing itself out, putting itself _sous rature_, like a repressed memory.[3]

In our quest for a map that will help us unravel the confused narrative, that will help us read, we find instead, not exactly a map of reading, but at least a pattern that suggests how reading proceeds, how meaning is produced. Strachey's intervention held out the promise of meaning, the promise of a map to Z---, the promise of linearity, a way of bypassing the detours and distortions of Freud's texts. But this promise leads us on another detour, leads us in fact to a dead end, an effaced map.

The Debt

Let us return to the Rat Man's account of the trip he did not take. Why, we may ask, does the Rat Man go to Vienna, and why does he feel compelled to go to Z---? For the same reason that we follow Strachey's footnote, as if it beckoned to us ("Ten o'clock train, sir?"). The Rat Man wants to reach the end. A packet has arrived for him, but a debt remains. In Vienna, under the influence of his friend, the Rat Man does send the _kronen_ to the post office at Z---. This is not to say that he repays the debt, for it will trouble him for some time to come. But the sum that the patient dispatches to Z--- is Freud's first clue in deciphering the narrative:

> It was this last statement which provided me with a starting-point from which I could begin straightening out the various distortions involved in his story. After his friend had brought him to his senses he had dispatched the small sum of money in question neither to Lieutenant A. nor to Lieutenant B., but direct to the post office. He must therefore have known that he owed the amount of the charges due upon the packet to no one but the official at the post office, and he must have known this before he started on his journey. It turned out that in fact he had known it before the captain made his request and before he himself made his vow; for he now remembered that a few hours before meeting the cruel captain he had had occasion to introduce himself to another captain, who had told him how matters actually stood. This officer, on hearing his name, had told him that he had been at the post office a short time before, and that the young lady there had asked him whether he

knew a Lieutenant L. (the patient, that is), for whom a packet had arrived, to be paid on delivery. The officer had replied that he did not, but the young lady had been of opinion that she could trust the unknown lieutenant and had said that in the meantime she would pay the charges herself. It had been in this way that the patient had come into possession of the pince-nez he had ordered. The cruel captain had made a mistake when, as he handed him over the packet, he had asked him to pay back the 3.80 _kronen_ to A., and the patient must have known it was a mistake. In spite of this he had made a vow founded upon this mistake, a vow that was bound to be a torment to him. In so doing he had suppressed to himself, just as in telling the story he had suppressed to me, the episode of the other captain and the existence of the trusting young lady at the post office (X, 172-73).

When the missing episode has been restored to the narrative, it becomes clear that the Rat Man's attempt to pay back A., his complicated plan to unite A. and B. at point Z. is itself a pointless detour, that all he was required to do in order to discharge the debt was to send the money directly to the post office. Both the journey to Z--- and the journey to Vienna are detours for what could have been accomplished by a simple letter.

Having restored the confused narrative and inserted the crucial episode, Freud notes: "When this correction has been made his behavior becomes even more senseless and unintelligible than before" (X, 173). The reconstruction of the missing episode clarifies nothing, for we have not yet got at the sense of the debt, of the vow, of the journey.

The debt is not discharged so easily. Even when the patient has remembered that the vow was made on false premises, premises he knew before the vow, this does not counteract its effect. For a long while, he will view his time in Vienna, in psychoanalysis, as just a stopping-off place before the real journey to Z---:

> [The patient's] determination to consult a doctor was woven into his delirium in the following ingenious manner. He thought he would get a doctor to give him a certificate to the effect that it was necessary for him, in order to recover his health, to perform some such action as he had planned in connection with Lieutenant A.; and the lieutenant would no doubt let himself be persuaded by the certificate into accepting the 3.80 _kronen_ from him... Many months later, when his resistance was at its height, he once more felt a temptation to travel to P--- after all, to look up Lieutenant A. and to go through the farce of returning him the money (X, 173).

The debt is not so easily discharged. The analyst himself is drawn

15

into the debt; the Rat Man seeks out a doctor who will supply him with a certificate, the ticket that would take him back to Z--- to fulfill the vow.

Yet Freud says that his role is different, that "there was no question of getting a certificate from me... all he asked of me was, very reasonably, to be freed of his obsessions" (X, 173). But perhaps repaying the debt and being freed of one's obsessions are not such different things. For Freud's role as analyst is to uncover the Rat Man's secret, restore the meaning of the compulsion, repay the debt of meaning, a meaning that was lost in the "indeterminateness" of the compulsion, in the formation of the compulsion itself, which seeks to disguise its own meaning.

In time, Freud will fill in the gaps, will tell us the meaning of the debt, of the obsession, of the rat torture --or rather, will lead us to discover it. But first, we must take another detour.

The Detour of Analysis

We have already followed Strachey on his quest for sense, on his journey to restore or repay the meaning that has been lost in the Rat Man's or in Freud's narrative. And now, following Freud's text more or less faithfully, we are again led in another direction. The section is called "Initiation into the Nature of the Treatment," and it is also an initiation of the reader:

> The reader must not expect to hear at once what light I have to throw upon the patient's strange and senseless obsessions about the rats. The true technique of psychoanalysis requires the physician to suppress his curiosity and leaves the patient complete freedom on choosing the order in which topics shall succeed each other during the treatment. At the fourth session, accordingly, I received the patient with the question: 'And how do you intend to proceed to-day?' (X, 173-74).

This question, "How do you intend to proceed to-day?" is Freud's version of that other question, "Ten o'clock train, sir?" which put the Rat Man on a train leading on a long detour that ends in Vienna. And indeed, the patient will not continue to discuss the rat obsession, but will lead Freud in a different direction, just as, at this point, Freud the writer will break off the narrative and will lead the reader through all the twists and turns of analysis, according to the "true technique of psychoanalysis."

In fact, these twists and turns constitute what Freud termed, in another place, the "preliminaries" one must take care of before a journey towards a cure can begin. But since, in this case, the "initiation into the treatment" follows on the Rat Man's narrative of his journey, interrupts the narrative, we may just as well see the section as a <u>detour</u> in the case history as well as in the analysis. And indeed, the analysis can proceed in no other way:

16

just as the Rat Man could not have cured his obsessional neurosis nor even discharged his "debt" by taking the train directly to Z---, the analysis could not have eventuated in a cure if Freud had pressed the Rat Man on this single strand of the neurosis.

The analysis can only proceed by detour, and, as in the obsessional journey, this detour will move toward an end of its own, altering irrevocably the journey itself. The Rat Man never arrives at Z---, for in the course of the detour (in Vienna), he realizes that his destination is not Z--- after all. In the same way, Freud's analysis reveals that the solution to the Rat Man's obsession does not lie simply within the elements of this first narrative.

Thus, it is surprising that in the introduction to the case history, Freud must apologize for the "fragmentary" and "aphoristic" nature of the text and explain that

> a programme of this kind seems to me to require some justification. For it might otherwise be thought that I regard this method of making a communication as perfectly correct and as one to be imitated; whereas in reality I am only accommodating myself to obstacles (X, 155).

So that, in spite of everything, Freud continues to privilege narrative and to consider the detour as a mere "accommodation" to an "obstacle," a method, above all, that should not be imitated. Despite a text that reveals the obsessional nature of narrative and the necessity of a detour that is no longer simply a derivation from a journey to which one must return, Freud clings to the ideal of a smooth and uninterrupted narrative.

The detour of analysis comprises thirty-five of the sixty-two pages that make up the "Extracts from the Case History." In it, various elements of the rat obsession, as well as other obsessions, are touched upon, considered, and dropped again. Towards the end of this long detour, Freud remarks that

> one day the patient mentioned quite casually an event which I could not fail to recognize as the precipitating cause of his illness.... He himself had no notion that he had brought forward anything of importance (X, 195).

Freud's remark follows a long section of "obsessional ideas," an almost random enumeration of the Rat Man's compulsions. It appears, then, almost casually in the text, inserts into the middle of the case history the precipitating cause, the premise or origin of the Rat Man's obsessional neurosis. By placing it here, Freud accomplishes two things: first, he reenacts the "casualness" with which the Rat Man introduces it "one day" (and, in fact, after the prominent position and startling detail of the rat story, one easily forgets the almost banal precipitating cause); secondly, he retains in the case history the <u>structural function</u> that the event

17

has in the analysis itself. For the discovery made on this <u>one day</u> leads to the "transferential relationship" with the analyst that is the condition for a successful analysis.[4] This transference makes possible the passage from the "preliminaries" to the journey of analysis itself. The precipitating cause, presented almost as casually by Freud as by the Rat Man, thus becomes the central moment in the analysis.

The Debt of Meaning

We can now begin the journey itself. "And now the path was clear to the solution of [the] rat idea (<u>dann war aber auch der Weg zur Auflösung der Rattenvorstellung frei</u>)" (X, 209). "The treatment had reached its turning-point" or, as Freud puts it, we are now "auf der Höhe der Kur." The term "Höhe" suggests that the analysis until this point has been an <u>upward</u> journey, and that the path leading to the solution of the rat idea entails a reversal of direction. Just where is the analysis heading?

It is at this point that "a quantity of material information... became available and so made possible a reconstruction of the whole concatenation of events" (X, 209-10). This is also the moment, we recall, when the patient is to "get hold of the material put before him" and thus become "independent of the physician's authority." In other words, in this last stage, the patient separates himself from the physician, escapes the authorship of the analyst, takes the elements brought out in the analysis and molds them into an autobiography, into a narrative self. This process, however, raises a number of difficulties. First, unlike the other episodes in the analysis, which Freud manages to replicate at a textual level in the case history, the physician cannot reproduce this phase of the analysis without negating it. For Freud is the <u>author</u> of the case history and must, therefore, continue to speak for the Rat Man, retain his authority over him. The last scene of analysis cannot be represented, except as a gap:

> It was impossible to unravel [the] tissue of phantasy thread by thread; the therapeutic success of the treatment was precisely what stood in the way of this. The patient recovered, and his ordinary life began to assert its claims: there were many tasks before him, which he had already neglected far too long, and which were incompatible with a continuation of the treatment. I am not to be blamed, therefore, for this gap in the analysis (X, 207-08n.).

If anyone is to be "blamed for this gap," it is, of course, the patient. Not this time, for "throwing confusion" over an episode in order to hide the meaning of his illness even from himself (this, we remember, was Freud's pretext for including the map) but rather, for <u>getting well</u>, for abandoning his "author" before the latter had elucidated all the details. By becoming the author of his own life, the Rat Man scurries away on his own journey, leaving the analyst with a gap in his text. A residual debt of meaning remains.

The above passage suggests something else: this second stage of the analysis, "the journey itself, " is also a detour, a detour from the larger journey of life, which the patient is now anxious to get back to. Indeed, Freud habitually recommends to his patient that he

> not take any important decisions affecting his life during the time of his treatment --for instance, not... choose any profession or definitive love-object-- but ...postpone all such plans until after his recovery (XII, 153).

It becomes more and more difficult to distinguish the journey from the detour, or to point to a journey that is not itself a detour from another journey.

In addition to the impossibility of representing the last phase of analysis, there is another problem involved in the Rat Man's attempt to make sense of his life, and in particular, to make sense of the obsessional journey. To put it simply, the compulsion has no meaning in itself. The obsession is a text and, what is more, an allegorical text whose function is to represent an earlier episode even while keeping it from becoming conscious. In the particular case we are dealing with, the allegory is not even autobiographical since it refers to an episode in the life of the Rat Man's father:

> One of his father's little adventures had an important element in common with the captain's request. His father, in his capacity as non-commissioned officer, had control over a small sum of money and had on one occasion lost it at cards. (Thus he had been a 'Spiel-ratte.') He would have found himself in a serious position if one of his comrades had not advanced him the amount. After he had left the army and become well-off, he had tried to find this friend in need so as to pay him back the money, but had not managed to trace him. The patient was uncertain whether he had ever succeeded in returning the money.... The captain's words, 'You must pay back the 3.80 kronen to Lieutenant A.,' had sounded to his ears like an allusion to this unpaid debt of his father's (X, 210-11).

At this point, the meaning of the debt rejoins what I have been calling the "debt of meaning." The financial debt cannot be discharged by the patient because, in fact, it reverts back to the father. The debt is not owed by the son, but by the father. Thus, the obsession to repay the debt, to fill up the lack, cannot be relieved by the simple act of returning a small sum.

In the same way, the debt of meaning, contracted by the Rat Man and by Freud, the obligation to explain what the obsession means, cannot be repaid by simply restoring the confused narrative to its original form, by filling in the ellipses and straightening out the distortions. The narrative must be brought to bear on another, prior scene. Just as Strachey's promise of meaning led eventually to a superannuated map, the meaning that the Rat Man searches for in his own life leads further back, to his father. The autobiographical obsession is "an identifica- tion with his father" (X, 211), that is, a "heterobiography," and the journey out (out of analysis, out of senselessness) is a journey back.

In order to make sense of his life, the Rat Man must re-turn to his father's life, to an unpaid debt contracted by the father. That is to say that an obsession cannot simply be an autobiographical text and that an autobiography cannot simply be a narrative of the self, a journey from one station to another, without, at the same time, an inscription of other selves, other journeys that threaten to lead the narrative on an endless detour.

Needless to say, the other elements in the compulsion --the two lieutenants, the woman at the post office, the indecision as to which direction to take-- all allude to other conflicts, other people, other episodes, in the lives of the Rat Man and of his father. I will not discuss them here.

The Birth of the Rat Man

We arrive, finally, at the "solution of the rat idea," at the meaning of the very short journey that two phantasmal rats take into the anus of their victim. Freud promises to give us "the briefest possible summary" (X, 210), the completion of this long-deferred or -detoured narrative, but he must, nevertheless, "follow the course of the analysis more closely," follow, that is, the detours and free associations that are characteristic of analysis. Freud explains that

> the idea of the punishment carried out by means of rats had acted as a stimulus to a number of [the patient's] instincts and had called up a whole quantity of recollections; so that, in the short interval between the captain's story and his request to pay back the money, rats had acquired a series of symbolic meanings, to which, during the period which followed, fresh ones were continually being added (X, 213).

In the "very incomplete account" (X, 213) that follows, Freud uncovers a chain of meanings that the signifier "rat" has taken on. This signifying chain, perpetuating itself through verbal bridges (Raten-Ratten, Spielratte)[5] and connotations (rats carry disease, therefore they signify prostitution, etc.) goes on for four pages.

> Yet, in spite of all this wealth of material, no light was thrown upon the meaning of his obsessional idea until one day... it became impossible to escape the inference

that... rats had another meaning still --namely, that of children (X, 215).

Now it happens that the woman whom the patient loves cannot bear children (any more than his own father could) and that the Rat Man's fondness for children was the reason that he hesitated to marry the lady. Freud thereby advances an interpretation of the obsession:

> When the captain had handed him the packet upon which the charges were due and had requested him to pay back the 3.80 kronen to Lieutenant A., he had already been aware that his 'cruel superior' was making a mistake, and that the only person he owed anything to was the young lady at the post office. It might easily, therefore, have occurred to him to think of some derisive reply, such as, 'Will I, though? ' or 'Pay your grandmother!' or 'Yes ! You bet I'll pay him back the money' --answers which would have been subject to no compulsive force. But instead, out of the stirrings of his father-complex and out of his memory of the scene from his childhood, there formed in his mind some such answer as 'Yes! I'll pay back the money to A. when my father and the lady have children!' or 'As sure as my father and the lady can have children I'll pay him back the money.' In short, a derisive affirmation coupled with an absurd condition which could never be fulfilled. But now the crime had been committed; he had insulted the two persons who were dearest to him --his father and his lady. The deed had called for punishment, and the penalty had consisted in his binding himself by a vow which it was impossible for him to fulfil and which entailed literal obedience to his superior's ill-founded request (X, 217-18).

Freud adds that the sanction

> was based upon the influence of two infantile sexual theories.... The first of these is that babies come out of the anus; and the second, which follows logically from the first, is that men can have babies just as well as women. According to the technical rules for interpreting dreams, the   notion of coming out of the rectum can be represented by the opposite notion of creeping into the rectum (as in the rat punishment) (X, 220).

The direction of the rats' journey has been reversed, and an understanding of the obsession can only come about when the proper direction is restored. And, since this understanding comes at the very end of the analysis, we can say that, in some sense, the trip to Z---, the detour to Vienna, the psychoanalysis itself with all the detours it entails, are all just an enormous detour that attempts to set the rats back on their proper course. The rats must get back out of the anus. From the compulsion itself to Freud's case history, each of the texts is an effort to convert the torture into birth, to signify this <u>impossible birth by the father</u>. And if, as the analysis shows, the patient is <u>himself</u> the rat, then it is his birth that we witness at the end of the case history.

When the meaning of the rat idea had been made clear, Freud assures us, "the patient's rat delirium disappeared" (X, 220). The obsession can only persist for as long as its meaning remains hidden: in this unusual case, the translation or interpretation of the obsession makes the "original text" vanish completely. The original compulsion-text, as we saw, was an impossible autobiography, the allegory of the impossibility of an autobiography that is not also a "heterography." The Rat Man suffers from an identification with his father, suffers from being trapped within the father, from sharing his identity. The autobio- graphics of analysis works to efface this hetero-autobiographical text, to bring about a rebirth, a separation from the father. And this separation from the father is also a separation from the analyst, who stands as author of the Rat Man's life until the latter can take control. When the journey is finally over, when the debt of meaning has finally been repaid, what else remains? The text can only conclude with an impossible birth.

The Rat Man recovers his health. He leaves the detour of analysis and rejoins the life he had neglected for so long. We can only contemplate the tragic irony of the directness with which, after so many detours, the Rat Man now proceeds to his destination. For in a final note, added in 1923, Freud writes: "The patient's mental health was restored to him by the analysis which I have reported upon in these pages. Like so many other young men of value and promise, he perished in the Great War" (X, 249).

CHAPTER II

FRAGMENTS OF DORA / FRAGMENTS OF FREUD

The Aesthetics of Analysis

Freud's clearest formulation of the relationship between narrative autobiography and mental health appears in a footnote near the beginning of "Fragment of an Analysis of a Case of Hysteria" (the case of Dora). Freud has been explaining the hysteric's characteristic difficulties in presenting her life in coherent verbal form. In his note, he offers the example of a healthy ideal:

> Another physician once sent his sister to me for psychotherapeutic treatment, telling me that she had for years been treated without success for hysteria (pains and defective gait). The short account which he gave me seemed quite consistent with the diagnosis. In my first hour with the patient I got her to tell me her history herself. <u>When the story came out perfectly clearly and connectedly in spite of the remarkable events it dealt with, I told myself that the case could not be one of hysteria</u>, and immediately instituted a careful physical examination. This led to the diagnosis of a not very advanced stage of tabes, which was later treated... with markedly beneficial results (VII, 16-17n., emphasis mine).

The clarity with which this patient tells her story, the clearsightedness with which she fits all the odd-shaped pieces together into a smooth narrative, has a compelling significance in the psychoanalytic setting. The patient's narrative of her life is proof of her mental health, of the existence of an integral self untouched by hysteria. The analyst's diagnosis is immediate, the proper treatment is prescribed; and physical health is restored.

This little success story stands in brilliant contrast to the "mutilated relics" of a life that the hysteric Dora offers Freud. In fact, Dora never does succeed in giving Freud a coherent account of her life. The analysis of Dora fails: the hysterical body-text resists interpretation, and after three months, Dora, in an act of revenge against Freud, unexpectedly leaves the analysis. Dora's story, as the title of Freud's case history indicates, remains a

23

fragment, the broken pieces (Bruchstücke) of a life that should have been restored, that should have, in addition, provided the writer/analyst with a complete and coherent narrative. What begins as the hysteric's incapacity to make sense of her life becomes a pressing problem for Freud the writer as well. A curious repetition marks the relation between the subject of analysis and the writer of her case history, between the patient's broken narrative and that of the scientist. "In face of the incompleteness of my analytic results," Freud claims,

> I had no choice but to follow the example of those discoverers whose good fortune it is to bring to the light of day after their long burial the priceless though mutilated relics of antiquity. I have restored what is missing, taking the best models known to me from other analyses; but, like a conscientious archaeologist, I have not omitted to mention in each case where the authentic parts end and my constructions begin (VII, 12, emphasis mine).

As the careful scientist, the archaeologist of knowledge, Freud not only publishes these priceless but mutilated relics, he also augments, shapes, and organizes them. Yet this work of restoration does not complete: Freud does not omit the scar that marks the difference between the relic and his construction. The relic retains its fragmented character: the construction, grafted onto it, only accentuates the appearance of incompleteness.

This work of restoration is not only an archaeological endeavour, but an aesthetic one as well. In his attempt to resolve the conflict in Dora's life, to shape her history into a story that makes sense, Freud appends a fictional "happy ending" to the failed analysis. The analyst assumes, with marked ambivalence, the role of Dichter. He assumes and repudiates the role, noting his inability to compensate for the fragmented form of the text, for the fragmented analysis that Dora has left in his hands. It is Dora, finally, who is to blame for this, and Freud the Dichter cannot master that act of revenge, the acting-out of an earlier moment in her life, that Dora carries out when she leaves the analysis in fragments.

Fragments of Dora

In the first pages of the "Fragment," Freud tells us that Dora's inability to produce a "smooth and precise" account of her life "possesses great theoretical significance." He attributes this inability to three factors:

> In the first place, patients consciously and intention-ally keep back part of what they ought to tell --things that are perfectly well known to them-- because they have not got over their feelings of timidity and shame (or discretion, where what they say concerns other people)

; this is the share taken by <u>conscious</u> disingenuousness. In the second place, part of the anamnestic knowledge, which the patients have at their disposal at other times, disappears while they are actually telling their story, but without their making any deliberate reservations: the share taken by <u>unconscious</u> disingenuousness. In the third place, there are invariably true amnesias, gaps in the memory into which not only old recollections but even quite recent ones have fallen-- and paramnesias, formed secondarily so as to fill in those gaps. When the events themselves have been kept in mind, the purpose underlying the amnesias can be fulfilled just as surely by destroying a connection, and a connection is most surely broken by altering the chronological order of events. The latter always proves to be the most vulnerable element in the store of memory and the one which is most easily subject to repression. Again, we meet with many recollections that are in what might be described as a first stage of repression, and these we find surrounded with doubts. At a later period the doubts would be replaced by a loss or a falsification of memory (VII, 16-17).

The first two factors (conscious and unconscious disingenuousness) concern the question of audience or, more exactly, the relationship between the patient and her audience-of-one (but also her eventual "biographer" of sorts), the analyst. The patient is reluctant, overly timid: she does not wish to tell everything about herself to a virtual stranger and, what is more, to a man.

This is also a question of social class, as Freud points out in <u>Studies in Hysteria</u>: his patients are, for the most part, from the upper classes, and this accounts for their shame in discussing personal, and especially, sexual matters with the physician. Nevertheless, by including this feature in the enumeration of the "theoretical significance" of the hysteric's confused narrative, Freud seems to be claiming that this disingenuousness is one of the symptoms of hysteria. It is, in any case, a symptom that the analyst makes every effort to cure. I shall have more to say about the relationship between analyst and patient, and in particular, about the problematic bond between Freud and Dora which accounts for the failure of the analysis. For it is precisely what Dora keeps back, as well as her reasons for doing so, that make all Freud's efforts futile.

The last factor that Freud mentions relates to memory and consists in three parts. There is, first, the problem of gaps or shady parts in the memory, events that are forgotten or in doubt; secondly, there is the effect of "paramnesia," the fictions that the unconscious constructs in order to fill in the gaps of memory; and finally, the scrambled chronology that makes finding connections, causal relations between events, virtually impossible. These problems, Freud insists, are not insignificant: they are <u>motivated</u> by the illness of hysteria. "That this state of affairs should exist in regard to the memories relating to the history of the illness is <u>a necessary correlate of the symptoms and one which is theoretically requisite</u>" (VII, 17-18, Freud's emphasis).

The therapist's role is to lead the patient to produce the narrative of her life:

> In the further course of the treatment the patient supplies the facts which, though he[1] had known them all along, had been kept back or had not occurred to his mind. The paramnesias prove untenable, and the gaps in his memory are filled in. It is only towards the end of the treatment that we have before us an intelligible, consistent, and <u>unbroken</u> [emphasis mine] case history. Whereas the practical aim of the treatment is to remove all possible symptoms and to replace them by conscious thoughts, we may regard it as a second and theoretical aim to repair all the damage to the patient's memory. These two aims are coincident. When one is reached, so is the other; and the same path leads to them both (VII, 18)[2]

In a quite literal sense, psychoanalysis is a workshop for autobiographers. The analyst's goal is to break down the repressed memories that have erected themselves into monuments of physical symptoms, and to replace these with conscious memories in verbal, narrative form. Success is measured by the patient's ability to produce such a narrative at the end of analysis. By this criterion, the analysis of Dora, which ends with her listening to Freud's version of her life, listening without a word before leaving for good, is unquestionably a failure. When Dora closes the door behind her, Freud is left with only the fragments of an analysis.

Fragments of Freud

It is by no means a matter of indifference to Freud that his case history, like Dora's life story, remains a fragment. Freud begins and ends the case history with lengthy explanations and excuses for the form of the text. These explanations sound strangely familiar. Freud begins by facing his accusers. Noting that he is now bringing forward "some of the material" upon which his earlier published findings are based, findings that concern the role of sexuality in the aetiology of the neuroses, Freud adds that

> I shall not escape blame by this means. Only, whereas before I was accused of giving no information about my patients, now I shall be accused of giving information about my patients that ought not to be given (VII, 7).

Having thus imagined an audience of accusers, Freud goes on to admit that they are not altogether in the wrong:

Even if I ignore the ill-will of narrow-minded critics such as these, the presentation of my case histories remains a problem which is hard for me to solve.... [Tlhe complete elucidation of a case of hysteria is bound to involve the revelation of... intimacies and the betrayal of... secrets. It is certain that the patients would never have spoken if it had occurred to them that their admissions might possibly be put to scientific uses (VII, 7-8).

Freud's next gesture, however, is to defend his practice:

In such circumstances persons of delicacy, as well as those who were merely timid, would give first place to the duty of medical discretion and would declare with regret that the matter was one upon which they could offer science no enlightenment. But in my opinion the physician has taken upon himself duties not only towards the individual patient but towards science as well.... Thus it becomes the physician's duty to publish what he believes he knows of the causes and structure of hysteria, and it becomes a disgraceful piece of cowardice on his part to neglect doing so (VII, 8).

These opening paragraphs are nothing other than a discussion of the problem of "disingenuousness" or "discretion" that Freud characterizes as a difficulty that his patient faces in relating her life. The characters have shifted --now it is the writer-analyst before a medical readership-- but the structure remains the same. Freud's strategy is to produce the accusations, to concur with them, appropriate them to a certain degree, only to chastise himself for this ill-founded discretion, this "disgrace-ful piece of cowardice." He also implicitly turns these self-accusations back on his readers, on those who are more timid than he.

Freud's next move is to turn his accusers' other claim, that he reveals too much, back onto the shoulders of his readers:

I am aware that --in this city, at least-- there are many physicians who (revolting though it may seem) choose to read a case history of this kind not as a contribution to the psychopathology of the neuroses, but as a roman à clef designed for their private delectation (VII, 9).

In order to foil such unscrupulous readers, Freud takes a number of precautions: he chooses a subject who is not known in Vienna; he keeps her identity from everyone but his friend Fliess; he waits four years after the analysis is terminated before publishing his case history; he changes the names of the parties involved; and he publishes the case in a "purely scientific and technical periodical [which] should... afford a guarantee against unauthorized readers of this sort" (VII, 8).

All these arguments take the form of a _tu quoque_. Freud will say, in reference to Dora, that "a string of reproaches against other people leads one to suspect the existence of a string of self-reproaches with the same content.... There is something undeniably automatic about this method of defending oneself" (VII, 35). It is clear that Freud is ambivalent about betraying Dora's secrets. He betrays her only to cover up that betrayal by changing her name, keeping her identity a secret. And he accuses his colleagues both of being _too_ discreet (in hesitating to publish case histories at all) and of not being discreet enough (in searching _his_ case history for the key to Dora's identity). All in all, Freud is uneasy about the revelations he makes about Dora's life. In short, he is disingenuous; he distrusts his readers; he hides his secret text away in a drawer for four years; and when he finally publishes it, he tells only what he wants to tell, keeping back the rest. When his readers object, he reacts violently, calling their behavior "shameful," "narrow-minded," "ill-willed," and "revolting." And in this, Freud's behavior resembles in every respect Dora's disingenuousness in telling her story to Freud. Let us not forget that Freud has labelled such behavior "hysterical."

The parallel between Freud and Dora does not end there. Freud goes on to list the "technical difficulties" involved in writing a case history, and immediately raises the problem of memory:

> I will now describe the way in which I have overcome the technical difficulties of drawing up the report of this case history. The difficulties are very considerable when the physician has to conduct six or eight psycho-therapeutic treatments of the sort in a day, and cannot make notes during the actual session with the patient for fear of shaking the patient's confidence and of disturbing his own view of the material under observation. Indeed, I have not yet succeeded in solving the problem of how to record for publication the history of a treatment of long duration. As regards the present case, two circumstances have come to my assistance. In the first place the treatment did not last for more than three months; and in the second place the material which elucidated the case was grouped around two dreams.... The wording of these dreams was recorded immediately after the session, and they thus afforded a secure point of attachment for the chain of interpretations and recollections which proceeded from them. The case history itself was only committed to writing from memory after the treatment was at an end, but while my recollection of the case was still fresh and was heightened by my interest in its publication. Thus the record is not absolutely --phonographically-- exact, but it can claim to possess a high degree of trustworthiness. Nothing of any importance has been altered in it except in some places the order in which the explanations are

given; and this has been done for the sake of presenting the case in a more connected form (VII, 9-10).

Freud's difficulties are the same in every detail as those of Dora: he mentions "amnesia" (his inability to keep the details of a long analysis in his head), paramnesias (the question of "trustworthiness") and "connectedness," the establishing of relationships between events. We note, however, that all these problems have been "overcome." It is as if, in these first pages, Freud is claiming to have mastered the material, to have succeeded where Dora failed, to have given a clear and connected account of the analysis.

Such claims do not square with other statements in the case history nor with the form of the text itself. In the first place, whereas Dora's gaps of memory are considered to be motivated by her illness, Freud's own forgetfulness is attributed to merely extraneous matters, to the limits of human memory and the impossibility of writing down Dora's words immediately. Contrary to the theory of repression developed in this and other texts by Freud, it is not forgetting, but rather <u>remembering</u>, that is here said to be motivated.[3]

Nor is Freud's claim to trustworthiness compatible with his "archaeological" practice of attaching "constructions" to the "mutilated relics" of Dora's memory, constructions that resemble suspiciously the patient's "paramnesias," as Freud himself will admit in his late essay, "Constructions in Analysis" (XXIII, 267-8). Although Freud downplays the role of paramnesias in the passage quoted above, we shall see that these fictional constructions are of important proportions.

Lastly, of course, the "connectedness" that Freud tries to bring about by rearranging the material is wholly relative, since Freud gives no fewer than three reasons for the <u>dis</u>connected, fragmented form of his text. First, he writes,

the treatment was not carried through to its appointed end, but was broken off at the patient's own wish when it had reached a certain point. At that time some of the problems of the case had not even been attacked and others had only been imperfectly elucidated.... [T]herefore, I can present only a fragment of an analysis....
There is another kind of incompleteness which I myself have intentionally introduced. I have as a rule not reproduced the process of interpretation to which the patient's associations and communications had to be subjected, but only the results of that process.... It would have led to nothing but hopeless confusion if I had tried to complete [both] task[s] at the same time....
For a third kind of incompleteness in this report neither the patient nor the author is responsible. It is, on the contrary, obvious that a single case history, even if it were complete and open to no doubt, cannot

provide an answer to <u>all</u> the questions arising out of the problem of hysteria.... It is not fair to expect from a single case more than it can offer (VII, 12-13).

Here, at the end of Freud's "Prefatory Remarks," the reasons for the text's incompleteness proliferate. This is not the last time that Freud will make excuses for the fragmented form. And, as we saw at several moments in the Rat Man analysis, Freud is most concerned with assigning the blame. His patient Dora is to blame for the first and most important kind of incompleteness, for her unforgivable act of walking out of the analysis before all the problems had been elucidated; Freud himself takes responsibility for the second factor in the text's incompleteness; as for the third factor, he implicitly blames the reader for not being "fair," for expecting too much from him. It is clear that Freud has a desire to master Dora's story, to form a complete and coherent narrative out of her life. This desire leads him to blame whomever he can for the failure, to blame Dora, himself, his readers. But this desire is not fulfilled: Freud can only repeat the fragmented form of a life that Dora presents to him, can only repeat her failure.

Freud as <u>Dichter</u>

This last statement is not quite exact. For at several points in the text, Freud will try to compensate for the fragmented text by creating fictional constructs that supplement Dora's account. The source of this model of compensation is no mystery. For towards the end of the section entitled "The Clinical Picture," where Freud relates Dora's history and circumstances, he explicitly compares his work to that of the literary writer (<u>Dichter</u>):

I must now turn to consider a further complication to which I should certainly give no space if I were a man of letters (<u>Dichter</u>) engaged upon the creation of a mental state like this for a short story, instead of being a medical man engaged upon its dissection. The element to which I must now allude can only serve to obscure and efface the outlines of the fine poetic conflict which we have been able to ascribe to Dora. This element would rightly fall a sacrifice to the censorship of a writer, for he, after all, simplifies and abstracts when he appears in the character of a psychologist. But in the world of reality, which I am trying to depict here, a complication of motives, an accumulation and conjunction of mental activities --in a word, overdetermination-- is the rule (VII, 59-60).

In taking his distance from the literary writer, Freud also offers his definition of the poet's task. Unlike the psychoanalyst, the scientist or archaeologist who must be concerned with "the world of reality," the poet simplifies, abstracts and censors in the

30

interest of producing the clear outlines of a "fine poetic conflict." Such an exercise is counter-productive for the analyst, who must learn to report reality with all its complications and overdeterminations, even if this means that his text is less coherent, more fragmented, than the poet's texts. But Freud's protest comes too late and is too weak to refute the evidence of his aesthetic practice. The statement occurs at the end of the psycho-history, and the "complication" is merely appended to the other ending. In fact, the words immediately preceding Freud's protest echo like the end of a chapter in a serial novel, announcing what is to come in a prophetic voice designed to build suspense: "Nevertheless Dora persisted in denying my contention for some time longer, until, towards the end of the analysis, the conclusive proof of its correctness came to light" (VII, 59). Like the onmiscient narrator, Freud the novelist holds out the denouement of his text to the reader, only to pull it back, to oblige the reader to await the next installment. (James Strachey, who evidently does not approve of Freud's practice, appends a note at this point, instructing the reader of the exact passage that resolves this conflict.) Freud's next sentence is the protest: "Wenn ich ein Dichter wäre..."

Freud's "contention," which Dora at first denies, is that the patient is actually in love with Herr K., the older man, husband of her father's lover, who tried to seduce her when she was fourteen and again several years later. As evidence in support of his claim, Freud refers to a cousin of Dora's, who had noticed Dora turn pale when Herr K. came into sight. Freud adds, "I explained to her that the expression of emotion and the play of features obey the unconscious rather than the conscious, and are a means of betraying the former" (VII, 59). By way of explanation, Freud adds in a footnote: "Compare the lines: 'Ruhig mag ich Euch erscheinen, / Ruhig gehen sehn.'" Thus, Freud uses Schiller's lines of poetry in support of the "fine poetic conflict" he himself has created, to argue that the girl's duplicity, her apparent indifference, masks, as in Schiller's ballet, her true feelings of love (see Strachey's explanatory footnote, VII, 59n). And yet, Freud claims that he is not a poet.

Freud not only contends that Dora is in love with Herr K., but that Herr K. is also in love with her. Contrary to Dora's belief, Freud claims that Herr K. was not merely treating Dora like the governess whom he seduced and then dismissed from his home; Freud believes that Herr K.'s proposition would have been followed by a more honorable proposal, a proposal of marriage, if only Dora had not responded so badly to his first advances. One begins to suspect that Dora's problem is that she has not read Pamela, that she is unfamiliar with the plot of the insistent and reckless male who tries to seduce a pure young girl, who, in turn, protects her virtue until the man finally does the honorable thing and marries her. Freud's every effort is to bring Dora's life to this happy conclusion.

Even after the analysis fails, he insists on writing not one, but two, happy endings. In his last session with Dora, Freud tells her:

> I am beginning to suspect that you took the affair with Herr K. much more seriously than you have been willing to admit so far. Had not the K.'s often talked of getting a divorce?...
> May you not have thought that he wanted to get divorced from his wife so as to marry you? .... I imagine that this was a perfectly serious plan for the future in your eyes. You have not even got the right to assert that it was out of the question for Herr K. to have had any such intention; you have told me enough about him that points directly towards his having such an intention. Nor does his behavior at L--- [the scene of the attempted seduction] contradict this view. After all, you did not let him finish his speech and do not know what he meant to say to you. Incidentally, the scheme would by no means have been so impracticable.... I know now... that you did fancy that Herr K.'s proposals were serious, and that he would not leave off until you had married him.
> Dora had listened to me without any of her u s u a l contradictions. She seemed to me moved; she said good-bye to me very warmly, with the heartiest wishes for the New Year, and--came no more (VII, 107-9).

Freud is being carried away by the fictions he has invented as a happy alternative to Dora's illness. From the claim that Dora is in love with Herr K. and wishes to marry him, Freud proceeds to make all the arrangements, assuring her of Herr K.'s good intentions, of the practicality of the plan, even of her father's consent. He is convinced that this is the most logical and tidy outcome of the "poetic conflict."

The scene ends dramatically with Dora's final exit, and Freud is left to ponder the alternative ending he has created, and to rewrite the other characters' parts:

> I do not know whether Herr K. would have done any better if it had been revealed to him that the slap Dora gave him by no means signified a final 'No' on her part, but that it expressed the jealousy which had lately been roused in her, while her strongest feelings were still on his side. If he had disregarded that first 'No,' and had continued to press his suit with a passion which left room for no doubts, the result might very well have been a triumph of the girl's affection for him over all her internal difficulties (VII, 110-11).

Freud knows very well how his story ought to end --with a bourgeois marriage, a happy resolution. Freud even returns to the events he has heard recounted and refashions them to his liking, in order to restore Dora's fragmented life, and also, in order to compensate for the fragmented form of the case history. That is not all. In a postscript, Freud makes one last attempt to resolve the conflict happily, in a marriage:

> Years have again gone by since her visit. In the mean-time the girl has married, and indeed --unless all the signs mislead me-- she has married the young man who came into her associations at the beginning of the analysis of the second dream. Just as the first dream represented her turning away from the man she loved to her father --that is to say, her flight from life into disease-- so the second dream announced that she was about to tear herself free from her father and had been reclaimed once more by the realities of life (VII, 122).

In a final footnote, Freud admits that his belief that Dora married the man alluded to in her dream "as I afterwards learnt, was a mistaken notion." Freud neatly ties up the loose ends by marrying Dora off, not to Herr K., but to a young man who appears in a minor role toward the end of the story. This imagined marriage organizes the case history into the classic structure of conflict and resolution: the first dream advances the conflict, shows Dora's flight into illness, away from love; the second dream introduces a new character, a young man of good family, who leads Dora back to health and happiness. But reality intrudes again in the footnote: Dora marries, not this young man, but someone else, and then only after many years, another bout with hysteria, another treatment with a different analyst.... The footnote undoes all Freud's efforts at coherence.

What goes wrong? Why, despite Freud's efforts to produce a smooth narrative, a happy ending that accounts for every detail, does the case history remain a fragment? We need to return to the "complication" that Freud mentions, the "overdetermination" that interferes with the "fine poetic conflict" that Freud has thus far developed.

> In the world of reality, which I am trying to depict here, a complication of motives, an accumulation and conjunction of mental activities --in a word, over-determination-- is the rule. For behind Dora's supervalent train of thought which was concerned with her father's relations with Frau K. there lay concealed a feeling of jealousy which had that lady as its object --a feeling, that is, which could only be based upon an affection on Dora's part for one of her own sex.... When Dora talked about Frau K., she used to praise her 'adorable white body' in accents more appropriate to a lover than to a defeated rival.... I never heard her speak a harsh or angry word against the lady, although from the point of view of her supervalent thought she should have regarded her as the prime author of her misfortunes (VII, 60-2).

What obscures the clear outlines of the "poetic conflict," the hidden love Dora holds for Herr K., is her unconscious love of another woman. To put it simply, Dora's homosexuality does not make a good story. It interferes with the telling, breaking up the coherence of the romantic conflict, and forces Freud back into the "world of reality."

The Roles of Transference

The same factors that contribute to the "fine poetic conflict" in Dora's life, as well as to the fragmenting of that conflict, also lead to difficulties within the analysis, in the relationship between analyst and patient, and to the eventual breaking off of the treatment. And once more, Freud offers several versions of what happened, and of what should have happened, in his case history. It is not surprising that Dora's relationship with the K.'s is replicated in her bond with the psychoanalyst. In fact, this is essential, an unavoidable result of the phenomenon Freud calls "transference" (Übertragung). In the case history, Freud defines transferences as the "new editions or facsimiles of the impulses and phantasies which are aroused and made conscious during the progress of the analysis. ... [T]hey replace some earlier person by the person of the physician" (VII, 116). In other words, Dora's relationship to Freud is necessarily the repetition of an earlier significant relationship. Freud explains that the operation of transference is both essential and extremely difficult to deal with:

> Transference is an inevitable necessity.... There is no means of avoiding it and... this latest creation of the disease must be combated like all the earlier ones. This happens, however, to be by far the hardest part of the whole task.... Transference is the one thing the presence of which has to be detected almost without assistance and with only the slightest clues to go upon (VII, 116).

This difficult task of detecting transferences must be carried out if the analysis is to be successful. The repetition of the earlier "edition" (the metaphor is a textual one) must not be allowed to go beyond a certain point; otherwise, the relationship between analyst and patient is put in jeopardy.

This is precisely what goes wrong in the Dora case. Freud does not discover Dora's transference until it is too late. He gives several versions of the nature of this transference, but what remains constant in these various and incompatible versions is Freud's self-reproaches. In the first version, Freud contends that Dora has transferred her love and anger toward Herr K. onto him:

> When the first dream came, in which [Dora] gave herself the warning that she had better leave my treatment just as she had formerly left Herr K.'s house, I ought to have

34

listened to the warning myself. 'Now,' I ought to have said to her, 'it is from Herr K. that you have made a transference on to me. Have you noticed anything that leads you to suspect me of evil intentions similar (whether openly or in some sublimated form) to Herr K.'s? Or have you been struck by anything about me or got to know anything about me which has caught your fancy, as happened previously with Herr K.?' Her attention would then have been turned to some detail in our relations, or in my person or circumstances, behind which there lay concealed something analogous but immeasurably more important concerning Herr K. And when this transference had been cleared up, the analysis would have obtained access to new memories, dealing, probably, with actual events (VII, 118-19).

Freud is once again creating happy endings for his failed analysis. It is important to note that the only way to deal successfully with a transference is to replace the repetition, the reimpression of an earlier text, with <u>commentary</u> on that text. Commentary is here the means of mastering the repetition. This is precisely what Freud reproaches himself for having failed to do:

But I was deaf to this first note of warning, thinking I had ample time before me, since no further stages of transference developed and the material for the analysis had not yet run dry. In this way the transference took me unawares, and, because of the unknown quantity in me which reminded Dora of Herr K., she took her revenge on me as she wanted to take her revenge on him, and deserted me as she believed herself to have been deceived and deserted by him. Thus she acted out an essential part of her recollections and phantasies instead of reproducing it in the treatment (VII, 119).

The analysis is broken off because Freud fails to recognize the transference that is taking place, fails to convert the theater of analysis (for Freud's metaphor of "acting out" is borrowed from the theater), the theater where Dora reenacts the scenes of her life, into a conmentary on that scene. By his own admission, Freud is to blame for being caught up in Dora's play-acting, for being cast in the role of Herr K., and for not recognizing this until it is too late.

Yet, on two other occasions, Freud reproaches himself for something else, for something quite different. Immediately after telling of Dora's final departure, Freud adds:

Might I perhaps have kept the girl under my treatment if I myself had acted a part, if I had exaggerated the importance to me of her staying on, and had shown a warm personal interest in her --a course which, even after allowing for my position as her physician, would have

35

been tantamount to providing her with the substitute for the affection she longed for? I do not know (VII, 109).

Despite Freud's explanation that "I have always avoided acting a part" (VII, 109), there is a note of regret here, an expression of sorrow at not having done all that it was possible to do to keep Dora. Freud is himself tempted to "act a part," to assume the role of Herr K., to effect a "counter-transference," precisely the response he warns against in the 1905 article called "Observations on Transference-Love."

The passage cited above is immediately followed by Freud's rewriting of Herr K.'s role: "Nor do I know whether Herr K. would have done any better... etc. Thus Freud juxtaposes the solution he might have found to Dora's departure with the solution his predecessor, Herr K., might have tried. It appears that Freud is identifying with Herr K., with a Herr K. who truly loves Dora, in order to express his own desire that Dora remain in analysis.

The confirmation of this hypothesis is found in another text, Psychopathology of Everyday Life. In attempting to demonstrate that even the apparently arbitrary choice of a name or number is determined by unconscious forces, Freud uses the example of the pseudonym he chooses for 'Dora' :

> With a view to preparing the case history... for publication I considered what first name I should give her in my account.... It might have been expected and I myself expected-- that a whole host of women's names would be at my disposal. Instead one name and only one occurred to me-- the name 'Dora.'
> I asked myself how it was determined. Who else was there called Dora? I should have liked to dismiss with incredulity the next thought to occur to me --that it was the name of my sister's nursemaid (Kinderfrau) ; but I have so much self-discipline or so much practice in analysing that I held firmly to the idea and let my thoughts run on from it. At once there came to my mind a trivial incident from the previous evening which provided the determinant I was looking for. I had seen a letter on my sister's dining-room table addressed to 'Fraülein Rosa W.' I asked in surprise who there was of that name, and was told that the girl I knew as Dora was really called Rosa, but had had to give up her real name when she took up employment in the house, since my sister could take the name 'Rosa' as applying to herself as well. 'Poor people,' I remarked in pity, 'they cannot even keep their own names!'.... When next day I was looking for a name for someone who could not keep her own, 'Dora' was the only one to occur to me. The complete absence of alternatives was here based on a solid association connected with the subject-matter that I was dealing with: for it was a person employed in someone else's house, a governess (Gouvernante), who

exercised a decisive influence on my patient's story, and on the course of the treatment as well (VI, 240-41).

When Herr K. makes advances to Dora, he tells her, "I get nothing out of my wife" (VII, 98). Dora knows that these are the same words that Herr K. used to seduce the governess who was subsequently treated badly and dismissed from the house. Thus, she suspects that she is being treated like Herr K.'s governess. When Dora decides to leave Freud's treatment, she makes the decision two weeks in advance. Freud responds to this news that "that sounds like a maidservant or a governess (<u>einem Dienstmäd-chen, einer Gouvernante</u>) --a fortnight's warning" (VII, 105). Thus, in leaving the analysis, Dora reenacts the role of the unfortunate governess and casts Freud once more in the role of Herr K. And Freud, by renaming his patient 'Dora,' the name of his sister's servant, accepts that role.

In the case history, Freud translates Dora's actions towards Herr K. into the following words: "Since you have treated me like a servant (<u>Dienstmädchen</u>), I shall take no more notice of you, I shall go my own way by myself, and not marry" (VII, 110n). Freud, of course, means "governess" and not "servant," since it is a governess whom Herr K. treated so badly. The error is significant, since it allows Freud to identify himself with Herr K., to inculpate himself, for it is Freud who is treating Dora like a <u>servant</u> by giving her the nursemaid's name. The reproach that Freud puts in Dora's mouth is not only directed against Herr K. but against himself as well.

Freud reproaches himself a third time for not preventing Dora from leaving. And, just as the second reproach is inconsistent with the first, the third reproach is incompatible with the other two. For Freud cannot, on the one hand, clear up the transference by converting it into commentary and, on the other, become an accomplice in the acting-out of the transferential relationship. Further, he can neither play the role of the beloved Herr K., nor analyze the role that Dora is asking him to play if, in fact, Herr K. is not loved. Yet that is precisely what Freud claims in a strange footnote appended to the "Postscript" of the text:

> The longer the interval of time that separates me from the end of this analysis, the more probable it seems to me that the fault in my technique lay in this omission: I failed to discover in time and to inform the patient that her homosexual (gynaecophilic) love for Frau K. was the strongest unconscious current in her mental life. I ought to have guessed that the main source of her knowledge of sexual matters could have been no one but Frau K. --the very person who later on charged her with being interested in those same subjects. Her knowing all about such things and, at the same time, her always pretending not to know where her knowledge came from was really too remarkable. I ought to have attacked this riddle and looked for the motive of such an extraordinary piece of repression.... Before I learnt the importance

of the homosexual current of feeling in psychoneurotics,
I was often brought to a standstill in the treatment of
my cases or found myself in complete perplexity (VII,
120n).

Dora is not only a frustrated Pamela who resents being treated like
a servant; she is also a vengeful lesbian, who loves not Herr K.
so much as his wife. And Dora's homosexuality not only doesn't
make a good story, it also makes for decidedly unpromising
circumstances in analysis. For if the strongest unconscious
current in Dora's mental life is homosexual, if her response to
Herr K.'s advances is, as Freud says, "Men are all so detestable
that I would rather not marry. This is my revenge" (VIII, 120),
then she can hardly form the necessary transference-love
relationship with the male analyst. Freud recognizes this problem
in his later case history of a female homosexual. Discovering that
"nothing resembling a transference to the physician had been
effected," or, to be more exact, that the patient "transferred to
me the sweeping repudiation of men which had dominated her," Freud
"broke off the treatment and advised her parents that... the
therapeutic procedure... should be continued by a woman doctor"
(XVIII, 164). If this is true for Dora's case as well, then the
analysis is broken off, remains incomplete, fragmented, for the
same reason that Freud's "fine poetic conflict" is disturbed: he
is unable to master Dora's homosexuality.

The Compulsion to Repeat

If, in our discussion of form, we were led to suspect that
the "Fragment of an Analysis of a Case of Hysteria" is itself a
hysterical text, we can now begin to understand the reasons. Freud
does not want Dora to leave. That is why he reproaches himself for
not discovering the transference in time, for not himself playing
a role, for underestimating Dora's homosexual tendencies. That is
why he tries to master Dora's story by becoming a _Dichter_, by
creating happy endings, by rewriting the roles of the characters.
That is, in fact, why Freud writes the case history in the first
place, and why his text has such a peculiar form. For there is
every indication that Freud has undergone a trauma, and that, in
writing of this trauma, he is repeating it in order to master it.

Let us look more closely at the "Postscript" to the Dora case,
where Freud discusses the phenomenon of transference. He writes:

What are transferences? They are new editions or
facsimiles of the impulses and phantasies which are
aroused and made conscious during the progress of the
analysis.... Some of these transferences have a content
which differs from that of their model in no respect
whatever except for the substitution. These then --to
keep the same metaphor-- are merely new impressions or
reprints. Others are more ingeniously constructed; their

content has been subjected to a moderating influence...
and they may even become conscious, by cleverly taking
advantage of some real peculiarity in the physician's
person or circumstances and attaching themselves to that.
These, then, will no longer be new impressions, but
revised editions (VII, 116).

Freud uses an extended metaphor to define "transferences," even
drawing our attention to the fact that it is a metaphor.
Transferences are the reimpressions or the reeditions, in short,
the <u>repetition</u>, of earlier, often hidden, texts. Now, this passage
appears in the "Postscript" to the case history, a case history
which had been written four years earlier, stored away in a drawer
until Freud finally decides to finish and publish it. This "Postscript" begins with the following words: "It is true that I have
introduced this paper as a fragment of an analysis; but the reader
will have discovered that it is incomplete to a far greater degree
than its title might have led him to expect" (VII, 112). Freud
goes on to repeat the same excuses for the text's incompleteness
that he had already given in the "Prefatory Remarks." He repeats
them at length, for more than two pages, as if he had not already
explained it all to us. One cannot fail to notice that the
metaphor Freud uses to define transference applies rather directly
to his "Postscript": it, too, is the repetition of an earlier,
previously hidden text. Can a text be a transference as well as
the other way around? Freud repeats Dora's analysis, repeats, as
we saw, her disingenuousness, her vengefulness towards her
audience, repeats the fragmented form of her life story in the
fragment of a case history.

Freud's text is a transference, or, to be more exact, it is
the compulsion to repeat Dora's transference. Freud's text remains
a fragment (<u>Bruchstück</u>) because the analysis is broken off
(<u>unterbrochen</u>), and the analysis is broken off because Freud fails
to master Dora's transference.[4]

The entire text reenacts the failed analysis: Freud becomes
Dora in an effort to take control of her story, to master her, to
take the active role in her departure. When Dora leaves, Freud
does nothing. But within the next two weeks, he writes a text, a
fragment of an analysis. He mistreats his audience, hurling
accusations at them, just as Dora mistreated him. He writes a
story with a happy ending, or two, or three, anything to keep Dora
from leaving him again, from leaving the analysis in fragments.
He explains repeatedly why his text is only a fragment in an
attempt to convert this repetition into a commentary, a mastery of
the repetition. Four years later, Freud again takes up his "Fragment"; he writes of transference, of what he should have done to
master the transference; he writes another happy ending, mastering
transference this time, mastering repetition itself.

Freud repeats. He repeats the analysis, but this time it is
he who is Dora and his audience who is Freud, the analyst who is
left behind, who must look on passively as Dora leaves. Freud
repeats without mastery, no more able to effect a cure in himself

39

than in his patient Dora. And in repeating the analysis, Freud's "Fragment of an Analysis of a Case of Hysteria" becomes, at the limit, an autobiographical text.

PART TWO

THE GENEALOGY OF PSYCHOANALYSIS

FOUNDATIONS

Ernest Jones' <u>Life and Work of Sigmund Freud</u> reports that the writing of <u>The Interpretation of Dreams</u> was so intimately connected with the first years of Freud's self-analysis that "one may legitimately bracket the two together."[1] Freud embarked upon the self-analysis in 1897 as a means of coping with the experience of his father's death. Thus, <u>The Interpretation of Dreams</u>, Freud's "magnum opus," toward which he showed the greatest confidence and considerable affection, is closely associated with the death of Jakob Freud and the son's reactiou to it. Jones does not, however, "give any account of the contents of such a wide-embracing book" in his biography since "it is the best known and most widely read of all Freud's works, and one cannot imagine anyone who is not familiar with it wishing to read a biography of him."[2]

Let us not assume too hastily that we are "familiar" with <u>The Interpretation of Dreams</u>, that we have read it, or that we truly "know" it. What can it mean, for instance, when the text that establishes Freud as the father of psychoanalysis issues from a work of mourning (<u>Trauerarbeit</u>) brought on by the father's death? To assume that we can already answer that question is to close the matter too quickly; it is to close the covers of a book that may have more to say about Jones' <u>Life and Work of Sigmund Freud</u> than the biography says about <u>The Interpretation of Dreams</u>. For in a sense, Jones' biography --the entire problem of biography and autobiography-- is already contained within Freud's text.

<u>The Interpretation of Dreams</u>, for example, provides a commentary on the dedication to Jones' book: "To Anna Freud, True Daughter of an Immortal Sire." Since immortality and its relation to the siring of true sons and daughters are the subject of some of the oddest and most difficult passages in Freud's text, Jones' dedication may be understood within that problematic. The three aspects that Jones has isolated --the death of Freud's father, the self-analysis, and the writing of a magnum opus-- not only form the foundations of the science of psychoanalysis, they also appear as major themes in Freud's texts. Freud's writings reflect upon the problem of founding a science on the basis of a self-analysis and consider the question of a magnum opus that will guarantee his immortality. In other words, these three apparently simple terms that Jones "brackets together" constitute Freud's autobiographics. Do we understand them as well as we believe?

CHAPTER III

SCREENED MEMORIES

The Rhetoric of Memory

What, for example, is a self-analysis? Jones replies that it was Freud's "most heroic feat.... What indomitable courage, both intellectual and moral, must have been needed!"[1] Freud's own answer is considerably less lofty; it is, in fact, as down-to-earth as a pun or a play on words, and the effect is equally comic.

In "Screen Memories" (1898), an essay with considerable significance for the theory of autobiography, Freud illustrates his discussion with a disguised autobiographical example that stages his own self-analysis. The content of the example is not indifferent, nor does it merely illustrate Freud's thesis. The personal and the theoretical are inextricably linked, and the autobiographical moment reveals the founding gesture of the text itself.

Freud begins by distinguishing between two kinds of memory: memory as "a connected chain of events," usually beginning between the ages of six and ten; and the "isolated recollections" of earliest childhood which "are often of dubious or enigmatic importance" (III, 303). Freud is particularly interested in this second group. He notes that

> there are some people whose earliest recollections of childhood are concerned with everyday and indifferent events which could not produce any emotional effect even in children, but which are recollected (too clearly, one is inclined to say) in every detail, while approximately contemporary events, even if, on the evidence of their parents, they moved them intensely at the time, have not been retained in their memory (III, 305-06).

Such memories seem to argue against our assumption that we remember what is important to us and forget what is indifferent. Even more surprising, these recollections often have a sharpness and clarity of detail that are missing from other memories. Freud goes on to cite two examples from a survey on memory carried out by two French researchers, V. and C. Henri: first, of a philology professor

> whose earliest memory, dating back to between the ages

43

of three and four, showed him a table laid for a meal and on it a basin of ice. At the same period there occurred the death of his grandmother which, according to his parents, was a severe blow to the child. But the professor of philology... has no recollection of this bereavement (III, 306).

"Another man," Freud continues, "reports that his earliest memory is an episode upon a walk in which he broke off a branch from a tree.... There were several other people present, and one of them helped him" (III, 306).

Freud does not immediately attempt to interpret the examples, but he does explain that such impressions, "screen memories" (Deckerinnerungen) as he calls them, acquire their significance by virtue of their relation to more important experiences, which, through repression, have been obliterated. Two psychical forces oppose each other in this process:

> One of these forces takes the importance of the experience as a motive for seeking to remember it, while the other-- a resistance-- tries to prevent any such preference from being shown. These two opposing forces do not cancel each other out.... Instead, a compromise is brought about... What is recorded as a mnemic image is not the relevant experience itself... [but rather] another psychical element closely associated with the objectionable one (III, 307).

In other words, the indifferent impression is retained as a memory, not on account of its own content but "due to the relation holding between [this] content and a different one which has been suppressed" (III, 307).

The relation, in this case, is one of contiguity: "The essential elements of an experience are represented in memory by the inessential elements of the same experience" (III, 307). To illustrate the functioning of screen memories, Freud draws upon "a common saying among us about shams, that they are not made of gold themselves but have lain beside something that _is_ made of gold" (III, 307). This is no different from the rhetorical figure of metonymy, which substitutes "crown" for "monarch" because a crown happens to be associated with a ruler.

Example

The screen memory, then, is a trope. Rather than pausing here to consider the consequences of this insight for a theory of autobiography, we shall take Freud's cue and consider a detailed example. For at this point in the text, Freud, no longer satisfied with generalities, interrupts the theoretical portion of his essay in order to provide us with an example which, he claims, is particularly well-suited to his purposes. "Its value," says Freud," is certainly increased by the fact that it relates to someone who is not at all or only very slightly neurotic" (III, 309). This well-chosen example, however, does not simply illustrate the theoretical discussion that precedes it; as we shall see, it introduces a new kind of screen memory, one in which the relation between the screen and the suppressed material is not metonymic, but _allegorical_.

The example begins like many of Freud's case histories with the author introducing the patient to his readers. The patient is "a man of university education, aged thirty-eight.... He has taken an interest in psychological questions ever since I was able to relieve him of a slight phobia by means of psychoanalysis" (III, 309). The patient has studied the Henris' investigations on memory and this prompts him to relate a screen memory of his own:

> The scene appears to me fairly indifferent and I cannot understand why it should have become fixed in my memory. Let me describe it to you. I see a rectangular, rather steeply sloping piece of meadow-land, green and thickly grown; in the green there are a great number of yellow flowers --evidently common dandelions. At the top end of the meadow there is a cottage and in front of the cottage door two women are standing chatting busily, a peasant-woman with a handkerchief on her head and a children's nurse. Three children are playing in the grass. One of them is myself (between the age of two and three); the two others are my boy cousin, who is a year older than me, and his sister, who is almost exactly the same age as I am. We are picking the yellow flowers and each of us is holding a bunch of flowers we have already picked. The little girl has the best bunch; and, as though by mutual agreement, we --the two boys-- fall on her and snatch away her flowers. She runs up the meadow in tears and as a consolation the peasant-woman gives her a big piece of black bread. Hardly have we seen this than we throw the flowers away, hurry to the cottage and ask to be given some bread too. And we are in fact given some; the peasant-woman cuts the loaf with a long knife. In my memory the bread tastes quite delicious --and at that point the scene breaks off (III, 311).

"Now," the patient asks Freud, "what is there in this occurrence to justify the expenditure of memory which it has occasioned me?" (III, 311). Freud answers with another question, asking

> since when he had been occupied with this recollection: whether he was of opinion that it had recurred to his memory periodically since his childhood, or whether it had perhaps emerged at some later time on some occasion that could be recalled (III, 312).

Thus prompted, the patient continues:

It seems to me almost a certainty that this childhood memory never occurred to me at all in my earlier years. But I can also recall the occasion which led to my recovering this and many other recollections of my earliest childhood. When I was seventeen and at my secondary school, I returned for the first time to my birthplace for the holidays.... I was the child of people who were originally well-to-do and who, I fancy, lived comfortably enough in that little corner of the provinces. When I was about three, the branch of industry in which my father was concerned met with a catastrophe. He lost all his means and we were forced to leave the place and move to a large town. Long and difficult years followed.... I never felt really comfortable in the town.... Those holidays, when I was seventeen, were my first holidays in the country .... I could compare the comfort reigning there with our own style of living at home in the town. But it is no use evading the subject any longer: I must admit that there was something else that excited me powerfully. I was seventeen, and in the family where I was staying there was a daughter of fifteen, with whom I immediately fell in love... but I kept it completely secret. After a few days the girl went off to her school.... I passed many hours in solitary walks through the lovely woods... and spent my time building castles in the air. These, strangely enough, were not concerned with the future but sought to improve the past. If only the smash had not occurred! If only I had stopped at home and grown up in the country and grown as strong as the young men in the house, the brothers of my love! And then if only I had followed my father's profession and if I had finally married her --for I should have known her intimately all those years!

The patient concludes by noting that the woman, whom he sees occasionally

is quite exceptionally indifferent to me. Yet I can remember quite well for what a long time afterwards I was affected by the yellow colour of the dress she was wearing when we first met, whenever I saw the same colour anywhere else (III, 312-13).

Freud now begins his interpretation by referring this last statement to a passing remark the patient had made in relating the screen memory, to the effect that he no longer liked the common dandelion.

Do you not suspect that there may be a connection between the yellow of the girl's dress and the ultra-clear yellow of the flowers in your childhood scene? (III, 313)

The patient agrees, then continues the story he has been relating:

> I now come to a second occasion which stirred up in me the impressions of my childhood.... I was seventeen when I revisited my birthplace. Three years later during my holidays I visited my uncle and met once again the children who had been my first playmates, the same two cousins, the boy... and the girl... who appear in the childhood scene with the dandelions (III, 314).

"And did you once more fall in love, " Freud asks, "--with your cousin this time?"

> No, this time things turned out differently. By then I was at the University and I was a slave to my books.... But I believe that my father and my uncle had concocted a plan by which I was to exchange the abstruse subject of my studies for one of more practical value, settle down, after my studies were completed, in the place where my uncle lived, and marry my cousin.... It was not until later, when I was a newly-fledged man of science and hard pressed by the exigencies of life... that I must have reflected that my father had meant well in planning this marriage for me (III, 314).

With this additional information, Freud is able to construct the meaning of the screen memory:

> The element on which you put most stress in your childhood scene was the fact of the country-made bread tasting so delicious.... This idea... corresponded to your phantasy of the comfortable life you would have led if you had stayed at home and married this girl... or, in symbolic language, of how sweet the bread would have tasted for which you had to struggle so hard in your later years. The yellow of the flowers, too, points to the same girl. But there are also elements in the childhood scene which can only be related to the <u>second</u> phantasy --of being married to your cousin. Throwing away the flowers in exchange for bread strikes me as not a bad disguise for the scheme your father had for you: you were to give up your unpractical ideals and take on a 'bread-and-butter' occupation (<u>Brotstudium</u>), were you not? (III, 315)

In this example, unlike the metonymic screen memory Freud discusses in the first portion of the essay, the screen memory is separated in time from what it disguises. Furthermore, the suppressed material is here not a memory, but a fantasy. The early childhood memory functions as an allegory for "the most momentous turning-points" in the patient's life, and symbols --bread and flowers-- represent "the influence of the two most powerful motive forces --hunger and love" (III, 316).

Once Freud has explained this, the patient goes on to add that

> the essence of [the screen memory] is its representation of love. Now I understand for the first time. Think for a moment! Taking flowers away from a girl means to deflower her (einem Mädchen die Blume wegnehmen, das heißt ja: deflorieren). What a contrast between the boldness of this phantasy and my bashfulness on the first occasion (III, 316).

As Freud explains, it is this last "coarsely sensual" element of the fantasy that accounts for the formation of the screen memory. In order for a screen memory to be formed, there must be some resistance to the material's finding more direct expression.

After they have discerned the meaning of the screen memory, Freud and his patient turn to consider its "genuineness." Freud admits that "there is in general no guarantee of the data produced by our memory," and compares the unconscious construction of such memories to "works of fiction" (III, 315). Nevertheless, he grants the possibility that the memory is genuine: "If so, you selected it from innumerable others of a similar or another kind because, on account of its content (which in itself was indifferent) it was well adapted to represent the two phantasies, which were important enough to you" (III, 315). It is not the question of authenticity that distinguishes screen memories from other recollections: a screen memory may or may not be fictional. What matters is the added meaning that the memory has taken on, its ability to function as an allegory. This may entail a reworking of the childhood memory; the details may be "remodelled" (III, 315) to better suit the thoughts seeking expression.

The patient, however, is not convinced by Freud's argument and suspects that the scene "has been unjustifiably smuggled in among my childhood memories" (III, 318). At this point, the analyst "must take up the defence of its genuineness", pointing out that

> it contains elements which have not been solved by what you have told me and which do not in fact fit in with the sense required by the phantasy.... For instance, your boy cousin helping you to rob the little girl of her flowers-- can you make any sense of the idea of being helped in deflowering someone? ... So the phantasy does not coincide completely with the childhood scene. It is only based on it at certain points. That argues in favour of the childhood memory being genuine (III, 318-19).

A certain effet de réel, a portion of the impression that seems to resist an allegorical interpretation, witnesses for the memory's authenticity.

At the end of their discussion, Freud and his patient decide to "amuse themselves" by interpreting the two short examples of screen memories taken from the Henris' study. They can make nothing of the basin of ice on the dinner table, but conclude that the second example, of the man who pulled off the branch of a tree, is probably a masturbation fantasy. In a reversal of roles, it is the patient who explains that "what provides the intermediate step between a screen memory and what it conceals is likely to be a verbal expression" (III, 319). In this case, the expression "to pull one out" (sich einen ausreiBen), a vulgar term for "to masturbate," is represented as a concrete image.

Memory and Autobiographics

In his concluding remarks, Freud nuances the distinction he had earlier made between "screen memories" and other sorts of recollections. These final reflections cannot fail to affect any theory of autobiography that assumes that the writer's task is to shape the raw material of his memories into a coherent, aesthetic form. For what Freud proceeds to demonstrate is that memories, all memories, are already a product of such a shaping activity.

Opposing the "simple view" that screen memories are an exceptional case and that most memories "arise simultaneously with an experience as an immediate consequence of the impression it makes and that thereafter they recur from time to time in accordance with the familiar laws of reproduction," Freud points out that certain features of memories "do not tally with this view" (III, 321). Most importantly, it seems that

> in the majority of significant and in other respects unimpeachable childhood scenes the subject sees himself in the recollection as a child, with the knowledge that this child is himself; he sees this child, however, as an observer from outside the scene would see him.... Now it is evident that such a picture cannot be an exact repetition of the impression that was originally received. For the subject was then in the middle of the situation and was attending not to himself but to the external world (III, 321).

We are no longer speaking of screen memories in the strict sense. These are rather "significant" and "unimpeachable" childhood memories, yet they share with screen memories the quality of being formed, given a plastic form, at a later period.

> This contrast between the acting and the recollecting ego may be taken as evidence that the original impression has been worked over. It looks as though a memory-trace from childhood had here been translated back into a plastic and visual form at a later date --the date of the

memory's arousal. But no reproduction of the original impression has ever entered the subject's consciousness (III, 321).

Mnemic images are not photographic copies of an original impression; they are rather psychic constructions that shape and give a visual form to memory-traces.

This insight breaks down the distinction Freud draws at the beginning of his essay, between screen memories and other childhood recollections. He goes so far as to inquire "whether we have any memories at all _from_ our childhood: memories _relating to_ our childhood may be all that we possess" (III, 322). Furthermore, such memories "show us our earliest years not as they were but as they appeared at the later periods when the memories were aroused," that is, when they were _formed_. And, he adds, "a number of motives, with no concern for historical accuracy, had a part in forming them, as well as in the selection of the memories themselves" (III, 322).

This final conflation of screen memories with memory-formation in general casts a different light on the project of writing an autobiography. Most importantly, it suggests that autobiographics, the process of making sense of one's life, begins long before the planning, writing, or communicating of a text. Memories are not the raw material that must be refined, organized, and represented in textual form; they are themselves already a text, an effect of organization, selection, signification, and (internal) visual representation. The formation of memories is already a means of making sense, and the sense one assigns to one's life determines both the form and the content of conscious memories.

Thus, memories are already works of fiction: the metonymic or allegorical--tropological--structure of screen memories extends, to a certain degree, to all memories. The making of fictions is then not restricted to the literary writer but is a fundamental human activity, essential in the constituting of selfhood or identity. This is not to say, of course, that the written or oral autobiography is then merely a reproduction of the autobiographics of memory. There are further distortions, censorships, organizing movements, and aesthetic effects at work in this transformation of memory into text.

No doubt this is analogous to the transformation of dream-images into the language the dreamer uses in waking life to report the dream. In effect, in The Interpretation of Dreams, Freud answers the objection that what we remember of a dream "has been mutilated by the untrustworthiness of our memory" and may be "not only fragmentary but positively inaccurate and falsified" (V, 512), by explaining that, though this is true enough, the distortions involved are, first, only the last in a series of distortions, and second, by no means arbitrary. The dream is already a product of distortion; the _Traumarbeit_ condenses, displaces, censors, and distorts the dream-thoughts. But this distortion is not arbitrary; it reveals the dream-thoughts in the very attempt to conceal them. In the same way, "the modifications to which dreams are submitted under the editorship of waking life... are associatively linked to the material which they replace, and serve to show us the way to that material, which may in its turn be a substitute for something else" (V, 515).

In fact, Freud adds, when he finds a patient's account of a dream particularly hard to follow, he asks him to repeat it. The patient rarely uses the same words the second time; but it is precisely the parts of the account that he alters that tips Freud off. "Under pressure of the resistance... he hastily covers the weak spots in the dream's disguise by replacing any expressions that threaten to betray its meaning by other less revealing ones. In this way he draws my attention to the expression which he has dropped out" (V, 515). The various distortions, in other words, determined as they are by an effort to conceal, reveal in their very act of concealing.

Hence, the "secondary revision" (sekundäre Bearbeitung) involved in recording a dream in simply a further stage of the Traumarbeit that produced, and distorted, the dream in the first place. It is precisely the Freudian notion of Arbeit in all its forms (Traum- and Trauerarbeit, Bearbeitung and durcharbeiten)[2] that blurs the traditional distinction between "original" and "copy."[3] If we apply this model to the process of transforming memories into an autobiographical text, we see that an autobiography is not simply the more or less faithful reproduction of a self or a life, for the self is already a product of such an Arbeit. And the distortions involved at both the psychical and textual level do not simply interfere with an ideal reproducibility. The distortions themselves have a positive, signifying function. The selection of one memory over another and the reshaping of certain elements make sense, that is, they have a meaning since they are determined by unconscious motives, and they produce a meaning, give meaning to one's life.

Self-analysis

The homology between psychical operations and the writing of a text allows for the comparison between, for instance, a compulsion and a narrative or between a screen and an example that is selected to illustrate an argument. This is an especially promising strategy in the case of "Screen Memories." For Freud's essay is of more than theoretical interest. Its additional significance lies in what James Strachey terms "an extraneous fact" which has "undeservedly overshadowed" the "intrinsic interest" of the paper (III, 302) : the lengthy example that Freud reports in "Screen Memories" is an autobiographical one and the "well-chosen" illustration is drawn from Freud's own memory. But this fact can hardly be said to be extraneous, especially when, as Strachey says, the notion of screen memory was "brought into focus" by Freud's working through of this particular memory and "the topic was closely related to several others which had been occupying his mind... ever since he had embarked on his self-analysis in the summer of 1897" (III, 301).

Self-analysis: Strachey attaches no particular importance to the word or to the image it might convey. But is not Freud's long autobiographical example precisely a "self-analysis," or, to be more precise, a staging or visual representation of the verbal expression, "self-analysis"? And once we know that the "only very slightly neurotic patient" is in fact Freud himself, can we continue to look at the essay, or at Strachey's and Jones' comments in the same way?

This knowledge has a decidedly comic effect on the whole proceeding. It is not merely that Freud is literally talking to himself, holding an analytic dialogue with himself. He actually makes a point of underlining the differences between analyst and patient, both by presenting the "analysis" in dialogue form, and by carefully noting which party is responsible for the various insights in the analysis.

-- "I thought it advisable to ask him since when he had been occupied with this recollection," reports Freud the analyst. "This question was all that was necessary for me to contribute.... The rest was found by my collaborator himself, who was no novice at jobs of this kind" (III, 312).

-- "I have not yet considered that point," replies Freud the patient. "Now that you have raised the question...." (III, 312).

-- "I see now that I shall have to tell you a whole big piece of my history," Freud the patient tells Freud the analyst. "You have brought it upon yourself by your question. So listen" (III, 312).

-- "It is no use evading the subject any longer," confesses Freud the patient to himself, the physician. "I must admit there was something else" (III, 313).

-- The analyst interrupts his patient with an interpretation and the patient gently rebukes him: "But I have not finished yet" (III, 314).

-- The analyst is bewildered: "In this childhood scene of yours love is represented far less prominently than I should have expected." And the patient corrects him: "No. You are mistaken. The essence of it is its representation of love" (III, 316).

-- Finally, the patient is disconcerted by the analyst's claim that there is "no guarantee" for the genuineness of his memory. But the analyst reassures him: "I see that I must take up the defence of its genuineness" (III, 318).

And so on. The roles of analyst and patient are carefully constructed to represent the distance between the two selves, the collaboration of one with the other.

The "auto-analysis" ends with a discussion of auto-eroticism. The analyst enlists the aid of his patient in interpreting the screen memories from the Henri survey. They consider the example "to amuse ourselves" (_zum Scherz_, as a jest) (III, 319), and conclude that the pulling off of a branch signifies masturbation, or rather _could_ signify masturbation. The problem is that the expression "sich einen ausreiBen" is German, and the subject of the Henri survey is presumably French:

> However, our interpretation remains a jest (_Übrigens bleibt die Deutung ein Scherz_), since we have no idea whether a Frenchman would recognize an allusion to masturbation in the words _casser une branche d'un arbre_ or in some suitably emended phrase (III, 320).

Perhaps the example does not _really_ represent masturbation. Freud draws attention to the fact that someone helps the child pull off the branch of a tree. In his own screen memory, we recall, the boy cousin helps him "deflower" the little girl. In both cases, an illicit sexual activity is disguised as innocent play. Now, in the playful staging of his self-analysis, Freud the analyst has his "patient" _help_ him interpret the screen memory, a parallel that might lead us to ask, impertinently, just what Freud is trying to "pull off," just what game he is playing with himself. Freud's playfulness in representing his self-analysis certainly contrasts with Jones' earnestness in speaking of the "courage" of the undertaking. How does Freud view his self-analysis and why does he represent it as play?

We have seen that the form of Freud's example resembles a screen memory in several ways. First, it presents the self as an other, just as, in a childhood scene, the subject sees himself "as an observer from outside the scene would see him." Freud the analyst observes Freud the patient. Secondly, Freud tells us that "the intermediate step between a screen memory and what it conceals is likely to be a verbal expression." I have been suggesting that the example is an elaborate staging of the expression, "self--analysis." What, then, does the example screen? First, of course, it conceals its own autobiographical nature. Freud concludes his example by saying: "This analysis, which I have reproduced as accurately as possible, will, I hope, have to some extent clarified the concept of a 'screen memory'" (III, 320). As accurately as possible? Does Freud say this as a jest? Freud not only changes the details of the analysis (his "cousin" is in fact his nephew; most of the chronology is inaccurate; etc.), he also neglects to mention that the example is autobiographical, and he presents the self-analysis as a dialogue between two people. We may well say of this example, as Freud says of memory-foundation, that

> simple inaccuracy of recollection does not play any considerable part here.... Close investigation shows rather that these falsifications... are tendentious --that is, that they serve the purposes of the repression and replacement of objectionable or disagreeable impressions.... A number of motives, with no concern for historical accuracy, had a part in forming them (III, 322).

This suggests that there is something "objectionable or disagreeable" either in the content of the screen memory or in the activity of self-analysis itself. In fact, both elements contribute to the formation of this "screened memory." For the content of the screen memory is simply a mirror image of what is disguised in the example.

The screen memory, we recall, represents a "what if": what if I had followed my father's profession, chosen a _Brotstudium_, married the woman my father chose for me? It represents a desire to escape the "exigencies of life" that Freud's choice of career forced upon him. It expresses the wish to be reconciled with his father, to go along with his father's plans for him. In short, the screen memory stages Freud's temptation not to break with the father, set out on his own, and found psychoanalysis.

Yet Freud chooses to go his own way in defiance of his father. We have already noted the importance of his self-analysis for the foundation of psychoanalysis. We can now begin to see why this self-analysis is represented in disguised form as a playful masturbation: it is a defiant and derisive gesture directed at the father.

It is important to remember here that a screen memory is a compromise-formation: that is, it is designed not only to screen but also to reveal, to retain as well as to repress a memory. It is significant that Freud censors his example, conceals its autobiographical nature; but it is just as significant that he includes the example in the first place. What Freud reveals is nothing less than the very condition for the writing of "Screen Memories" and the psychoanalytic texts that will follow. In going against his father's hope for him and in refusing the love interest that his father has chosen for him, Freud can become the father of psychoanalysis. And this desire, barely alluded to in the form of the autobiographical example of "Screen Memories" finds full expression in other writings of the same period.

CHAPTER IV

THE INTERPRETATION OF DREAMS AS WORK OF MOURNING

Prefaces

On March 23, 1900, Freud writes his friend Wilhelm Fliess in Berlin:

> I heard with great satisfaction that your interest in my dream-child (<u>Traumkind</u>) is unabated.... I have now come down on the side of being very grateful to you for standing godfather to it.... It has been a consolation to me in many a gloomy hour to know I have this book to leave behind.[1]

This is the blessing Freud bestows on his favorite child, <u>The Interpretation of Dreams</u>: it will be a comfort to its father, the hope of the father for immortality. And it is not only the theoretical insight, the originality of the text that determines Freud's affection and esteem for the dream-child. Certain "subjective" considerations, only recognized after the child has been sent out into the world, play a part in the value Freud attaches to <u>The Interpretation of Dreams</u>.

In the original preface, indeed, Freud expresses his uneasiness about "the broken threads which so frequently interrupt my presentation" (IV, xxiii). One of the reasons for the fragmented form lies in the choice of material. Freud considers several possible sources of material on which to demonstrate his method of dream interpretation. Either he can discuss the dreams already appearing in published works, dreams from unknown sources; or he can report the dreams of his neurotic patients; or lastly, he can work on his own dreams. Each of these alternatives has its drawbacks but, Freud tells us, the first two options are precluded entirely: the first, on account of the nature of dream interpretation, which depends upon the associations of the dreamer; the second, because of certain complications that make the neurotic's dreams unsuitable as examples of the normal dream processes. Thus, Freud has <u>no choice</u> but to report his own dreams, even though he has considerable resistance to doing so.

This argument might at first appear cogent, were we not alerted to a characteristic protest. Explaining his reluctance to record his dreams, Freud writes:

55

But if I was to report my own dreams, it inevitably
followed that I should have to reveal to the public gaze
more of the intimacies of my mental life than I liked,
or than is normally necessary for any writer who is a man
of science and not a poet [Poet]. Such was the painful
but unavoidable necessity (IV, xxiii-ix).

We have already seen in both <u>Studies in Hysteria</u> and "Fragment of
an Analysis of a Case of Hysteria" why Freud's protest that he is
no poet cannot be taken at face value. In <u>The Interpretation of</u>
<u>Dreams</u>, too, we will have reason to consider the literary as
central to Freud's textual practice. But the argument, in
addition, contains a serious flaw: it presents as exclusive options
what are, in fact, complementary possibilities, <u>all of which</u> Freud
exploits in <u>The Interpretation of Dreams</u>. For Freud's text
includes literally dozens of dreams reported by his patients, as
well as by his children and friends. He also considers, from time
to time, dreams by people unknown to him. So that the preface
seriously distorts the actual content of the text. Why is Freud
so intent on convincing us that he had no choice? What is at stake
in the presentation of his dreams that leads Freud to justify his
action with an explanation that is blatantly false?

Freud ends his first preface by confessing that "I have been
unable to resist the temptation of taking the edge off some of my
indiscretions by omissions and substitutions" (IV, xxiv), and then
makes a plea for the reader's indulgence, begging "that anyone who
finds any sort of reference to himself in my dreams may be willing
to grant me the right of freedom of thought --in my dream-life, if
nowhere else" (IV, xxiv). Freud is in a "difficult situation" (IV,
xxiv). He does not want to reveal the intimacies of his life: he
only wants to be a conscientious scientist and to communicate to
his readers his findings on the functioning of the mind. He must
overcome, as much as possible, his personal reticence in order for
the work of scientific discovery to go forward. Certainly, his
readers will understand his predicament and treat him with
indulgence.

The second preface, written ten years later, tells a different
story. His readers have not been kind. Not that they have
objected to Freud's indiscretions, taken offense at the slandering
of his friends in the dreams he reports; rather, they have not
bothered to read his book at all. They have ignored or rejected
the son he sent out into the world:

My psychiatric colleagues seem to have taken no trouble
to overcome the initial bewilderment created by my new
approach to dreams.... The attitude adopted by reviewers
in the scientific periodicals could only lead one to
suppose that my work was doomed to be sunk into complete
silence (IV, xxv).

As the opposition, or rather the obliviousness, to his book becomes evident, Freud's esteem and affection for it increase. He explains that

> in the sphere of dream-life I have been able to leave my original assertions unchanged. During the long years in which I have been working at the problems of the neuroses I have often been in doubt and sometimes been shaken in my convictions. At such times it has always been the Interpretation of Dreams that has given me back my certainty. It is thus a sure instinct which has led my many scientific opponents to refuse to follow me more especially in my researches upon dreams (IV, xxv-vi).

Freud chastises his colleagues for overlooking the theoretical significance of his text; the personal nature of its content is no longer, and not yet, at issue. No longer, since the issue was already raised in the first preface; and not yet, because it surfaces again in the next paragraph. Freud admits that "this book has a further subjective significance for me personally --a significance which I only grasped after I had completed it. It was, I found, a portion of my own self-analysis, my reaction to my father's death..." (IV, xxvi). For this reason, Freud says "I felt unable to obliterate the traces of the experience" (IV, xxvi). The Interpretation of Dreams commemorates the death of the father and Freud's reaction to it. The material of the book, examples that ought to be indifferent in themselves, have a particular significance to Freud, since they record an important experience in his life. But lest we begin to catch a glimpse of what is at stake in the chastisement of his colleagues, his reason for being so disappointed that his cherished son is rejected by them, Freud immediately adds that the "subjective significance" is only important to him and that "to my readers... it will be a matter of indifference upon what particular material they learn to appreciate the importance of dreams and how to interpret them" (IV, xxvi).

Freud tries to enforce a strict distinction between the personal importance the material of The Interpretation of Dreams has for him and the theoretical significance of his discovery of the method of dream interpretation. One phrase, however, threatens to blur the careful distinction. The book, says Freud, records his reaction to his father's death, "that is to say, to the most important event, the most poignant loss, of a man's life" (IV, xxvi). The death of the father is not simply Freud's personal loss, a loss that happens, on this occasion, to affect him deeply. The death of the father is an event of general significance, a poignant loss for any man. The "personal" aspect of The Interpretation of Dreams is not simply autobiographical: it records the outcome of the Oedipal drama, a drama of mythical and universal importance, that is played out by every son. What Freud does not even whisper is that the outcome of the Oedipal drama may be related to the later reception of The Interpretation of Dreams, as

57

it is recorded in the later prefaces.

In 1911, for example, Freud expresses his pleasure at a "new turn of events" that made a third edition necessary after "scarcely more than a single year" (IV, xxvii). In 1914, he notes that an English translation has appeared and that Otto Rank has "contributed two self-contained chapters to the [German] text" (IV, xxviii). In 1918, he mentions that a Hungarian translation is about to appear (IV, xxix); and in 1921, he explains that the sixth edition has a "new task to perform. If its earlier function was to offer some information on the nature of dreams, now it has the no less important duty of dealing with the obstinate misunderstandings to which the information is subject" (IV, xxix-xxx). In 1929, Freud reports that his <u>Gesammelte Schriften</u> have appeared in print, and that French, Swedish, and Spanish translations of <u>The Interpretation of Dreams</u> have been published. And in the final "Preface to the Third (Revised) English Edition," Freud underlines the important role that psychoanalysis plays in "American intellectual life" and concludes that <u>The Interpretation of Dreams</u> contains "the most valuable of all the discoveries it has been my good fortune to make. Insight such as this falls to one's lot once in a lifetime" (IV, xxxii).

"<u>Viresque adquirit eundo</u>" ("And it gathers strength in going"), as Montaigne wrote of his own "book of the self."[2] <u>The Interpretation of Dreams</u>, Freud's cherished son whom he sends out into the world, establishes Freud as the father of psychoanalysis, extends his influence to every corner of the world. The book that works through the death of Freud's father establishes Freud's right to call himself "father." That is why we should not be too quick to conclude that when Freud speaks of his father's death in the second preface, he is merely referring to a man named Jakob Freud who passed away in 1896. Such an assumption should lead us to overlook a passage in the first chapter of his book which, though it precedes any mention of Freud's biological father, yet already sounds like a death knell.

<u>Glocken</u>

'I dreamt... that one spring morning I was going for a walk and was strolling through the green fields till I came to a neighbouring village, where I saw the villagers in their best clothes, with hymnbooks under their arms, flocking to the church. Of course! It was Sunday, and early morning service would soon be beginning. I decided I would attend it; but first, as I was rather hot from walking, I went into the churchyard which surrounded the church, to cool down. While I was reading some of the tombstones, I heard the bell-ringer climbing up the church tower and at the top of it I now saw the little village bell which would presently give the signal for the beginning of devotions. For quite a while it hung there motionless, then it began to swing, and suddenly its peal began to ring out clear and piercing that--so clear and piercing that it put an end to my sleep. But what was ringing was the alarm-clock.

Here is another instance. It was a bright winter's day and the streets were covered with deep snow. I had agreed to join a party for a sleigh-ride; but I had to wait a long time before news came that the sleigh was at the door. Now followed the preparations for getting in --the fur rug spread out, the foot-muff put ready-- and at last I was sitting in my seat. But even then the moment of departure was delayed till a pull at the reins gave the waiting horses the signal. Then off they started, and, with a violent shake, the sleigh bells broke into their familiar jingle --with such violence, in fact, that in a moment the cobweb of my dream was torn through. And once again it was only the shrill sound of the alarm-clock (der schrille Ton der Weckerglocke).

And now yet a third example. I saw a kitchenmaid, carrying several dozen plates piled on one another, walking along the passage to the dining-room. The column of china in her arms seemed to me in danger of losing its balance. "Take care," I exclaimed, "or you'll drop the whole load." The inevitable rejoinder duly followed: she was quite accustomed to that kind of job, and so on. And meanwhile my anxious looks followed the advancing figure. Then --just as I expected-- she stumbled at the threshold and the fragile crockery slipped and rattled and clattered in a hundred pieces on the floor. But the noise continued without ceasing, and soon it seemed no longer to be a clattering; it was turning into a ringing --and the ringing, as my waking self now became aware, was only the alarm-clock doing its duty' (IV, 27-28).

The above passage is already a quotation in Freud's text. He borrows it from F. W. Hildebrandt for his first chapter on "The Scientific Literature Dealing with the Problems of Dreams." The chapter is a result of comprehensive bibliographical scholarship, an exercise that Freud despised and abandoned in his later texts. The conclusion of this long and painstaking review of Freud's predecessors is, in essence, that no one has come close to understanding the function and significance of dreams. In fact, scientists have not even caught up with "lay opinion," the "ancient and jealously held popular belief" that dreams have a meaning; they have failed even to recognize that dreams can be interpreted (IV, 96, 100). Thus, in quoting the works of scientists and philosophers in his first chapter, Freud is not unlike the subject of Hildebrandt's first dream who reads the names and inscriptions on tombstones, considering the texts of dead authors who have nothing to say.[3]

In the second chapter, Freud will let the bells ring out, the bells that mark the end of the scientists' dark ignorance, and celebrate the discovery of the true method of dream interpretation. Freud announces the discovery in a tone of jubilation:

59

> We find ourselves in the full daylight (_Klarheit_) of a
> sudden discovery. Dreams are not to be likened to the
> unregulated sounds that rise from a musical instrument
> struck by the blow of some external force instead of by
> a player's hand; they are not meaningless; they are not
> absurd.... They are psychical phenomena of complete
> validity (IV, 122).

Dreams are pieces of music, not the cacophony of unregulated blows to a keyboard, nor clattering sounds on the threshold of consciousness. They are musical scores that can be interpreted, and Freud's jubilation at this discovery announces the brightness, the _Klarheit_, of day. Thus, Freud's discovery is a _Weckerglocke_ that tears through the cobweb of the scientists' sleep. But what is the relation of this jubilant mood to the impatient tone with which Freud dismisses his predecessors? What is the link between the _Weckerglocke_ of discovery and the _Totenglocke_, passing-bell or death knell, that commemorates the passing of Freud's ignorant forefathers?

Both _Weckerglocken_ and _Totenglocken_ mark the passage from one state to another, and both chime in the space between the two states. As Hildebrandt's dreams show, the ringing of an alarm clock may be incorporated into the dream, may prolong the dream for a moment before finally putting an end to it. In the same way, a death knell sounds after a death but before the body has been laid to rest. It commemorates, keeps the memory alive for a moment longer. And Freud's quotation of Hildebrandt's dreams fulfills the same function. The chiming effect of the quotation marks the death of Freud's scientific forefathers. Freud quotes in order to bury his predecessors, bury them at the threshold of his book. The quotation is also a knell.[4]

It is no surprise, then, that in two postscripts to the first chapter, Freud drives the last nails into the coffin and seals the tomb. In 1909, he explains that he has not extended his discussion of the pertinent literature on dreams to include works published in the period between the first and second editions, since "to continue the task would have cost me an extraordinary effort" (IV, 93). Besides, few of these new works have taken into account Freud's dream book and "if there were such a thing in science as a right to retaliate, I should certainly be justified in disregarding [their] literature." Freud's only response to these writers is "to suggest their reading the book again --or perhaps, indeed, merely to suggest their reading it" (IV, 93). Thus, Freud retaliates against his scientific colleagues by turning his back on them, declaring them legally dead.

By 1914, however, the situation has turned around. The Interpretation of Dreams has at last found its audience and "has raised a whole series of fresh considerations and problems" (IV, 95). But, since Freud himself has become a predecessor, "I cannot give an account of these works... before I have expounded those views of my own on which they are based" (IV, 95). As the recognized father of dream interpretation, Freud's own predecessors are now safely buried away. Final stroke of the Totenglocke.

The Work of Mourning

The jubilant mood in which Freud announces his findings, bringing dream interpretation to the light of day, even as he sounds the death knell for his scientific forefathers, is in keeping with the theoretical content of one of his later essays, "Mourning and Melancholia." The loss of a loved one, Freud tells us, will provoke one of three possible reactions. In order of severity these are: normal mourning, pathological or obsessional mourning, and melancholia. The term "mourning" (Trauer) generally refers to a loss through death, though it may also be "the loss of some abstraction... such as one 's country, liberty, an ideal, and so on" (XIV, 243). The death of a loved one may also bring on melancholia, but often the loss in this case is "of a more ideal kind" (XIV, 245). It may result, for example, from being jilted by a loved one; at times, indeed, "one feels justified in maintaining the belief that a loss... has occurred, but one cannot see clearly what it is that has been lost" (XIV, 245).

In all three reactions to a loss, the disappearance of the "libidinal object" is perceived as a threat to the ego and the process of mourning (or of melancholia) works to detach the self from the lost object. "This demand," writes Freud, "arouses understandable opposition" (XIV, 244).

> Normally, respect for reality gains the day (den Sieg behält). Nevertheless its orders cannot be obeyed at once. They are carried out bit by bit, at great expense of time and cathectic energy, and in the meantime the existence of the lost object is psychically prolonged. Each single one of the memories and expectations in which the libido is bound to the object is brought up and hypercathected, and detachment of the libido is accomplished in respect of it.... When the work of mourning is completed the ego becomes free and uninhibited again (XIV, 244-45, emphasis mine).

Freud adds that "the ego, confronted as it were with the question of whether it shall share [the lost object's] fate, is persuaded by the sum of the narcissistic satisfactions it derives from being alive to sever its attachment to the object that has been abolished" (XIV, 255). In other words, "mourning impels the ego to give up the object by declaring the object to be dead and offering the ego the inducement of continuing to live" (XIV, 257).

We are then justified in comparing the work of mourning to a death knell. The Trauerarbeit chimes for each individual memory, investing then detaching libidinal energy, like the stroke and resonance of a bell. The work of mourning prolongs the existence of the object, but only to rid the ego of it in the end. With every chime, the loved one dies a bit; the mourner detaches himself from the object, triumphs over the object, and allows himself to go on living. The death knell tolls for the benefit of the mourner; the work of mourning rescues him from the danger of death. Like the Weckerglocke, the work of mourning marks the passage from darkness to light.

In "Mourning and Melancholia," Freud attempts to "throw some light on the nature of melancholia by comparing it with the normal affect of mourning" (XIV, 243). It becomes evident, however, that even this "normal affect" is not entirely comprehensible; in particular, "we do not even know the economic means by which mourning carries out its task" (XIV, 255). This enigma concerning the economy of pain makes it impossible to explain why melancholia should sometimes be accompanied by "mania --a state which is the opposite of it in its symptoms" (XIV, 253), while normal mourning includes no manic phase.

Freud believes that he can explain mania by comparing it to the similar normal states of "joy, exultation or triumph" which result when "a large expenditure of psychical energy, long maintained or habitually occurring, has at last become unnecessary, so that it is available for numerous applications and possibilities of discharge" (XIV, 254). Thus, energy that has been "bound" is suddenly released. In the case of the melancholic, Freud speculates, "the ego must have got over the loss of the object... and thereupon the whole quota of anticathexis which the painful suffering of melancholia had drawn to itself from the ego and 'bound' will have become available" (XIV, 254-55). Mania, then, represents a liberation of the energy involved in the work of melancholia, a phase of freedom from, or triumph over, the object.

"This explanation certainly sounds plausible," Freud admits, but it does not explain the absence of a manic phase in normal mourning, which also entails a total absorption of the ego's energy until the loss of the object is overcome. "Why, then, after it has run its course, is there no hint in its case of the economic condition for a phase of triumph?" (XIV, 255) The answer to this question must lie in the distinction between mourning and melancholia. Freud explains that normal, "profound" mourning resembles in every respect but one the pathological condition of melancholia. It involves "the same painful frame of mind, the same loss of interest in the outside world... the same loss of capacity to adopt any new object of love... and the same turning away from any activity that is not connected with thoughts of [the loved one]" (XIV, 244). If the ambivalence of the love relationship is especially pronounced, it may lead the mourner (like the melancholic) to form "self-reproaches to the effect that [he] himself is to blame for the loss of the loved object, i.e., that he has willed it" (XIV, 251). In this instance, the obsessional nature of the self-reproaches transforms normal mourning into "pathological mourning" (XIV, 250). The condition of melancholia is even more complex. Not only does it entail a loss of interest in the outside world and self-reproaches for having willed the object's disappearance, it also involves "an extraordinary diminution" in self-regard (XIV, 246-47). Whereas for the mourner, it is the world that seems poor and empty, since it no longer contains the loved object, for the melancholic, it is the ego that seems empty. Freud explains that "the analogy with mourning led us to conclude that he has suffered a loss in regard to an object; what he tells us points to a loss in regard to his ego" (XIV, 246). The loss of self-respect characteristic of mourning indicates that there has been "an _identification_ of the ego with the abandoned object" (XIV, 249). In melancholia, in other words, the ego itself is split: one part identifies itself with the lost object and the other part, a critical agency, reproaches the ego that has been split off as if it were the libidinal object. All the ambivalence that the ego feels for the lost object is directed against itself. "Thus the shadow of the object fell upon the ego" (XIV, 249).

Since it is this identification of the ego with the lost object that distinguishes melancholia from both normal and pathological mourning, it must be this characteristic that accounts for the manic phase proper to melancholia. The work of melancholia, according to this hypothesis, would require a greater investment of energy than the corresponding work of mourning; the conflict within the ego would act like "a painful wound" that draws a tremendous amount of energy to itself. When the work of melancholia comes to an end, that surplus of energy, no longer necessary, would be released in a phase of mania.

Freud, however, is not satisfied with this explanation either and leaves the question unresolved. As long as the economics of pain remains a mystery, the manic phase of melancholia lies beyond comprehension. For this reason, Freud finds it necessary to "call a halt and to postpone any further explanation of mania." At this moment of irresolution, "Mourning and Melancholia" breaks off.

In his "Editor's Note," James Strachey points out that although Freud rarely made use of the analogy between mourning and melancholia apart from this essay, he did address the problem in an early draft. In fact, Strachey notes, "we find [here] one of the most remarkable instances of Freud's pre-vision" (XIV, 240). The passage is among the drafts that Freud sent to Fliess and was written some eighteen years before "Mourning and Melancholia":

> Hostile impulses against parents (a wish that they should die) are also an integral part of neuroses. They come to light consciously in the form of obsessional ideas. In paranoia the worst delusions of persecution (pathological distrust of rulers and monarchs) correspond to these impulses. They are repressed at periods in which pity for one's parents is active --at times of their illness or death. One of the manifestations of grief (_Trauer_) is then to reproach oneself for their death (cf. what are described as "melancholias") or to punish oneself in a hysterical way by putting oneself into their position with an idea of retribution.... It seems as though in sons this death-wish is directed

63

against their father and in daughters against their mother.[6]

The most striking difference between this early draft and "Mourning and Melancholia" (which dates from 1915) is that, whereas in the later essay the "libidinal object" is unspecified, here it is clearly a parent who has died (a footnote informs us that this is the "first hint of the Oedipus complex"). The draft was written on May 31, 1897, just six months after the death of Freud's father and at the very beginning of the self-analysis. Not surprisingly, Freud's first consideration of the problem of mourning comes as a result of the loss of his own father. And, to judge from the distinctions he makes in the essay of 1915, Freud's reaction to that death was not "normal" mourning, but melancholia.[7] For the work of mourning, as it develops in The Interpretation of Dreams, includes a clear phase of mania --of megalomania, to be exact.

Ambition

One of the first disagreeable discoveries Freud makes about his unconscious when he turns to analyze his dreams is that he possesses "a pathological ambition which I did not recognize in myself and believed was alien to me" (IV, 192). This boundless ambition finds its clearest expression in dreams about his father. Freud reports a long dream he had while on a train journey. The fourth and last episode of this dream proceeded:

> Once more I was in front of the [train] station, but this time in the company of an elderly gentleman. I thought of a plan for remaining unrecognized; and then saw that this plan had already been put into effect. It was as though thinking and experiencing were one and the same thing. He appeared to be blind, at all events with one eye, and I handed him a male glass urinal (which we had to buy or had bought in town). So I was a sick-nurse and had to give him the urinal because he was blind. If the ticket-collector were to see us like that, he would be certain to let us get away without noticing us. Here the man's attitude and his micturating penis appeared in plastic form. (This was the point at which I awoke, feeling a need to micturate.) (IV, 210-11)

Claiming that he will not give a "detailed analysis" of this part of the dream but will "merely pick out the elements leading to the two childhood scenes on whose account alone I embarked upon a discussion of this dream" (IV, 215), Freud explains: "It will rightly be suspected that what compels me to make this suppression is sexual material; but there is no need to rest content with this explanation" (IV, 215). The explanation may be correct, but one need not be satisfied with it, since it answers the wrong question. The important question for dream interpretation is not what Freud conceals from his readers, but what he has concealed from himself, that is, "the motives for the <u>internal</u> censorship which hid the true content of the dream from myself" (IV, 215). Freud then reveals to his readers what he has until now concealed even from himself: the dream analysis showed that the episodes were "impertinent boastings, the issue of an absurd megalomania which had long been suppressed in my waking life" (IV, 215).

After this brief explanation, Freud returns to "the material relating to the two childhood scenes which I have promised my readers (<u>den zwei versprochenen Kinderszenen</u>)" (IV, 215). This promised material concerns, precisely, promises:

> It appears that when I was two years old I still occasionally <u>wetted the bed</u>, and when I was reproached for this I <u>consoled</u> my father by promising to buy him a nice <u>new red</u> bed in N., the nearest town of any size. This was the origin of the parenthetical phrase in the dream to the effect that we had bought or had to buy the urinal in town: one must keep one's promises (<u>was man versprochen hat, muB man halten</u>) (IV, 216).

Freud had promised to buy his father a new bed to replace the one he had wetted; in his dream, he buys a urinal so that an elderly man can urinate. But what precisely is the meaning of the imperative, "One must keep one's promises," that Freud appends so curiously to his interpretation? Are we to conclude that buying the urinal in the dream fulfills the promise Freud made to his father as a child?

Freud tells us that "this promise of mine exhibited all the megalomania of childhood.... We have... learned from the psychoanalysis of neurotic subjects the intimate connection between bed-wetting and the character trait of ambition" (IV, 216). The act of wetting the bed is already a sign (a promise?) of ambition and Freud's promise to buy his father a new bed, a promise that apparently tries to compensate for wetting the bed, is in fact an additional expression of megalomania. The compensation for the wrongdoing merely supplements the original act.

Freud goes on to relate the second scene from childhood that played a role in the dream:

> When I was seven or eight years old there was another domestic scene, which I can remember very clearly. One evening before going to sleep I disregarded the rules that modesty lays down and obeyed the calls of nature in my parents' bedroom while they were present. In the course of my reprimand, my father let fall the words: 'The boy will come to nothing.' This must have been a frightful blow to my ambition, for references to this scene are constantly recurring in my dreams and are always linked with an enumeration of my achievements and successes, as though I wanted to say: 'You see, I <u>have</u> come to something' (IV, 216).

Once more, there is a micturition, a reprimand, and a compensation. Freud explains that this childhood scene "provided the material for the final episode of the dream, in which --by revenge, of course-- the roles were interchanged" (IV, 216). The blind old man represents Freud's father (who suffered from unilateral glaucoma) and the dream expresses the triumph over his father in two ways: first, by making him submit to the same humiliation that the son had to endure, when, as a child, he was reprimanded for urinating in front of his father; and secondly, by telling him that his son has after all made something of himself. "In the reference to his glaucoma I was reminding him of the cocaine, which had helped him in the operation, as though I had in that way kept my promise... and I revelled in allusions to my discoveries in connection with the theory of hysteria, of which I felt so proud" (IV, 216-17). Freud discovered the anaesthetic properties of cocaine and contributed to its widespread use in the treatment of glaucoma: thus, when he alludes to his father's glaucoma in the dream, he is telling his father that he has kept his ambitious promise.

The father's reprimand, "The boy will come to nothing," is actually a misinterpretation of the micuturition, which means, precisely, "I have ambition. I will amount to something." Freud's response to the reprimand is to enumerate his successes, which repeats the very thing that he was reprimanded for. When Freud expresses his ambition and the fruits of that ambition, he is once more micturating in front of his father.

In a lengthy footnote appended to his analysis of the dream, Freud offers "some further interpretive material," that is, he continues to enumerate his successes for his reader:

> The phrase '<u>thinking and experiencing were one and the same thing</u>' had a reference to the explanation of hysterical symptoms, and the '<u>male urinal</u>' belonged to the same connection. I need not explain to a Viennese the principle of '<u>Gschnas</u>'. It consists in constructing what appear to be rare and precious objects out of trivial and preferably comic and worthless materials (for instance, in making armour out of saucepans, wisps of straw and dinner rolls) --a favourite pastime at bohemian parties here in Vienna. I had observed that this is precisely what hysterical subjects do: alongside what has really happened to them, they unconsciously build up frightful or perverse imaginary events which they construct out of the most innocent and everyday material of their experience. It is to these phantasies that their symptoms are in the first instance attached and not to their recollections of real events, whether serious or equally innocent. This revelation had helped me over a number of difficulties and had given me particular pleasure. What made it possible for me to refer to this by means of the dream-element 'male urinal' was as follows. I had been told that at the latest '<u>Gschnas</u>'-night a poisoned chalice belonging to Lucrezia

Borgia had been exhibited; its central and principal constituent had been a male urinal of the type used in hospitals (IV, 217).

Thus, the "male urinal" alludes to one of Freud's achievements, the discovery that the functioning of hysteria resembles the "principle of 'Gschnas.'" This principle would seem to apply equally to the formation of dreams, since they too take the indifferent impressions of the "dream-day" (the day preceding the night of the dream) and fashion them into a dream language that expresses significant conflicts in the dreamer's life. In fact, Gschnas is a rather apt description of The Interpretation of Dreams itself, a magnum opus built out of autobiographical incidents and apparently absurd dreams. We already know that Freud's understanding of the functioning of dreams was also a revelation that "helped me over a number of difficulties and had given me particular pleasure."

In a more direct way, the dream-element "cocaine" alludes to the writing of The Interpretation of Dreams. This allusion is spelled out in another dream Freud reports:

> I had written a monograph on a certain plant. The book lay before me and I was at the moment turning over a folded coloured plate. Bound up in each copy there was a dried specimen of the plant, as though it had been taken from a herbarium (IV, 169).

In his lengthy analysis of the dream, Freud explains that "I really had written something in the nature of a mondgraph on a plant, namely a dissertation of the coca-plant" (IV, 170). He goes on to underline the importance that this discovery had in his father's glaucoma operation. The very next element alludes to The Interpretation of Dreams:

> I saw the monograph which I had written lying before me. This again led me back to something. I had had a letter from my friend [Fliess] in Berlin the day before in which he had shown his power of visualization: 'I am very much occupied with your dream-book. I see it lying finished before me and I see myself turning over its pages.' How much I envied him his gift as a seer! If only I could have seen it lying finished before me! (IV, 172, Strachey's brackets)

Thus, the dream expresses his wish to see The Interpretation of Dreams finished, to add this contribution to the one he had already made on cocaine.

The dream-element "coloured plate," in addition, alludes to two memories that combine the idea of "book" with "father." The first episode occurred during Freud's early childhood:

> It had once amused my father to hand over a book with

coloured plates... for me and my eldest sister to destroy.... The picture of the two of us blissfully pulling the book to pieces... was almost the only plastic memory that I retained from that period of my life.... I had recognized that the childhood scene was a 'screen memory' for my later bibliophile propensities (IV, 172-73).

In the early scene, the father actually encourages his son's interest in books (in reading and writing them but especially, in destroying them. Freud adds parenthetically that this was "not easy to justify from the educational point of view." Yet Freud's treatment of books by other authors, in the first chapter of The Interpretation of Dreams, for instance, indicates that Freud had learned his lesson well.)

In the later scene, dating from his adolescence, Freud reports that his father was not always amused at his son's interest in books: "When I was seventeen I had run up a largish account at the bookseller's and had nothing to meet it with; and my father had scarcely taken it as an excuse that my inclinations might have chosen a worse outlet" (IV, 173). Freud is reprimanded for having too much to do with books; since it is through books that Freud will realize his ambitions, we again have a parallel to the micturition scene. The conflict over books also recalls the situation reported in "Screen Memories," where Freud goes against his father's wishes and continues his studies. In that instance, it is clear that the "worse outlet" that his adolescent "inclinations" might have found is the company of women. It appears that the choice for Freud is often between love and books (his means of achieving ambition).

In case he has not given us enough clues to indicate that the botanical monograph dream expresses his defiant wish to prove to his father that he has amounted to something by writing The Interpretation of Dreams, Freud concludes the discussion by saying:

I can assure my readers that the ultimate meaning of the dream, which I have not disclosed, is intimately related to the subject of the childhood... memory of my father, when I was a boy of five, giving me a book illustrated with coloured plates to destroy (IV, 191).

I will not attempt to reconstruct the "ultimate meaning" that Freud has chosen to conceal; no doubt the concealment itself is part of the meaning.

The male urinal dream is actually the fourth and last episode of a long dream Freud reports. The second and third episodes are interpreted much later in The Interpretation of Dreams, and serve as a sequel of sorts to the fourth part. The section is entitled "Absurd Dreams," and, as Freud explains, all the dreams considered in this section "deal (by chance, as it may seem at first sight) with the dreamer's dead father" (V, 426). Here is the third of the four episodes:

> I was driving (Ich fahre) in a cab and ordered the driver to drive me to a station (zu einem Bahnhof zu fahren). 'Of course I can't drive with you along the railway line itself' I said, after he had raised some objection, as though I had overtired him. It was as if I had already driven with him for some of the distance one normally travels by train (mit der Bahn fahrt) (V, 432).

Several days before Freud had this dream, he had made a trip with his brother on a train. The brother accompanied him to the railway station, but "jumped out shortly before we got there, at the suburban railway station adjoining the main line terminus, in order to travel to Purkersdorf by the suburban line" (V, 432). At that time, Freud remarked to his brother "that he might have stayed with me a little longer by travelling to Purkersdorf by the main line instead of the suburban one" (V, 432). He adds that

> this led to the passage in the dream in which I drove in the cab for some of the distance one normally travels by train. This was an inversion of what had happened in reality.... What I had said to my brother was: 'you can travel on the main line in my company for the distance you would travel by the suburban line' (V, 432-33).

Freud introduces an "absurdity" into the dream by replacing "suburban line" with "cab" and makes it "scarcely possible to disentangle" the events of the dream. Since there seemed to be no reason for this confusion, Freud concludes that he "must have arranged the whole of this enigmatic business in the dream on purpose" (V, 433). This calculated absurdity in the dream should be translated by the clause, "It is absurd.. " and this judgment understood to apply to the notion of "fahren." This term in the dream alludes to two riddles that Freud had heard several evenings before. They ran as follows:

> Der Herr befiehlt's
> Der Kutscher tut's.
> Ein jeder hat's
> Im Grabe ruht's.

> Der Herr befiehlt's
> Der Kutscher tut's
> Nicht jeder hat's
> In der Wiege ruht's.

Strachey translates:

> With the master's request
> The driver complies:
> By all men possessed.

In the graveyard it lies.

With the master's request
The driver complies :
Not by all men possessed
In the cradle it lies. (V, 433-34)

The solution of the riddles relies on a pun involving compounds of "fahren" and "kommen." The answer to the first is "Vorfahren," both "drive up" and "ancestry." Similarly, the answer to the second riddle is "Nachkommen," "follow or come after" and "progeny." The dream thought expressed here is: "It is absurd to be proud of one's ancestry; it is better to be an ancestor oneself" (V, 434), and the judgement that something is absurd translates into an absurdity in the dream.

Freud concludes that an absurd dream often has "criticism or ridicule as its motive" and that it is no accident that such dreams so often deal with a dead father. "In such cases, the conditions for creating absurd dreams are found together in characteristic fashion" (V, 434-35). The authority that the father exerts over his children leads them to resent him and to seek out his weaknesses in order to criticize him; but the "filial piety" they feel toward him, especially after his death, "tightens the censorship which prohibits any such criticism from being consciously expressed" (V, 435).

In the "male urinal" dream, Freud humiliates his father by making him micturate in front of his son, just as the son had been humiliated when he micturated before the father. The father is placed in the position of the son. In the "fahren" dream, however, Freud puts himself in the position of his father: he desires to triumph over his father by becoming an ancestor himself.

Freud's ambition is represented as micturition in another dream, but this time, the enumeration of his accomplishments is not an attempt to prove to his father that he has amounted to something, but rather to leave his children with a legacy:

A hill, on which there was something like an open-air closet: a very long seat with a hole at the end of it. Its back edge was thickly covered with small heaps of faeces of all sizes and degrees of freshness. There were bushes behind the seat. I micturated on the seat; a long stream of urine washed everything clean; the lumps of faeces came away easily and fell into the opening. It was as though at the end there was still some left (V, 468-69).

Freud interprets:

The most agreeable and satisfying thoughts contributed to bringing the dream about. What at once occurred to me in the analysis were the Augean stables which were cleansed by Hercules. This Hercules was I. The hill and bushes came from Aussee, where my children were stopping at the time. I had discovered the infantile aetiology of the neuroses and had thus saved my own children from falling ill.... The stream of urine which washed everything clean was an unmistakable sign of greatness. It was in that way that Gulliver extinguished the great fire in Lilliput.... Gargantua, too, Rabelais' superman, revenged himself in the same way on the Parisians by sitting astride on Notre Dame and turning his stream of urine upon the city (V, 469).

In this second dream of micturition, the father has disappeared. Or rather, Freud himself has become a father, a mighty father patterned on Hercules and the two giants, Gulliver and Gargantua. It is as if Freud had taken to heart the admonition of his dream: "It is absurd to be proud of one's ancestors, it is better to be an ancestor oneself." The micturition is no longer a defiant promise made to the father, an expression of the son's ambition: it expresses the fulfillment of the ambition, the washing away of the neuroses, the legacy that Freud leaves to his children. This second micturition, then, fulfills the promise of the first: Freud has amounted to something, has taken the place of the father, and has left a legacy to his children.[8]

This legacy is a text, progeny of another sort, the dream-child that Freud speaks so fondly of in his letter to Fliess. In yet another dream, Freud reports:

Old Brücke must have set me some task; STRANGELY ENOUGH [SONDERBAR GENUG], it related to a dissection of the lower part of my own body, my pelvis and legs, which I saw before me as though in the dissecting-room, but without noticing their absence in myself and also without a trace of any gruesome feeling. Louise N. was standing beside me and doing the work with me.... I was then once more in possession of my legs and was making my way through the town. But (being tired) I took a cab.... Finally I was making a journey through a changing landscape with an Alpine guide who was carrying my belongings. Part of the way he carried me too, out of consideration for my tired legs. The ground was boggy; we went round the edge; people were sitting on the ground like Red Indians or gipsies --among them a girl. Before this I had been making my own way forward over the slippery around with a constant feeling of surprise that I was able to do it so well after the dissection. A t last we reached a small wooden house at the end of which was an open window. There the guide let me down and laid the wooden boards, which were standing ready, upon the window-sill, so as to bridge the chasm which had to be crossed over from the window. At that point I really became frightened about my legs, but instead of the expected crossing, I saw two grown-up men lying on wooden benches that were along the walls of the hut, and what

> seemed to be two children sleeping beside them. It was
> as though what was going to make the crossing possible
> was not the boards but the children. I awoke in a mental
> fright (V, 452-53).

The section of The Interpretation of Dreams in which this dream appears deals with the nature of judgements made in the course of a dream. Thus, Freud begins by explaining that what appears to be a judgement about the the task Brücke had assigned him, the expression "strangely enough," is in fact merely an allusion to a conversation from his waking life concerning a "strange book," H. Rider Haggard's She. In this conversation, his friend Louise N. asks to borrow a book so that she will have something to read. He offers her Haggard's book, explaining that it is "full of hidden meaning... the eternal feminine, the immortality of our emotions" (V, 453). But Louise N. is already familiar with the book and asks instead for something Freud himself has written. Freud replies: "My own immortal works have not yet been written." His friend then asks, somewhat sarcastically, "Well, when are we to expect these so-called ultimate explanations of yours which you've promised even we shall find readable?" This prompts Freud to reflect

> on the amount of self-discipline it was costing me to
> offer the public even my book upon dreams --I should have
> to give away so much of my own private character in it.
> The task which was imposed on me in the dream of carrying
> out a dissection of my own body was thus my self-analysis
> which was linked up with my giving an account of my
> dreams (V, 454-55).

The dream expresses a number of autobiographical themes already familiar to us: once more, the self-analysis (represented, as in "Screen Memories," in plastic form) is a means of producing an immortal work, a means of founding psychoanalysis. The quest for immortality, despite Freud's resistance to revealing his inner self, is carried out by way of a self-analysis and its publication as The Interpretation of Dreams. The desire for immortality must pass through autobiography. Yet the self-analysis, the condition for attaining immortality, is also a hindrance toward that goal. In the dream, Freud is unsure how far his legs, which have just been dissected, will carry him. He is not sure that he will attain immortality on such a shaky support.

Freud points out that "numerous elements of the dream were derived" from Rider Haggard's novel She. Most importantly, the novel treats the question of immortality:

> The end of the adventure in She is that the guide,
> instead of finding immortality for herself and the
> others, perishes in the mysterious subterranean fire.
> A fear of that kind was unmistakably active in the
> dream-thoughts, the 'wooden house' was also, no doubt,
> a coffin.... Accordingly, I woke up in a 'mental

> fright,' even after the successful emergence of the idea
> that children may perhaps achieve what their father has
> failed to --a fresh allusion to the strange novel in
> which a person's identity is retained through a series
> of generations for over two thousand years (V, 454-55).

In this allusion to a second sort of "immortal works," human children, Freud identifies with Kallikrates, the protagonist of She who, through a series of reincarnations, retains his identity over thousands of years, continually renewing his search for "an undiscovered region" (V, 454). For Freud, this is the "underworld" of the unconscious. Thus, his dream is an interpretation of a literary text, a sort of "dreamer-response" criticism that locates Freud's "identity theme" (to use Norman Holland's term) in Haggard's text. But this identity theme is here precisely a _desire for identity_, a desire for an immortal self that will live on, identical to itself across the generations.

Freud also alludes to the female protagonist of Haggard's novel, Ayesha or She-who-must-be-obeyed, the woman who has found the secret of eternal youth and waits two thousand years for her beloved Kallikrates to return. For Freud, Ayesha represents "the eternal feminine" and her constancy to Kallikrates demonstrates "the imnortality of our emotions." This last expression brings to mind Freud's own theory of the timelessness of the unconscious, which accounts for the frequent recurrence of infantile wishes in dreams.[18] This suggests that Ayesha, the guide who carries Freud when his own legs fail him, represents the science of the unconscious, of psychoanalysis, that transcends Freud's self--analysis. I shall return to this question later.

In this dream of self-dissection, as in the dream of the open-air closet, Freud's father has disappeared. The selfanalysis, and the "immortal" text that follows from it, are a boon for Freud's children. Freud has become a father. But the model that Freud chooses in becoming a father is not his own father, but larger-than-life, mythical ancestors: Hercules, Gargantua, Gulliver, Kallikrates. Freud turns to literature for a model on which to shape his own greatness. On the pattern of the literary epic or quest novel, Freud fashions himself into a hero, the protagonist of an epic: the story of psychoanalysis. The conflict between Freud the son and Jakob Freud the father is rewritten on a grand scale as Freud becomes the father of psycho- analysis. The personal struggle is made universal.

In this movement from the personal to the universal, literature plays a central role. On the one hand, Freud writes himself _into_ literature, finds a worthy self in the heroic models of literature. On the other hand, Freud _rewrites literature_, rewrites the texts and myths in terms of psychoanalysis. In some sense, psychoanalysis is the translation of a literary discourse into a scientific one. A dialectical relation, then, between Freud and literature: in becoming great, Freud becomes a literary hero; but as the father of psychoanalysis, Freud rewrites literature in scientific terms.

Typical Dreams

This dialectic between Freud and literature, the personal and the universal, is most evident in the section of <u>The Interpretation of Dreams</u> called "Typical Dreams." It is also in this section that Freud's motives for writing his **magnum opus** appear in their clearest form, though couched in the language of universality.

In the first edition (1900), typical dreams are considered an anomaly, almost a contradiction in terms, since "as a general rule, each person is at liberty to construct his dream-world according to his individual peculiarities and so to make it unintelligible to other people" (IV, 241). <u>The Interpretation of Dreams</u> posits a universal <u>grammar</u> of dreams, the <u>Traumarbeit</u> that converts latent dream-thoughts into the manifest content of the dream. The signifiers or dream elements are not themselves universal: they vary from person to person and indeed, from night to night. These signifiers stem from two sources: the childhood memories of the dream and the impressions (often of the most indifferent kind) of the dream-day. In some ways, then, Freud's <u>Interpretation of Dreams</u> is the most autobiographical of texts, since even the language that is used to write about the self (Freud's dream-language) is produced from the memories and impressions of his life.

In "complete contrast" to this general rule, Freud tells us, "there are a certain number of dreams which almost everyone has dreamt alike and which we are accustomed to assume must have the same meaning for everyone" (IV, 241). In such dreams, not only the grammar but the language of the dream is shared by all dreamers. Freud considers only four typical dreams in his first edition: dreams of being naked; dreams of the death of a loved one; examination dreams; and dreams of flying. Of this last category, Freud is obliged to confess that he is unable to supply a full interpretation because "I myself have not experienced any dreams of the kind" (IV, 273). Thus, even in the analysis of these dreams of universal significance, Freud must rely on his personal experience. And in fact, the three types of dreams that Freud does deal with reelaborate the thematics or autobiographics of <u>The Interpretation of Dreams</u> which we have been discussing. F r e u d first considers dreams of being naked. The dream is only "typical" if the dreamer feels shame at being undressed and if, paradoxically, the observers in the dream pay no attention to the dreamer, ignore him or meet him with solemn expressions. In other words, it is a typical dream if the dreamer, like Freud in the prefaces of <u>The Interpretation of Dreams</u>, is uneasy about revealing too much, even while the audience chooses to ignore what he reveals. This dream, adds Freud, is accompanied by a desire to flee and, at the same time, an incapacity to do so. It would be a typical dream, for example, if, because of a bizarre "self-analysis" that consisted in dissecting one's own pelvis, one found oneself unable to advance a step further in order to cover oneself.

Freud, of course, does not use these examples, does not take the small step that would bridge the chasm between dreams of nakedness and his own practice of revealing and concealing in The Interpretation of Dreams. But what does a dream of nakedness signify? Freud tells us that the dream represents a memory from childhood, but that memory has been "recast in a form designed to make sense of the situation," and, as a result, the scene is "deprived of its original meaning and put to extraneous uses" (IV, 243). In particular, the dreamer's moral feelings of shame, his modest but futile efforts to hide himself, actually disguise the wish fulfillment latent in the dream, the wish, that is, to reveal himself: "It is only in our childhood that we are seen in inadequate clothing both by members of our family and by strangers --nurses, maid-servants and visitors; and it is only then that we feel no shame at our nakedness" (IV, 244). On the contrary, Freud adds, "children frequently manifest a desire to exhibit. One can scarcely pass through a country village in our part of the world without meeting some child of two or three who lifts up his little shirt in front of one --in one's honour, perhaps" (IV, 244).

Freud concludes that "dreams of being naked are dreams of exhibiting" (IV, 245). But they are dreams of exhibiting in two senses: first, as we have seen, because the shame one feels at being naked conceals the desire to be naked; but also because such dreams are the repetition of childhood memories, and "impressions of earliest childhood... strive to achieve reproduction, from their very nature and irrespectively perhaps of their actual content... their repetition constitutes the fulfillment of a wish" (IV, 245). In other words, the dream has succeeded in exhibiting a memory to the dreamer and that repetition fulfills a wish. The desire to expose oneself is also the desire for autobiography.

This casts a considerably different light on the moral tone of Freud's prefaces, his efforts to conceal himself or to make excuses for revealing himself, the accusations he hurls at his audience. In this view, Freud's shame would express a desire for autobiography and the appeal for indulgence would be merely a plea to be noticed.

In essence, Freud confirms this interpretation a few pages later. In the final paragraph of his discussion of the dream of nakedness, the first typical dream to be discussed, he notes:

> In a psycho-analysis one learns to interpret propinquity in time as representing connection in subject-matter. Two thoughts which occur in immediate sequence without any apparent connection are in fact part of a single unity which has to be discovered; in just the same way, if I write an 'a' and a 'b' in succession, they have to be pronounced as a single syllable 'ab' (IV, 247)[11]

Immediately following this paragraph, Freud turns to consider a second typical dream, without any apparent connection to the first. "Dreams of the Death of Persons of Whom the Dreamer is Fond,"

75

subsection β of the section called "Typical Dreams," immediately follows subsection α "Embarrassing Dreams of Being Naked." This is the only time in The Interpretation of Dreams that Freud uses Greek letters to designate subsections of his text; he thereby disguises, but just barely, the fact that he has written "a" and "b" in immediate sequence and that we ought to be able to discover a "single unity."

The connection is not difficult to find. The first two prefaces of the text have already juxtaposed the embarrassment of revealing too much and the subjective importance of The Interpretation of Dreams as a self-analysis dealing with the death of the father. What Freud wants to reveal is the work of mourning, the death and the analysis that made it possible for him to triumph over his father. He wants to micturate in front of his readers, to reveal the megalomania that has made this triumph possible.

The dream of the death of a loved one is only typical if, in the dream, the dreamer feels grief at the loss. "The meaning of such dreams," Freud explains, "as their content indicates, is a wish that the person in question may die" (IV, 249). Having made this claim, Freud fully expects his readers to object, since it is shocking to think that anyone would wish a loved one to die. Freud therefore seeks out the "broadest possible foundation" for such a claim, the universal basis for the wish. This leads him to consider the infantile source of such a wish, and in particular, the child's wish that a sibling or parent will die. Having explained the dynamics of sibling rivalry, the child's desire for the exclusive possession of his parents' love, he goes on to consider a crime even more terrible than wishing for a sibling's death: "How are we to explain [the child's] deathwishes against his parents, who surround him with love and fulfil his needs and whose preservation that same egoism should lead him to desire?" (IV, 255). In order to explain what appears to be a "monstrous" idea, Freud makes the observation that "dreams of the death of parents apply with preponderant frequency to the parent who is of the same sex as the dreamer: that men, that is, dream mostly of their father's death and women of their mother's" (IV, 256). It appears as though "a sexual preference were making itself felt at an early age: as though boys regarded their fathers and girls their mothers as their rivals in love, whose elimination could not fail to be to their advantage" (IV, 256). In this first formulation of the rivalry between parent and child, a strict symmetry is respected: the boy child is his father's rival for possession of the mother, and the girl child wants to be rid of her mother in order to possess the father. Freud follows this claim with a great deal of supporting evidence, drawn for the most part from observation of children and the analysis of neurotics. Based on his extensive experience, he is able to assert that, at least in "the minds of most children," a rivalry exists between the child and the parent of the same sex for the possession of the other parent.

In support of this last claim, Freud introduces a literary text into evidence.

This discovery is confirmed by a legend that has come down to us from classical antiquity: a legend whose profound and universal power to move can only be understood if the hypothesis I have put forward in regard to the psychology of children has an equally universal validity. What I have in mind is the legend of King Oedipus and Sophocles' drama which bears his name (IV, 261).

Freud calls upon <u>Oedipus Rex</u> not only to confirm his hypothesis but to establish its <u>universal</u> basis. We are no longer concerned with Freud's particular relation to his father, nor even with an idea in the minds of "many children": Sophocles' play argues for a psychic structure of universal validity.

But the movement between Freud and literature is double, dialectical, since it is only Freud's psychoanalytic theory that can account for the play's enduring power to move audiences, a power that has baffled critics and would-be playwrights for generations. Psychoanalysis has the solution. Sophocles' drama represents the fulfillment of every child's wish; Oedipus' destiny "moves us only because it might have been ours --because the oracle laid the same curse upon us before our birth as upon him" (IV, 262). Psychoanalysis holds the key to <u>Oedipus Rex</u>, just as <u>Oedipus Rex</u> holds the key to the phenomenon that will become known as the "Oedipus complex." Freud needs the literary text in order to establish the universality of the conflict he has been describing; but, in using Oedipus for his own purposes, Freud provides the definitive interpretation, the "deepest layer" (IV, 266) of the text's significance.

The resolution of the dialectic between psychoanalysis and literature is the establishment of a psychoanalytic concept, "Oedipus complex," which is from then on considered as a universal constituent of the psyche. Yet, when Freud moves from the evidence of experience to the universal level as represented in the literary text <u>Oedipus Rex</u>, a strange thing happens. The symmetry between boys and girls disappears. Freud concludes his discussion of Sophocles' play by affirming: "It is the fate of all of us, perhaps, to direct our first sexual impulse towards our mother and our first hatred and our first murderous wish against our father" (IV, 262). All of "us," that is, who are men. The daughter has disappeared from consideration, and with her the mother as rival. The distinction between the daughter who desires the father and the mother who possesses him vanishes. Only the mother as object remains. The rivalry is between men, and woman is the object of desire.

This effacement of woman as subject occurs at precisely the moment when Freud moves from the empirical to the universal, from the struggle between particular children and parents (between Freud and his father, for example) to the universal struggle given the name of Oedipus complex. It is also this moment that will establish Freud as the father of psychoanalysis. The importance of this passage for the history of psychoanalysis can hardly be overestimated. A footnote to the 1919 edition of The Interpretation of Dreams explains that the Oedipus complex "throws a light of undreamt-of importance" on the evolution of religion, morality, and the human race. It thus assures Freud's claims to greatness and establishes him as father of a new lineage which, alas, also includes some rebellious sons. In a rare allusion to his detractors, Freud appends a footnote to this section in 1914: "None of the findings of psycho-analytic research has provoked such embittered denials, such fierce opposition --or such amusing contortions-- on the part of critics as this indication of the childhood impulses towards incest which persist in the unconscious" (IV, 263n). Why, at this particular moment, when Freud assumes his place as the father of psychoanalysis, assumes a role that will lead his sons to oppose him, does woman as subject disappear?

To put it another way: does psychoanalysis have a mother as well as a father? More likely, psychoanalysis is the mother, mother and daughter both, the object that the father possesses, just as the Urvater (primal father) of Totem and Taboo keeps all the women for himself and so brings about the sons' murderous jealousy (XIII, 141-46). In that rivalry between father and sons, woman as subject has no place. The foundation of psychoanalysis as object, the establishment of Freud as father, takes place at the expense of woman as subject. Neither the daughter of Oedipus nor the daughter of psychoanalysis has a place here. We will have to examine the results of this disappearance of woman at a later point.

But we have not yet discussed the last group of typical dreams, the dream that one has failed an important examination. In our discussion of the first two groups that Freud cites, we were led to draw a connection between the dreams of nakedness and Freud's practice of revealing and concealing in the prefaces, and to conclude that his manifestation of shame in fact expressed a desire to expose; in the treatment of the dreams of the death of a loved one, we concluded that what Freud wants to reveal is his murderous desire toward his father, a desire that culminated in Freud's taking the place of his father and, in fact, in his becoming the mighty father of the noble lineage of psychoanalysis. Where, then, do examination dreams fit into this autobiographics?

Freud tells us that the dreams generally occur when "we feel the burden of responsibility," when, that is, "the dreamer has some responsible activity ahead of him next day and is afraid there may be a fiasco" (IV, 274). The characteristic feature of such dreams is that one only fails the examinations in the dream that one passed successfully in waking life. The dream, then, offers a consolation by reproducing a scene from the past where "great anxiety has turned out to be unjustified and has been contradicted by the event" (IV, 274). The dream assures the dreamer: "Don't be afraid of tomorrow! Just think how anxious you were before your Matriculation, and yet nothing happened to you. You're a doctor, etc., already" (IV, 274). In other words, an examination dream tells the dreamer that, despite the tremendously difficult task ahead, he will in fact amount to something.

More Typical Dreams

The Interpretation of Dreams is one of the few texts that Freud updated from one edition to the next. The most striking difference between the 1900 edition and later revisions lies in the number of typical dreams discussed, and in the development of the notion of "dream symbolism." Freud admits that although he recognized the existence of symbols in dreams from the beginning, it was only "by degrees and as my experience increased" that he understood its "extent and significance." Freud's treatment of dream-symbols grows with every edition. In fact, the section called "Representation by Symbols in Dreams--Some Further Typical Dreams" did not even appear until the 1914 edition, when it was constructed from new material and from material added to other sections of the 1909 and 1911 editions. Symbolism is the one aspect of dreams that Freud had virtually overlooked in the first edition, and the one issue that he consistently has more to say about as the years pass.

In the first edition, that is, Freud had discounted the "dream-books" that assign a fixed meaning to particular dream elements. He considered dream-language to be private, to vary with the individual and the dream. In later editions, however, he reintroduces fixed symbols, and, what is more, posits a universal language that is characteristic of "unconscious ideation" and common to "folklore... popular myths, legends, linguistic idioms, proverbial wisdom and current jokes" (V, 351). Freud adds that "things that are symbolically connected to-day were probably united in prehistoric times by conceptual and linguistic identity. The symbolic relation seems to be a relic and mark of former identity" (V, 352). Freud is positing no less than an original and motivated language, where signified and signifier are joined by a relation of identity.

Thus, in the later editions, Freud's private language of dreams is supplemented by a symbolic, universal language. What starts out as the most autobiographical of texts expands to include the universal basis of language itself. As Freud becomes the father of psychoanalysis, the language of dreams is progressively universalized.

The section on "Representation by Symbols" has another peculiarity: among the "Further Typical Dreams," we find several lengthy passages quoted from Freud's followers, most of whom pay homage to The Interpretation of Dreams. Otto Rank (V, 369-71, 388-92), Alfred Robitsek (V, 373-77), Hans Sachs (V, 378-81), and Ernest Jones (V, 401) all contribute dreams to Freud's text. This friendly citationality contrasts with Freud's harsh treatment of his own predecessors in the first chapter.

The later editions of The Interpretation of Dreams witness to the fact that the book succeeds at the task Freud set for it: it fulfills his ambition, makes of him a great man, transforms the personal struggle between Freud and his father into a universal

Oedipal struggle that he, as the father of psychoanalysis, can uncover. The 1900 edition is a defiant promise of greatness, a child's micturition before the father. In the later editions, the ambition comes to coincide with the fulfillment of the ambition: the stream of urine washes everything clean. From this act issues the lineage of psychoanalysis.

Rebellious Sons, Immortal Daughter

The Interpretation of Dreams, like the dream, is a wish fulfillment : it presents Freud as the unrivaled Urvater of psychoanalysis. In fact, however, Freud's own sons are as rebellious as he was, and the history of their rebellion is recorded in On the History of the Psycho-Analytic Movement (1914). Freud begins by asserting that "psycho-analysis is my creation [Schöpfung]; for ten years I was the only person who concerned himself with it" (XIV, 7). And, although Freud recognizes that he is no longer alone in his devotion to psychoanalysis, he still feels justified in maintaining that "even to-day no one can know better than I do what psychoanalysis is, how it differs from other ways of investigating the life of the mind, and precisely what should be called psychoanalysis and what would better be described by some other name" (XIV, 7, emphasis mine).

The occasion for these comments is Freud's decision to deal with what he terms "a cool act of usurpation" by several of his former followers, by regaining control of the psychoanalytic Jahrbuch, which had fallen into the hands of C. J. Jung. In this rivalry for the Jahrbuch, "psychoanalysis" functions as a proper name. Freud reserves the right to bestow the name on those worthy of it, and to withdraw the name and the father's blessing from those who rebel against him.

Freud looks back nostalgically on the days when he was the only psychoanalyst, when "like Robinson Crusoe, I settled down as comfortably as possible on my desert island" (XIV, 22). In this "glorious heroic age," Freud was unrivaled: he did not feel pressed to publish, was free from worries about "doubtful priority," and had no obligations to read other publications in the field, since there were none to read. Thus, his rights as father were unquestioned and he was in sole possession of the object psychoanalysis.

Nevertheless, Freud does admit to having three predecessors of sorts, three men who at least had an intuition of the role that sexuality plays in the etiology of the neuroses. Breuer, Charcot, and Chrobak, three men who command Freud's "deepest respect," "had all communicated to me a piece of knowledge which, strictly speaking, they themselves did not possess" (XIV, 13). The fathers hand over to the son an object that they do not possess. What can this mean? Freud goes on to relate the three conversations. Breuer had confided to him, speaking of nervous illnesses, that "these things are always secrets d'alcôve!" In the second episode, Freud overhears Charcot saying: "Mais, dans des cas pareils c'est toujours la chose génitale, toujours... toujours... toujours."

Freud adds: "I know that for a moment I was almost paralyzed with amazement and said to myself: 'Well, but if he knows that, why does he never say so?'" (XIV, 14). And in the final instance, Chrobak takes Freud aside and

> told me that the patient's anxiety was due to the fact that although she had been married for eighteen years she was still _virgo intacta_. The husband was absolutely impotent.... The sole prescription for such a malady, he added, is familiar enough to us, but we cannot order it. It runs: 'Rx Penis normalis dosim repetatur!' (XIV, 14-15).

Freud concludes this tribute to his predecessors with the words:

> I have not of course disclosed the illustrious parentage [_erlauchte Abkunft_] of this scandalous idea in order to saddle other people with the responsibility for it. I am well aware that it is one thing to give utterance to an idea once or twice in the form of a passing _aperçu_, and quite another to mean it seriously.... It is the difference between a casual flirtation and a legal marriage with all its duties [_Pflichten_] and difficulties. 'Epouser les idées de...' is no uncommon figure of speech, at any rate in French (XIV, 15).

In other words, Breuer, Charcot, and Chrobak have failed to perform their conjugal duties: they have merely flirted with an idea. They have not "strictly speaking" possessed the object, and psychoanalysis remains a _virgo intacta_. The illustrious parents now pass on to Freud the virgin they have failed to possess. Freud then becomes the father of psychoanalysis ("Psycho-analysis is my creation") and the legal husband. Mother and daughter are identical.

As the husband/father of psychoanalysis, Freud has two wayward sons, Alfred Adler and C. J. Jung. Freud believes that Adler clearly suffers from the Oedipus complex and reports that he once heard Adler announce : "Do you think it gives me such great pleasure to stand in your shadow my whole life long?" Dominated by personal ambition, Adler is given to "petty outbursts of malice which disfigure his writings" and "an uncontrolled craving for priority" (XIV, 51). Adler's efforts to escape from the father's shadow even lead him to usurp his father's ideas and claim them as his own. Adler's saving grace, however, is his willingness to sever his ties with the father. In his "striving... for a place in the sun," Adler leaves Vienna, severs all ties with psychoanalysis, and gives his new theory the name of "Individual Psychology." Freud concedes that

> there is room enough on God's earth, and anyone who can has a perfect right to potter about [_herumtummle_] on it without being prevented; but it is not a desirable thing for people who have ceased to understand one another and

have grown incompatible with one another to remain under the same roof. Adler's "Individual Psychology" is now one of the many schools of psycho-logy which are adverse to psycho-analysis and its further development is no concern of ours (XIV, 32).

Psychoanalysis is clearly a family matter. Father and son are no longer compatible; they no longer get along and so should not live under the same roof. The son wants to seek his own place in the sun, and the father has no choice but to withdraw the name and the blessing and send him out to do what he will on "God's earth."

Adler at least is decent enough to renounce all claim to his father's blessing, and to simply go his own way. Jung and his Swiss followers are a more difficult case. First, they refuse to renounce the name of "psychoanalysis" (at least at the time Freud was writing <u>On the History of the Psycho-Analytic Movement</u>. Shortly thereafter, Jung adopted the name "Analytical Psychology"). What is even more distressing to the father of psychoanalysis is that the theoretical assumptions of his young son, or rather, of his son Jung, argue that the Oedipus complex, the son's usurpation of the father's place, works toward the progress of civilization. Thus, "with Jung, the appeal is made to the historic right of youth to throw off the fetters in which tyrannical age with its hidebound views seeks to bind it." But, Freud objects:

> Jung's argument... rests on the too optimistic assumption that the progress of the human race, of civilization and knowledge, has always pursued an unbroken line; as if there had been no periods of decadence, no reactions and restorations after every revolution, no generations who have taken a backward step and abandoned the gains of their predecessors. His approach to the standpoint of the masses, his abandonment of any innovation which proved unwelcome, make it <u>a priori</u> improbable that Jung's corrected version of psycho-analysis can justly claim to be a youthful act of liberation (XIV, 59).

In other words, Jung's own relation to his predecessor Freud is the best counterargument to Jung's optimistic theory about the progress of the human race. The younger generation does not always surpass its ancestors; it is just as likely to regress, abandon the advances of earlier generations. Freud concludes: "After all, it is not the age of the doer that decides this but the character of the deed" (XIV, 59-60). That is to say, it is not enough to be <u>jung</u>.

Freud's third objection to Jung is that he abstracts away from the sexual content of psychoanalytic discoveries, which claim that cultural phenomena --religion, myth, rituals, etc.-- are the manifestations of sublimated sexual drives. Freud once more uses a genealogical analogy. In this extended "simile," Freud is no longer the father and Jung the rebellious son; or rather, in addition to <u>this</u> father/son relationship, there is the comparison of psychoanalytic theories to the search for a lineage. Freud's theory posits that ethics and religion are descended _from_ sexual complexes, from, in a further complication of the metaphor, the Oedipus complex, the relation of father to son. Jung, however, wants to claim a more noble lineage for ethics and religion. Freud compares Jung's theory to the _parvenu_ who "boasts of being descended from a noble family living in another place" and who, when confronted with the disagreeable news that his parents live in the neighborhood and are "quite humble people" asserts that they are in fact "of noble lineage and have merely come down in the world; and he procures a family-tree from some obliging official source" (XIV, 61).

In the same way, Jung reverses the genealogy of cultural phenomena and asserts that the family-complex is a descendant of more noble lineage, a co-heir and not an ancestor of myth and religion. What occupies the place of "father" in Freud's theory becomes the son in Jung's, and the son, in usurping the father's place, claims a more venerable ancestry. Of course, this is not far from Freud's owm method of becoming a father, the father of the noble lineage of psychoanalysis, in _The Interpretation of Dreams_. Where Freud differs from Jung, however, is in the founding principle of his science. Freud becomes a great man, founds a lineage, by redefining the notion of "lineage" itself, by revealing the antagonism of father and son, and by tracing the role that this antagonism plays in the history of the human race. Freud becomes a great man, a mighty father, by revealing the humbleness of mankind's origins.

Nevertheless, despite the primary importance that the rivalry between father and son has for both the development of the individual and for civilization at large, Freud wants to deny that the rivalry between himself and his followers has any serious consequences for the future of psychoanalysis. Thus, after his lengthy discussions of the rebellions of Adler and Jung, Freud reaffirms his faith in psychoanalysis and explains that such rebellions pose no real threat to it:

> Some people may be inclined to fear that this secession is bound to have more momentous consequences for analysis than would another, owing to its having been started by men who have played so great a part in the movement and have done so much to advance it. I do not share this apprehension. Men are strong so long as they represent a strong idea; they become powerless when they oppose it. Psychoanalysis will survive this loss and gain new adherents in place of these (XIV, 66).

Freud is confident that psychoanalysis will remain untouched by the controversies within the movement; he is certain that his science will retain its identity over time. In other words, for Freud, psychoanalysis is an ideal object that is unaffected by the errors that men might make.

That is why Jung's continued use of the term "psychoanalysis" is the most threatening of all his rebellious acts. Freud compares this use to "the famous Lichtenberg knife." Jung "has changed the hilt, and he has put a new blade into it; yet because the same name is engraved on it we are expected to regard the instrument as the original one" (XIV, 66). If "psychoanalysis" names an ideal object, then it ought not to be susceptible to the sort of tampering that Jung inflicts. Freud has engraved a name on his creation and he expects the name and the object to retain their relation of absolute proximity. Only that will guarantee psychoanalysis' survival.

"Psychoanalysis" is a proper name, but it is not a patronym: Freud does not get it from his father, nor does he use it to designate himself. "Psychoanalysis" is the name of the object, and that object ought to retain its identity in passing from one generation to the next. We begin to see why Freud found Rider Haggard's She such a strange and fascinating book, full of hidden meanings, and why he incorporated the story into a dream that expressed his own desire for immortality. For She is the tale of a love object, Ayesha, who retains her identity across thousands of years, who waits unaltered by time for every subsequent reincarnation of her beloved Kallikrates. In this ideal world that Freud dreams of, the rivalry between father and son is rendered void, not only because, in the community that Ayesha rules "descent is traced only through the line of the mother, and... individuals... never pay attention to, or even acknowledge, any man as their father," granting the title "Father" to only one "titular male parent in each tribe"[12] but also because Ayesha, the potential object of such rivalry, can never be possessed, but is destined to remain a virgin.

It is not hard to guess that Ayesha, figure of the eternal feminine and of psychoanalysis, is also aletheia, the figure of truth. This is in fact made explicit in Haggard's text. The narrator tells us that Ayesha, who veils her unearthly beauty lest any man gaze upon her and fall hopelessly in love, may have originally gotten the idea of the veil from a statue located not far from the little community she rules. The statue represents "the winged figure of a woman of... marvellous loveliness and delicacy of form" whose "perfect and most gracious form was naked, save... the face, which was thinly veiled." Engraved on the pedestal of the statue are the words:

> Is there no man that will draw my veil and look upon my face, for it is very fair? Unto him who draws my veil shall I be, and peace will I give him, and sweet children of knowledge and good words.'
> And a voice cried, 'Though all those who seek after thee desire thee, behold! Virgin art thou, and Virgin shalt thou go till Time be done. No man is there born of woman who may draw thy veil and live, nor shall be. By Death only can thy veil be drawn, oh Truth! ' A n d Truth stretched out her arms and wept, because those who sought her might not find her, nor look upon her face to

face.[13]

It is no wonder that Haggard's book, whose message is that "Time hath no power against Identity"[14] fascinated Freud. It supplied him with an image of eternal fidelity that fulfills his wish for a science that would survive him. We also begin to understand why woman as subject has no place in Freud's theories, and why she disappears at the very moment that Freud posits the Oedipus complex as a universal feature of mental life. For if woman is a subject, and thus involved in the same rivalry for the possession of an object, she can hardly function as the "eternal feminine," as the ideal object that retains its identity across generations. Woman as subject cannot play the role of an ideal psychoanalysis that remains untouched despite the rivalry between father and son. For psychoanalysis to be the ideal, unchanging, immortal science that Freud desires, the daughter must be identical to the mother. Freud's own immortality depends upon this immortal daughter.

In a letter to Ernest Jones, Freud makes it clear that it is the name of "psychoanalysis" that will be passed from generation to generation: "I am sure in a few decades my name will be wiped away and our results will last."[15] Thus, the last stage of Freud's ambition is to wipe away his own name, and to leave behind only that of his immortal daughter, psychoanalysis.

PART THREE

THE SELF AND THE SIGN

CHAPTER V

THE SELF AND THE SIGN

Derrida and Autobiography

The preceding analysis of The Interpretation of Dreams raises a number of theoretical questions about the status of autobiography in relation to scientific discourse and, in particular, to the development of psychoanalysis. Jacques Derrida's "Spéculer--sur 'Freud'" addresses these very issues by focusing on the autobiographical aspects of one of Freud's later texts, Beyond the Pleasure Principle (1920). Derrida asks first:

> Comment une écriture autobiographique, dans l'abîme d'une auto-analyse non terminée, peut-elle donner sa naissance à une institution mondiale? La naissance de qui? de quoi? Et comment l'interruption ou la limite de l'auto-analyse, coopérant à la mise 'en abyme' plutôt qu'elle ne l'entrave, reproduit-elle sa marque dans le mouvement institutionnel, la possibilité de cette remarque ne cessant alors de faire les petits, multipliant la progéniture de ses clivages, conflits, divisions, alliances, mariages, et recoupements? (CP, 325).[1]

In fact, Freud addresses this same question in On the History of the Psycho-Analytic Movement: discussing two "secessions" from the movement, he admits that access to psychoanalytic knowledge is limited by the particular repressions of the psychoanalyst making the inquiry so that "he cannot go beyond a particular point in his relation to analysis" (XIV, 48). This critique applies a fortiori to Freud since it is he who constructed the field of inquiry in the first place. Even the most extensive self-analysis cannot uncover the unconscious: there is always a part of the self that remains foreign, that is not recovered by a self-reflexion. And this remainder, these unconscious desires, fears, and complexes that Freud cannot see in himself mark his theory and become part of the science of psychoanalysis. When the observer is part of the thing observed, when a self looks at "the self," a certain shadow or blind spot is incorporated into the observation. Derrida contends that this blind spot or abyss is then inherited by all those who claim Freud as predecessor.

In the next paragraph, Derrida explains that, given the role that Freud's autobiographics plays in the development of psychoanalysis, "il faudrait reprendre le processus à l'envers et recharger sa prémisse apparente: qu'est-ce que l'autobiographie si tout ce qui s'ensuit... est alors possible?" (CP, 325-26). How does this seemingly unusual case of a disguised autobiography that founds a science require us to rethink not only the category of science but also that of autobiography? What is the relation between the "private" or even "literary" writings of an author and his scientific and philosophical texts? Or, even more fundamental, what is the relation of the self to writing in general? If, as Derrida believes, the structure of writing has a peculiarly ambiguous relation to both the self and to life, then the notion of auto-bio-graphy has to be reconsidered.

Derrida's "Spéculer--sur 'Freud,'" which I shall discuss at length in Part Five, is important for the study of autobiography for a number of reasons. First, it analyzes the role of autobiography in <u>Beyond the Pleasure Principle</u> and its position in the history of psychoanalysis. Second, this analysis proceeds through Derrida's confrontation with one of the major influences on his thinking and writing and stages the curious relationship between Freud and Derrida. Third, <u>La Carte Postale</u>, the volume in which "Spéculer--sur 'Freud'" appears, provides a general critique of the state of psychoanalysis in France and reflects upon Derrida's place within that movement. Far from a disinterested observer of the scene, Derrida is one of the major participants in a quarrel over the meaning and importance of Freud's texts. <u>La Carte Postale</u> places Derrida's autobiographics within the context of Freud's legacy, and so provides a sequel of sorts to the genealogy traced in the preceding chapter. We may, then, identify three connections between Freud and Derrida: Freud is, first, the object of Derrida's deconstructive reading; second, a major influence in Derrida's own thinking; and third, an ancestor whose legacy is the locus of a rivalry between Derrida and other French thinkers, notably psychoanalyst Jacques Lacan. As a philosopher, Derrida's claim to Freud's legacy seems less than assured and, in fact, in the last section of <u>La Carte Postale</u> he speaks of his marginal position in the psychoanalytic movement. As we shall see, Derrida's strategy is not so much to assert his claims to that legacy as to call into question the notion of a legacy itself.

Although Freud occupies an increasingly central role in Derrida's writings, (and we shall later have occasion to examine certain parallels between Freud's autobiographics and Derrida's), Derrida also owes a great deal to the philosophical tradition. It is only within the general problematic of structural linguistics, Husserlian phenomenology, and speech act theory that his critique of Freud and theory of autobiography are comprehensible. For, although "Spéculer--sur 'Freud'" is the most extensive discussion of the problem of autobiography, it is clear that Derrida has recognized as central the problem of the self and its relation to writing from his first texts. Derrida's theoretical framework calls into question any theory of autobiography that is founded on the notion of representation, on the sincerity of the author's intentions, the value of the proper name or signature: in short, on the integrity of the self, in every sense of the word.

Furthermore, Derrida's critique of the self has focused on autobiographies on several occasions. Most notably, Claude Lévi-Strauss' Tristes Tropiques and Jean-Jacques Rousseau's Les Confessions are central to Derrida's discussion of their ideas. Derrida follows his reading of the Confessions with a reflection on his methodology and specifically addresses the question of a "psycho-biographical" approach to philosophy. Freud is, then, never far from the scene: his radical rethinking of the self is a problem that Derrida encounters on many occasions. In certain ways, in fact, "Spéculer--sur 'Freud'" is Derrida's effort to face the difficulties that he had only partially recognized in the earlier texts. Thus, before turning to consider Derrida's theory and practice of autobiographics and their relation to Freud, we need to outline the general problem of the self and language as it appearas in Derrida's other texts.

Signs of Death: Language as Other

In La Voix et le Phénomène, Derrida approaches the question of the relation between the self and the sign by applying Edmund Husserl's general principles of language to the particular sign $\underline{I}$. Husserl argues, first, that the occurrence of a sign is not an "event" "si événement veut dire unicité empirique irremplaçable et irréversible. Un signe qui n'aurait lieu qu'une fois ne serait pas un signe" (VP, 55). Since the sign must be repeated in order to be recognizable as a sign, the repetition is what constitutes the sign's "ideality,"[2] its capacity to retain its identity in various circumstances and at various moments. The identity of the sign is ideal, but Husserl distinguishes this notion of meaning or Bedeutung from the Platonic Idea by affirming that the ideality "n'existe pas dans le monde et elle ne vient pas d'un autre monde" (VP, 58). Rather, it is constituted by the particular acts of repeating the sign. The Bedeuteung is not lodged within any particular use of the sign; rather, every occurrence of the sign appears in relation to this ideal Bedeutung.

Husserl argues, secondly, that the sign must be able to function in the absence of the speaker, and the of speaker's intuition of the referent. This capacity is structurally necessary for language to be language. One need not have the object present, or even the intuition of the object in mind in order to understand an utterance. Even if the referent is an impossible object, the utterance still makes a certain sense: "Si nous ne pouvions comprendre ce que veut dire 'cercle carré'... comment pourrions-nous conclure à l'absence d'objet possible?" (VP, 102). One understands well enough to know that the utterance refers to an impossible obiect. But this lack of a referent (Gegenstandslosigkeit) does not indicate a total lack of meaning (Bedeutungslosigkeit).

Given the ideal nature of the Bedeutung, one may even say that this Gegenstandslosigkeit can occur even when the object one is

89

apparently referring to is present. It is not only that one need not see the window in order to understand what "I see the window" means; since the meaning is always ideal, the utterance never refers merely to the particular referent or context: "Il est impliqué structurellement dans mon opération que le contenu de cette expression soit idéal et que son unité ne soit pas entamée par l'absence de perception hic et nunc" (VP, 103). One must distinguish between the contenu of the expression (the ideal Bedeutung) and the objet (referent).

The sign depends upon repetition to constitute it as a sign; therefore, if it were tied to a particular context or situation, if it vanished with that context, it would not be a sign. This is not only true of the written text, "nom courant de signes qui fonctionnent malgré l'absence totale du sujet, par (delà) sa mort" (VP, 104), but the spoken word as well: if the words I speak are understandable, it is because they are re-cognizable, a repetition of the same words used by someone else, and repeatable, capable of signifying in the future. One must conclude that the sign is not tied to the object nor to the subject of the utterance, that it functions as if referent and speaker were absent: the sign exists in spite of the object and does not depend upon it; and it exists before any particular subject who uses it and continues to exist after his death. And this capacity to function in the absence of the subject and the object is the condition of signification: language would not be language if it could not function in--the-absence-of.

All this is recognized by Husserl. When he turns to consider the particular example of the first-person pronoun I, however, he refuses to be constrained by his premises about the function of language in general. Derrida explains that Husserl seems to think that "pour celui qui parle, cette Bedeutung, comme rapport à l'objet (Je...) est 'réalisée.' 'Dans le discours solitaire, la Bedeutung du Je se réalise essentiellement dans la représentation immédiate de notre propre personnalité'" (VP, 105-06). Derrida points out that the notion that the intuition of an object (in this case, of oneself in a moment of self-presence) could completely "realize" the use of the sign does not follow from Husserl's premises: "Est-ce que l'apparition du mot Je dans le discours solitaire... ne fonctionne pas déjà comme une idéalité?" (VP, 106). The ideal nature of the Bedeutung makes it impossible that any particular occurrence of a sign (of the sign I) can completely "realize" its meaning.

Derrida goes on to point out that even the sign I must be able to function in the absence of a particular subject, must retain its meaning "même si ma présence empirique s'efface ou se modifie radicalement" (VP, 106). Further, it must be able to function independently of the speaker's intuition of the object, that is, of himself. "Que j'aie ou non l'intuition actuelle de moi-même, 'je' exprime; que je sois ou non vivant, je suis 'veut dire'... Et l'on n'a pas besoin de savoir qui parle pour le comprendre, ni même pour l'émettre" (VP, 106-07). There is nothing to guarantee that when I say "I," I have an intuition of the "objet visé," that is,

90

of myself. On the contrary, that intuition is structurally unnecessary, even superfluous for the functioning of the sign.

Noting that Husserl's own premises lead one to question his conclusions about the _I_, Derrida asks:

> Est-ce que Husserl ne contredit pas ce qu'il affirmait de l'indépendance de l'intention et de l'intuition remplissante en écrivant: 'Ce qui constitue chaque fois sa _Bedeutung_ (celle du mot _Je_) ne peut être tiré que du discours vivant et des données intuitives qui en font partie. Quand nous lisons ce mot sans savoir qui l'a écrit, nous avons un mot, sinon dépourvu de _Bedeutung_, du moins étranger à sa _Bedeutung_ normale.' Les prémisses de Husserl devraient nous autoriser à dire exactement le contraire (VP, 107).

If the _I_ is a sign, then its _Bedeutung_ cannot be simply occasional, shifting with the particular context in which it appears: that _Bedeutung_ must be ideal. If the _I_ is a sign, then one need not see or know the object to which it refers in order to understand what the _I_ means. "Quand le mot _Je_ apparaît, l'idéalité de sa _Bedeutung_, en tant qu'elle est distincte de son 'objet,' nous met dans la situation que Husserl décrit comme anormale: comme si _Je_ était écrit par un inconnu" (VP, 107). The condition for understanding any particular _I_, including the _I_ I use to refer to myself, is the ideality of its _Bedeutung_, the fact that the _I_ does not refer to the particular referent, but can and has been repeated without its meaning being used up. For this reason, Derrida maintains, the ideal _Bedeutung_ of the _I_ has a "valeur structurellement testamentaire."

> La _Bedeutung_ 'je suis' ou 'je suis vivant'.... n'est ce qu'elle est, elle n'a l'identité idéale propre à toute _Bedeutung_ que si... je puis être mort au moment où elle fonctionne.... L'énoncé 'je suis vivant' s'accompagne de mon être-mort et sa possibilité requiert la possibilité que je sois mort.... L'anonyme du _Je_ écrit, l'impropriété du _j'écris_ est, contrairement à ce que dit Husserl, la 'situation normale' (VP, 108).

It is of course clear that a written text can survive its author, that an autobiography, for example, can declare "I am alive" when the author is in fact dead. But Derrida extends this eventuality to every instance of language, including speech and the interior monologue. Language, even the language I use to describe myself, is always other. When I say "I," I designate myself with a word that does not only designate myself, a word whose meaning is ideal and so apart from any empirical object. To say "I" is to enter into relation with one's own death, since the sign _I_ does not require one's existence.

Language and the Constitution of the Self

Language, then, is always other: it precedes the self, functions as if the self were absent. But is there a self independent of the sign? Husserl wants to maintain that in the "discours intérieur dans la vie solitaire de l'âme," signs have no indicative or communicative function, that they function as "pure expressions." The use of signs when speaking silently to oneself would be merely a fictional representation of communication, because the self has no need of signs to communicate with itself. For Husserl, the subject is already in a state of perfect, immediate presence to itself. And this immediate self-presence that has no need for the sign becomes the foundation for intuition and perception in general. "Chaque fois que Husserl voudra marquer le sens de l'intuition originaire, il rappellera qu'elle est l'expérience de l'absence et de l'inutilité du signe" (VP, 67).

As Derrida points out in a chapter entitled "La Voix qui Garde le Silence," however, "la structure de la vie intérieure est ici simplifiée" (VP, 79) because, in fact, the self needs language in order to come to consciousness in the first place. Rather, one comes to consciousness through "auto-affection," and more specifically, through the experience of a "pure" auto-affection that consists in hearing oneself speak. Husserl privileges the experience of hearing one's own voice over other forms of auto-affection because it appears to combine the two features necessary for the formation of subjectivity: on the one hand, speech is "un médium de signification universelle" which consists of ideal, repeatable signs; on the other hand, this experience seems to take place immediately, "sans aucun détour par l'instance de l'extériorité du monde, ou du non-propre." As "l'être auprès de soi dans la forme de l'universalité," speech is the foundation of subjectivity and of consciousness. "La voix est la conscience" (VP, 89).

Husserl maintains that in the experience of hearing oneself speak, there is no loss of self, no need of passing through the world, as there is in other forms of auto-affection. In the experience of seeing oneself (a part of one's body or one's reflection in a mirror) or of touching oneself, there is a loss of self involved in the coming to consciousness, for the body one perceives is at first in the world, exterior to oneself. The body is first perceived as something foreign to oneself (non-propre) before being recognized as one's own. Similarly, in the experience of seeing oneself write, the exteriority of the sign makes itself felt, whereas in speaking, the signifier vanishes as soon as one has pronounced it.

But can it really be said that the voice, in pronouncing conventional, universal signs does not pass through the world? We have already seen how, for Derrida, "la possibilité de l'écriture habitait le dedans de la parole" (VP, 92). The ideal nature of the Bedeutung makes all language, even speech, foreign to the one who uses it. Furthermore, in recognizing that the subject is produced by this particular use of language, Husserl undermines his own claim that there is a "vie solitaire de l'âme" that can do without signs. Husserl must repress the origin of subjectivity in order to maintain this interiority of the self that is immediate to itself since "dès qu'on admet que l'auto-affection est la condition de la présence à soi, aucune réduction transcendantale pure n'est possible" (VP, 92). The "vie solitaire" only exists as a result of the moment of consciousness that establishes the difference between the self and the world, the inside and the outside. And that moment of consciousness depends upon language.

Derrida concludes: "L'auto-affection n'est pas une modalité d'expérience caractérisant un étant qui serait déjà lui-même (autos). Elle produit le même comme rapport à soi dans la différence d'avec soi, le même comme le non-identique" (VP, 92). Consciousness arises in the gap between \self and self, in the experiencing of oneself as other, non-propre. Language opens this gap, is both the condition for and the impossibility of identity.

Language, as the difference between self and self, not only constitutes the subject, it also produces as an effect a desire for the presence that is lost in the very movement of coming to consciousness (GR, 100 and passim). "Cela veut dire... que ce désir porte en lui le destin de son inassouvissement" (GR, 206). Writing, and particularly the writing of an autobiography, then becomes a futile and never-ending attempt to reappropriate what was lost from the beginning of subjectivity. Derrida writes of Jean-Jacques Rousseau:

> Dans les Confessions, au moment où Jean-Jacques tente d'expliquer comment il est devenu écrivain, il décrit le passage à l'écriture comme la restauration, par une certaine absence et par un type d'effacement calculé, de la présence deçue de soi dans la parole. Ecrire alors est le seul moyen de garder ou de reprendre la parole puisque celle-ci se refuse en se donnant (GR, 204).

Writing tries to fill the space that speech has opened up, but it only succeeds in opening the space wider, opening the self to the decentering effect of language and narrativity. In "Spéculer--sur 'Freud,'" Derrida will call this the space of autobiography.

Lejeune and the Subject of Autobiography

It is important to recognize at this point that the desire expressed by Husserl for an *I* that, in the interiority of the self, would be entirely realized by one's "propre personnalité," that one's identity would fill the *I*, that the *I* would not be, even a little bit, someone or something else, has formed the basis of a number of theories of autobiography. It is, most notably, the foundation of Philippe Lejeune's project in Le Pacte Autobiographique (1975). In his generic definition of autobiog-raphy, Lejeune argues that the author of an autobiography must be identical with both the narrator and the main character of the text, adding that "il n'y a ni transition ni latitude. Une identité est, ou n'est pas. Il n'y a pas de degré possible, et tout doute entraîne une conclusion négative."[3] Whatever the differences in age, perspective, or relation to the reader, the author, his narrator, and the main character of the autobiography must remain identical to one another: this requirement assumes as its precondition a self-identical subject. We see that, given Derrida's theory of a language before and beyond the self, a self that is "le même comme le non-identique," Lejeune's categorical statement that "une identité est, ou n'est pas" and that "tout doute entraîne une conclusion négative" excludes any possible text from the genre of autobiography.

Lejeune's insistence on the integrity of a self-identical subject arises from his desire to ground autobiography in the honesty and sincerity of the author's intentions. Reacting against Bertrand-Delpech's claim that Olivier Todd's L'Année du crabe is autobiographical despite the author's use of "pseudonymes transparents," Lejeune complains:

> Si Ross, c'est Todd, pourquoi porte-t-il un autre nom? Si c'était lui, comment se fait-il qu'il ne l'ait pas dit? Qu'il le laisse coquettement deviner, ou que le lecteur le devine malgré lui, peu importe. L'auto-biographie n'est pas un jeu de devinette, c'est même exactement le contraire. Manque ici l'essentiel, ce que j'ai proposé d'appeler le pacte autobiographique.[4]

If Lejeune's notion of "identity" is necessarily founded on the immediacy of a subject present to itself, this is very quickly supplemented by an exterior sign that would guarantee the intention. The reader does not have immediate access to the author's intentions; therefore, Lejeune makes an appeal to the institutional value of the signature and the proper name. Todd's identity with the character whose life he recounts must be made explicit by the use of the same name by author and character. What is inaccessible at a textual level (Todd's private intention to give a true account to his reader) must be guaranteed by the proper name of the author,

> seule marque dans le texte d'un indubitable hors-texte, renvoyant à une personne réelle, qui demande ainsi qu'on lui attribue, en dernier ressort, la responsabilité de l'énonciation de tout le texte écrit.[5]

The empirical existence of the author who bears the same name as the narrator and the main character of the autobiography thus becomes the means of authenticating the "pact."

Lejeune makes it clear that by "personne réelle," he means a person "dont l'existence est attestée par l'état civil et vérifiable."[6] It is thus to a legal contract assumed by the author and guaranteed not only by the signature but by the State that Lejeune must eventually have recourse.

This appeal to the law is an effort to reduce what Derrida calls the "anonyme du Je écrit." In an earlier work on autobiog-

94

raphy, in fact, Lejeune was obliged to admit that "sur le plan de l'analyse interne du texte," autobiography and the autobiographical novel are indistinguishable since "tous les procédés que l'autobiographie emploie pour nous convaincre de l'authenticité de son récit, le roman peut les imiter, et les a souvent imités."[7] In Le Pacte Autobiographique, Lejeune is able to revise this statement and thus to reassert the "authenticity" proper to autobiography by founding it on the proper name as it appears on the title page. That name not only "signs" the pact, it also guarantees that the "'je' ne se perd pas... dans l'anonymat" since "chacun se nommera 'je' en parlant; mais pour chacun, ce 'je' renverra à un nom unique, et que l'on pourra toujours énoncer."[8] Everything comes to depend on the proper name, the signature, and eventually, on the legal status of the subject as author.

We are left with the question, however, of whether that legal function corresponds to a self-identical subject that precedes it, or whether it is itself the constituting of a legal subject. Lejeune raises briefly the problem of the institutional function of language, only to "conjure" it away. The issue is raised, significantly, within the context of the problem of fictionality:

> Quand la Berma joue Phèdre, qui dit 'je'? La situation théatrale peut certes remplir la fonction des guillemets, signalant le caractère fictif de la personne qui dit 'je.' Mais ici, le vertige doit commencer à nous prendre, car l'idée effleure alors même le plus naïf, que ce n'est pas la personne qui définit le 'je,' mais peut-être le 'je' la personne.... Conjurons pour l'instant ce vertige. Ce que nous frôlons ici... [c'est] l'évidence que la première personne est un rôle.[9]

A few pages later, Lejeune in effect summarizes Derrida's theory of autobiography (though Derrida is not named), only to conclude with a remarkable statement:

> S'il n'y a pas de personne en dehors du langage, comme le langage c'est autrui, il faudrait en arriver à l'idée que le discours autobiographique, loin de renvoyer, comme chacun se l'imagine, au 'moi' monnayé en une série de noms propres, serait au contraire un discours aliéné, une voix mythologique par laquelle chacun serait possedé.... S'ouvrirait alors --toute psychologie et mystique de l'individu demystifiés-- une analyse du discours de la subjectivité et de l'individualité comme mythe de notre civilisation.[10]

Having thus not only drawn the logical conclusions from Derrida's theory of language but also outlined the project of autobiographical critique that follows from such conclusions, Lejeune stops short of putting it into effect, adding: "Chacun sent bien d'ailleurs le danger de cette indétermination de la première personne, et ce n'est pas hasard si on cherche à la neutraliser en la fondant sur le nom propre."[11] Lejeune thus admits that his theory of autobiography is formulated in order to ward off a danger, a danger so real and present that one need not even name it since everyone can sense it. What is perhaps most remarkable in this appeal to "bon sens" and claim to unanimity is Lejeune's rhetorical use of the impersonal pronoun "on" to refer to himself : at the very moment that he warns of the danger in the "indétermination de la première personne," Lejeune opts for universality over individuality.

Signature as Speech Act

Lejeune's conclusion about the proper name is of course no argument against Derrida's theory of language; it is merely a defensive gesture that seeks to neutralize a danger. It is precisely such defensive gestures and the desire that they express that have been the object of Derrida's critique of the "metaphysics of presence." Lejeune's theory of autobiography is part of this metaphysics for it denies the otherness of language and grounds autobiography in an entirely self-conscious subject. For, as Derrida shows in two essays on "speech act theory," the notions of proper name and of signature that Lejeune expounds are rooted in self-presence.

In "Signature Evénement Contexte," Derrida criticizes English philosopher J. L. Austin for continuing to adhere to a traditionally metaphysical notion of consciousness even while his theory mounts an attack on some of the most widely-held assumptions of that metaphysics. Austin's How to do Things with Words introduces a class of utterances called "performatives." Unlike "constatives," performatives "do not 'describe' or 'report' or constate anything at all;" rather, "to utter the sentence (in, of course, the appropriate circumstances) is not to describe my doing of what I should be said in so uttering to be doing or to state that I am doing it: it is to do it."[12] Among these appropriate circumstances are social or legal institutions whose existence gives the "speech act" its meaning. Austin's first example is that of the words "I do" as uttered in the course of a marriage ceremony. These words do not report on a marriage: they bring one about. But it is, of course, only the institution of marriage and the laws that govern it that allow for any particular marriage to take place.

In the course of How to do Things with Words, Austin extends and refines his definition of speech acts, arguing finally that every utterance has a performative as well as a constative function. As a result of this blurring of the initial categories, Austin is led to speak of the "force" of utterances in general:

> Saying something will often, or even normally, produce certain consequential effects upon the feelings, thoughts, or actions of the audience, or of the speaker, or of other persons: and it may be done with the design, intention, or purpose of producing them.[13]

Derrida believes that Austin "a fait éclater le concept de communication comme concept purement sémiotique, linguistique, ou symbolique" (MP, 383) since "communiquer, dans le cas du performatif... ce serait communiquer une force par l'impulsion d'une marque" (MP, 382). For this reason, Austin's theory is a powerful critique of metaphysical notions of language. Derrida criticizes Austin, however, for positing a notion of context (on which the success or "happiness" of the speech act depends) as "exhaustivement définissable," and in particular for depending upon the

> conscience libre et présente à la totalité de l'opéra-tion, [le] vouloir-dire absolument plein et maître de lui-même: juridiction téléologique d'un champ total dont l'intention reste le centre organisateur (MP, 384).

For Austin (as for Lejeune), the sign of this intention, this consciousness present to itself, is to be found, in written texts, in the signature of the author. Arguing against the absolute purity of the performative, Derrida explains that Austin "ne doute pas que la source d'un énoncé oral... soit présente à l'énonciation et à l'énoncé" and that "l'équivalent de ce lien à la source dans les énonciations écrites soit simplement évident et assuré dans la signature" (MP, 390-91). But, as he points out,

> pour fonctionner, c'est-à-dire pour être lisible, une signature doit avoir une forme répétable, itérable, imitable; elle doit pouvoir se détacher de l'intention présente et singulière de sa production. C'est sa mêmeté qui, altérant son identité et sa singularité, en divise le sceau (MP, 392).

For this reason, what makes possible the signature's success (its readability and its authenticity) also renders impossible its "rigoureuse pureté" (MP, 392). The signature only guarantees the identity of the signer through a dependence on repetition and therefore difference (a signature, in order to be valid, must be both the "same" and different from every other signature of the signer). Derrida calls this structure, the general structure of language, "iterability." The signature is only recognizable in a particular circumstance because it is the repetition, the alteration of an earlier signature.

Furthermore, the signature cannot guarantee the full intentions of the signer, since "l'absence essentielle de l'intention à l'actualité de l'énoncé, cette inconscience structurelle... interdit toute saturation de contexte" (MP, 389). The essential otherness of language that Derrida analyzed in La Voix et le Phénomène, the capacity of language to function in the absence of a particular speaker's intentions, keeps the signature from fulfilling the role assigned to it, that of guaranteeing the full intentions of the author.

Nevertheless, as Derrida points out, "les effets de signature

sont la chose la plus courante du monde" (MP, 391, emphasis mine).
He describes his own project as within a

> déploiement historique de plus en plus puissant d'une
> écriture générale dont le système de la parole, de la
> conscience, du sens, de la présence, de la vérité, etc.,
> ne serait qu'un effet et doit être analysé comme tel.
> C'est cet effet mis en cause que j'ai appelé ailleurs
> logocentrisme (MP, 392).

In other words, the intention, consciousness, autonomous presence
of a self that is presumed to lie behind the signature as its cause
or source is in fact an effect produced by the mark or signature.
The signature is itself a performative since it produces effects;
more radically, it is a "speech act" in the limited sense since it
constitutes the self as a legal subject.

Self as SARL

Derrida analyzes the "signature effect," the juridical and
legal status of the signature and of the copyright in "Limited Inc
a b c." The essay is a response to John Searle's "Reply" to
"Signature Evénement Contexte" and it begins by analyzing Searle's
decision to copyright his essay. According to Derrida, this
decision stems from a desire to assert his own status of author of
the text that bears his name, and from the fear that his article
will be stolen, plagiarized, or misrepresented. This fear, in
turn, arises from Searle's obscure knowledge of the iterable
structure of language, which makes his "Reply" not only immediately
expropriable but also already expropriated. This is especially
evident in Searle's case since he is claiming to speak the truth,
a truth that, in principle, everyone has access to:

> Si Searle dit vrai quand il dit qu'il dit le vrai, l'ob-
> viously true, alors le copyright est sans effet, sans
> interêt: tout le monde pourra, aura d'avance pu,
> reproduire ce qu'il dit. Le sceau de Searle est d'avance
> volé. D'où l'angoisse et la compulsion à cacheter... le
> vrai" (LI, 3).

As Derrida goes on to show, the copyright appearing in the
corner of the first page of Searle's "Reply" is in part falsified
by the first footnote (appended to the title of the paper) which
acknowledges the author's debt to D. Searle and H. Dreyfuss.
"Voilà que le 'vrai' copyright devrait revenir... à un Searle
divisé, multiplié, conjugué, partagé. Quelle signature compli-
queé!" (LI, 3) Derrida adds that Dreyfuss is an old friend of his
who had learned from Derrida himself: "'Je' prétends donc aussi au
copyright de la Reply" (LI, 3).

But it is not merely the debt Searle owes to a small number
of individuals for the ideas developed in his "Reply" that calls
into question the validity of the copyright: for Derrida, what is
at stake is the entire philosophical tradition which Searle has

inherited and which has put words and concepts into his mouth:

> Quelle est la nature du débat qui semble s'ouvrir ici? Où, ici? Ici? Est-ce un débat? A-t-il lieu? S'ouvre-t-il? Depuis quand? <u>Depuis Platon</u>, souffle le souffleur promptement dans les coulisses, et l'acteur répète <u>depuis Platon</u> (LI, 2, emphasis mine).

In this passage, Derrida characterizes his debate with Searle as one dating back to Plato, part of a much larger context. Yet Derrida further characterizes his own role as, precisely, a role: he is the actor who mouths the words of an anonymous <u>souffleur</u>. What Derrida criticizes in Searle is something not proper to "him" but belonging to "Western metaphysics" or "logocentrism." This philosophical influence continues to work on both Searle <u>and</u> Derrida.

Searle tries to characterize the Derrida-Austin debate as taking place between "two prominent philosophical traditions" (Anglo-Saxon and Continental); Derrida counters by asking if Searle "n'est... pas plus continental et parisien que moi?" and explains "<u>Signature Evénement Contexte</u> analyse les prémisses métaphysiques de la théorie anglo-saxonne --et foncièrement moralisante-- du performatif" adding that Searle's "prémisses et sa méthode relèvent de la philosophie continentale et sous une forme ou sous une autre, elles sont très présentes en France" (LI, 10-11). As Derrida does not hesitate to point out, these metaphysical premises dating back at least as far as Plato are also part of the "self" that writes "Signature Evénement Contexte" and "Limited Inc."

The last section of "Signature Evénement Contexte" deals with the question of the signature and concludes:

> (<u>Remarque</u>: le texte--écrit--de cette communication--orale--devait être adressé à l'Association des societés de philosophie de langue française avant la séance. Tel envoi devait donc être signé. Ce que j'ai fait et contrefais ici. Où? Là. J. D.
>
> J. Derrida (MP, 393)

In "Limited Inc," Derrida returns to the significance of this signature and makes a surprising claim: "Je suis prêt à.... jurer que cette signature n'est pas de ma main" (LI, 6). This confession is not merely meant to cast doubt on the "authenticity" of the signature and thus of the authorship of "Signature Evénement Contexte," nor to illustrate that the iterable structure of language makes forgery, imitation, etc. always a possibility, but also to show Derrida's complicity with traditional philosophy. For "Signature Evénement Contexte" was signed by Derrida's "other hand," a hand he cannot control:

> Je voulais seulement marquer... que cette autre main, peut-être, et nulle autre, avait dicté la Reply aux trois + n auteurs... et que la question du "copyright," en

> dépit ou à cause de son lieu marginal ou hors texte...
> ne devait plus être éludée, dans aucun de ses aspects:
> juridico-économique, politique, éthique, phantasmatique
> ou pulsionnel, etc (LI, 6).

The copyright's function is essentially legal and economic: it protects against "plagiarism," the theft of "one's own" ideas, and is part of the larger political structure that determines the rights of the "legal subject." The signature, as it functions on a legal contract, a lease, or a check has the same purpose. Derrida is suggesting that the determination and continued existence of these legal structures correspond to a desire (metaphysical in its origin) for identity, the proper, a self untouched by the other. The legal structure exists to protect against the reemergence of the difference from self that constitutes the self in the first place. The legal subject is a construct that disguises the indeterminacy and the heterogeneity of the self, and in disguising them, gives the self its power.

There is no question that, from a legal standpoint, Jacques Derrida is the author of "Signature Evénement Contexte" (and of Marges de la Philosophie in which it appears as the last essay, the signature thus validating the entire text) and that the signature performs its normal function in that context. Derrida is taken for responsible and answerable for his texts and those texts are seen as representative of their author. In colloquia and interviews, Derrida is asked to answer criticism of his texts; seminars, university courses, articles and books are dedicated to the work of Derrida. All of this assumes that the proper name "Derrida" means something; that the signature designates Derrida as responsible; and that his texts have a natural relation to him. We shall examine certain consequences of this "signature effect" in the next chapter.

Derrida is not arguing that the signature is without effect, that, because the self is divided from the beginning, it cannot function as Searle claims. Rather, he argues that the signature effect is produced by the signature itself and is not governed by the intentions of the signer. Whatever the intentions at the moment of signing, whether or not the signer maintains those intentions, the signature and the text function. It follows that whatever force a text exerts cannot be controlled by the author or determined in advance. The text functions independently of these intentions. For these reasons, Derrida advances a notion of the subject as "Sarl," the French acronym for "société à responsabilité limitée," the equivalent of the American term "incorporated" or the British "limited." These terms are legal titles that authorize a group of individuals to function as a single, legal entity. The word "incorporated," affixed to a name or group of names does not refer to an entity but rather constitutes it as such. And, like the legal subject, Sarl is part of an institution that distributes and governs power or force.

Derrida is led to conclude:

100

John R. Searle et 'moi-même' ne signons pas ici. Nous ne sommes que des 'prêtes-noms.' Dans ce simulacre de confrontation, nous sommes des 'fronts' : j'aime ce mot, j'ai appris dans un film de Woody Allen sur des événements datant du mac-carthysme qu'il signifiait 'prête-nom,' masque, substitut pour un sujet clandestin (LI, 9).

Woody Allen's character in "The Front" represents several writers who, because of political censorship (the blacklisting of suspected communists) cannot sign their own names to their writings and so enlist Allen as a "front." The political overtones of the analogy are entirely to the point. The law demands a signature, calls forth the sort of subterfuge that makes Woody Allen's character both cooperate with and subvert the system. Derrida is in a similar position. He sees the "confrontation" between himself and Searle as between "la tradition et son autre, autre qui n'est même pas 'son' autre" (LI, 43), adding: "Ce que ces 'fronts' représentent, de surcroît ce qui pèse sur eux au-delà de cet étrange chiasme, ce sont des forces non-philosophiques" (LI, 10). In signing his name, Derrida comes to represent forces that are outside philosophy, forces that Western metaphysics has repressed, in particular the force of writing (_écriture_), that is, the capacity of language to function in the absence of the subject, his intentions, and the referent. But in _signing_ his name, Derrida also produces a signature effect, a proper name that functions within the metaphysics of presence. That is why the signature appended to _Marges_ is not simply an ironic gesture or a game: even when he has "deconstructed" the signature, Derrida's own signature does not cease to function within a legal context. And this responds to his desire, or to the desire of "l'autre main" that Derrida inherits from philosophy.

Autobiography and Metaphysics

As might be expected, Derrida's readings of autobiographies do not stress the uniqueness of the life being recounted, nor the pact the author establishes with the reader, but rather focus on the self's relation to the otherness of language. In _De la Grammatologie_ (1967), for example, Derrida grants a central place to Jean-Jacques Rousseau's _Confessions_ in his discussion of Rousseau's attitude toward _writing_.

In order to demonstrate the ambivalence of this attitude, Derrida traces Rousseau's use of the term "supplement" across a number of his texts. In Rousseau, the word "supplement" appears as the articulation of two terms : writing is the supplement of speech, culture is the supplement of nature, masturbation is the supplement of normal sexuality. Reading _Les Confessions_ within the network of Rousseau's other texts (in particular the treatise on education _Emile_ and the _Essai sur l'Origine des Langues_), Derrida traces the strange logic of the supplement: "Le concept de supplément... abrite en lui deux significations dont la cohabitation est aussi étrange que nécessaire" (GR, 208). On the one hand, the supplement is a surplus, added on to something that is already complete, "une plénitude enrichissant une autre plénitude." On the other hand, however, "le supplément supplée. Il ne s'ajoute que pour remplacer. Il intervient ou s'insinue à-la-place-de; s'il comble, c'est comme on comble un vide." But in either case, whether it substitutes for something or is added onto something, "le supplément est extérieur, hors de la positivité à laquelle il se surajoute, étranger à ce qui, pour être par lui remplacé, doit être autre que lui" (GR, 208). It is for this reason that the supplement is dangerous: it is added onto something that should need no addition, that ought to be sufficient to itself; and it usurps the place of that to which it is added. Evil and dangerous, the supplement threatens the innocence and the integrity of whatever it attaches to. Nevertheless, Rousseau's attitude toward the supplement in its various forms (writing, masturbation, etc.) is not entirely negative. He recognizes, at least at some level, that writing can only supplement speech if speech is in some way already "infirme." In fact, Rousseau chooses to retreat from society and social intercourse in order to write because "moi présent, on n'aurait jamais su ce que je valais" (quoted in GR, 205). Thus, Rousseau's physical presence leads to misunderstandings and his decision to "se cacher" and to write is "la plus grande réappropriation symbolique de la présence" (GR, 208). Writing provides a surplus: by giving up human society, Rousseau manages to "me faire reconnaître dans l'idéalité de la vérité et de la valeur" (GR, 205). What his spoken word cannot accomplish is made possible by writing.

In the same way, and perhaps more spectacularly, masturbation, the supplement of normal sexuality, is dangerous but "ne l'est point autant, pense ici Jean-Jacques Rousseau, que l'habitation des femmes" (GR, 223). In fact, "menace terrifiante, le supplément est aussi la première et plus sûre protection: contre cette menace elle-même" (GR, 222-23). Rousseau writes: "J'appris ce dangereux supplément qui trompe la nature et sauve aux jeunes gens de mon humeur beaucoup de désordres aux dépens de leur santé, de leur vigueur et parfois de leur vie (quoted in GR 215). This formulation expresses all the ambivalence that Rousseau feels toward the supplement: it rescues one from certain disorders even while it threatens with others. In fact, Rousseau explains that he eventually gave up sexual relations with Thérèse because he felt that the activity "empirait sensiblement mon état; masturbation, "le vice équivalent dont je n'ai jamais pu bien me guérir m'y paraissait moins contraire" (GR, 224).

Finally, Rousseau fears that "la jouissance elle-même" involved in heterosexualitY would be deadly:

> Jouir! .... Si jamais une seule fois en ma vie j'avais
> goûté dans leur plénitude toutes les délices de l'amour,
> je n'imagine pas que ma frêle existence y eût pu suffire,

je serais mort sur le fait (quoted in GR, 223).

The supplement protects against this deadly plenitude as if "l'hétéro-érotisme ne peut etre vécu... qu'à pouvoir acceuillir en soi sa propre protection supplémentaire" (GR, 223). Masturbation, a vice that Rousseau fears will ruin his health, also protects against a greater danger, the danger involved in "l'habitation des femmes." Rousseau always regards the supplement with ambivalence, fearing it yet employing it as a protection against the very thing that it supplements, because the former is both desired and feared, and the supplement "transgresse et à la fois respecte l'interdit" (GR, 223).

Derrida concludes his discussion of Rousseau's Confessions with a reflection on his own methodology of reading. He concludes that, despite its focus on Rousseau's sexuality, the method "n'est... rien moins que psychanalytique" (GR, 228). The psychoanalytic reading assumes both "l'identité à soi du texte" and its simple referentiality that allows one to pass beyond the text to its true content "du côté du pur signifié," two assumptions that Derrida is led to question in the course of his analysis of Rousseau's autobiography.[14] Moreover, the term "supplement" that appears in Les Confessions is not "Rousseau's" word, but belongs to a long linguistic and metaphysical tradition.

> Cela pose la question de l'usage du mot 'supplément' : de la situation de Rousseau à l'intérieur de la langue et de la logique qui assurent à ce mot ou à ce concept des ressources assez surprenantes pour que le sujet présumé de la phrase dise toujours, se servant de 'supplément,' plus, moins, ou autre chose que ce qu'il voudrait dire. ... L'écrivain écrit dans une langue et dans une logique dont, par définition, son discours ne peut dominer absolument le système, les lois et la vie propres. Il ne s'en sert qu'en se laissant d'une certaine manière et jusqu'à un certain point gouverner par le système (GR, 226-27).

If Derrida's terminology and methods are Freudian, his goal is not to account for the "anomalies" of Rousseau's philosophy by appealing to an individual unconscious, but rather to analyze the structure of philosophy, to point to what has been "repressed" in metaphysics itself. The proper name "Rousseau" represents only one articulation of this general structure. Without subscribing to a Jungian notion of a "collective unconscious," Derrida sees individual repression as the product of a larger cultural or social repression, one that, in Western society at least, includes the repression of writing and of difference:

> La répression logocentrique n'est pas intelligible à partir du concept freudien de refoulement; elle permet au contraire de comprendre comment un refoulement individuel et original est rendu possible dans l'horizon

103

d'une culture et d'une appartenance historique (ED, 294).

Thus, what appears most "autobiographical" in Rousseau, the expression of his personal desires, is inherited from the philosophy of presence, passed on through a language that Rousseau cannot fully master.

This issue is taken up again in Derrida's discussion of structural anthropologist Claude Lévi-Strauss. Derrida begins the last section of his discussion of Lévi-Strauss with two epigraphs:

> Sans jamais remplir son projet, le bricoleur y met toujours quelque chose de soi.
> La pensée sauvage.

> Son système est peut-être faux; mais en le dévéloppant, il s'est peint lui-même au vrai.
> J. -J. Rousseau, Dialogues. (quoted in GR, 173)

Both quotations suggest the role of the autobiographical in the philosophical text. But as Derrida goes on to show, the autobiographics is more genealogical than individual. Lévi-Strauss presents himself as the modern disciple of Rousseau: he inherits, not Rousseau's text, but his discourse, which Derrida defines as "la représentation actuelle, vivante, consciente d'un texte dans l'expérience de ceux qui l'écrivent ou le lisent" (GR, 149). In Lévi-Strauss, there is a "rousseauisme déclaré et militant" and Derrida asks:

> Dans quelle mesure l'appartenance de Rousseau à la métaphysique logocentrique et à la philosophie de la présence... assigne-t-elle des limites à un discours scientifique?" (GR, 155).

In inheriting Rousseau's discourse, Lévi-Strauss also inherits a share of the logocentrism that Derrida makes clear is a desire, a desire for presence.

> Présence à soi, proximité transparente dans le face-à-face des visages et l'immédiate portée de voix, cette détermination de l'authenticité sociale est donc classique[,] rousseauiste.... Dans son laboratoire, ou plutôt dans son atelier, l'ethnologue dispose donc aussi de ce rêve, comme d'une pièce ou d'un instrument parmi d'autres [qui sert] le même désir obstiné dans lequel l'ethnologue 'met toujours quelque chose de soi' (GR, 200).

Lévi-Strauss' desire for an innocent world free from corruption leads him to privilege speech over writing and to admire societies that are "sans écriture." Derrida argues that this desire is

104

inherited from philosophy, from Rousseau but leading back once more to Plato. It is one of the tools that Lévi-Strauss borrows in developing a system by the method he calls "bricolage." Lévi-Strauss claims that the bricoleur, unlike the ingénieur, does not make his tools to fit the task but rather borrows them, using whatever happens to be at hand to fit his purposes. Derrida adds that one of these tools is language, a language that is "déjà là." Derrida further explains that the notion of ingénieur "relève de la théologie creationniste" (GR, 201). Everyone is in effect a bricoleur since

> le discours le plus radical, l'ingénieur le plus inventif et le plus systématique sont surpris, circonvenus par une histoire, un langage, etc., un monde... auquel ils doivent emprunter leurs pièces (GR, 201).

This formulation, of course, implicates Derrida as well as Lévi-Strauss: he too depends on the borrowed tools of language, philosophical logic, and history, and so he too is a mouthpiece or front for the logocentric desire. Derrida goes on to suggest a remedy for this problem:

> Dans le meilleur des cas, le discours bricoleur peut s'avouer lui-même, avouer en soi-même son désir et sa défaite, donner à penser l'essence et la necessité du déjà-là

and use the borrowed tools "pour détruire l'ancienne machine" (GR, 201). Derrida adds that:

> à supposer qu'on conserve, par bricolage, l'idée de bricolage, encore faut-il savoir que tous les bricolages ne se valent pas. Le bricolage se critique lui-même (GR, 201).

Thus, Derrida offers a model of self-criticism to combat the inherited desire lodged in philosophical discourse. Derrida's later texts, and especially Glas and "Envois" will adopt this paradigm of self-criticism in a manner that resembles, or at least mimes, autobiography. But these later texts also point to the limits of self-criticism and self-analysis: when Derrida takes up the theory of autobiography in 1980, he focuses on the "inanalysé de Freud" (CP, 297), the unconscious that is not recovered by self-analysis, the desire that is not only overlooked by self-criticism but actually expressed in the form of a self-criticism. It then becomes clear that the "meilleur des cas" is not the final response to bricolage but a further bricolage that only partly succeeds in destroying the "ancienne machine."

105

PART FOUR

AUTOBIOGRAPHICS AS <u>RESTE</u>:

DERRIDA'S <u>GLAS</u>

GLAS AND THE LOGIC OF THE UNCONSCIOUS

It is tempting to mark the publication of _Glas_ in 1974 as a turning-point in Derrida's development as a writer.[1] With _Glas_ and the later texts, the issues of the self, of language, and of the desire for presence are often raised within the context of Derrida's position in the structures he is describing. Thus, Derrida's signature is brought into play in his discussion of the signature; his desire for presence staged in assessing the weight of the history of metaphysics; and his theses concerning the functioning of language illustrated by his use of language. In contrast to the relatively traditional form of _De la Grammatologie_ and the essays on Husserl, Derrida's later texts experiment with various writing styles and their form and logic sometimes seem foreign to the conventions of philosophical discourse. This is not to say, however, that Derrida simply abandons the rigors of philosophical argument in these later writings: _Glas_ contains sustained discussions and expositions of Hegel, Kant, Freud, Saussure and Genet. It is simply that, in addition to or alongside the philosophical critique, there is another story being told, that of a self's relation to language and to the ancestry of philosophy. Thus, like _The Interpretation of Dreams_, _Glas_ is a theoretical text that is also a disguised autobiography.

In fact, the parallels in theme, method, and structure between _Glas_ and _The Interpretation of Dreams_ are striking. Both are a _Trauerarbeit_, the struggle between a son and the father he tries to commemorate and to bury. Derrida's biological father makes a brief but significant appearance; as in _The Interpretation of Dreams_, however, the struggle involves intellectual forefathers as well. In both texts, the autobiographics develops from the interpretation of chosen examples; in _Glas_, it is texts rather than dreams that are interpreted. And finally, both are constructed on the principle of _Gschnas_, pieced together out of disparate elements, combining the trivial with the all-important. The logic that brings these diverse elements together is the logic of the unconscious or of dreams: it is in the juxtaposition and association of the various pieces that a pattern of meanings begins to take shape. Thus, in that other story that Derrida tells in _Glas_, the logical relations between elements, characteristic of philosophical discourse, are replaced by relations of contiguity.

The similarities between _Glas_ and _The Interpretation of Dreams_ are by no means coincidental. Freud's influence pervades Derrida's text, and Derrida both analyzes and enacts Freud's notion of mourning. Furthermore, the "logic" that Derrida adopts in tracing various motifs in Jean Genet's texts is that of Freud's fetishist who, like the dreamer, chooses signifiers that express several, often contradictory, desires. Derrida's rereading of Freud's article on fetishism is translated into a fetishistic writing that structures _Glas_.[2] As we shall see, this textual fetishism is virtually indistinguishable from the structure of dreams.

In "Fetishism," Freud explains that the fetish is ultimately a phallic symbol but that the phallus in question is not "any chance penis" but rather "the woman's (the mother's) penis that the little boy once believed in and... does not want to give up" (XXI, 152-53). In Freud's view, to give up the belief that the mother has a penis is to face the possibility of one's own castration. In other words, the little boy, on discovering that his mother does not have a penis, concludes: she has been castrated; therefore, _it can happen to me_. To circumvent this disagreeable conclusion, the fetishist refuses to admit that women have no penis. Or rather, he retains the belief but he also gives it up:

> Yes, in his mind the woman _has_ got a penis, in spite of everything; but this penis is no longer the same as it was before. Something else has taken its place, has been appointed its substitute, as it were, and now inherits the interest which was formerly directed to its predecessor (XXI, 154).

Freud adds that the fetish becomes a "memorial" to the fear of castration and that "an aversion... to the real female genitals remains a _stigma indelebile_ of the repression that has taken place" (XXI, 154).

Toward the end of this short essay, Freud gives an example of a fetish that, Derrida claims, calls into question his earlier assertion that the fetish invariably symbolizes the mother's phallus. Freud prefaces the example with the words: "In very subtle instances both the disavowal and the affirmation of the castration have found their way into the construction of the fetish itself" and goes on to say:

> This was so in the case of a man whose fetish was an athletic support-belt (_Schamgürtel_) which could also be worn as bathing drawers. This piece of clothing covered up the genitals entirely and concealed the distinction between them. Analysis showed that it signified that women were castrated and that they were not castrated; and it also allowed of the hypothesis that men were castrated, for all these possibilities could equally well be concealed under the belt (XXI, 156).

Thus, the fetish may symbolize both the mother's phallus and the absence of a phallus, both castration and non-castration. As it happens, the French translation of the article of clothing that bears this multiple meaning (_Schamgürtel_) is _gaine_, a term whose etymology leads back to "vagina," that is, to the very term that is excluded (averted) in the opposition between castration and non-castration. What Derrida calls "l'argument de la gaine," then, is an argument that constantly reverses itself into its opposite or that combines contradictory possibilities into a single, undecidable term, a term that can no longer refer unequivocally to a single signified.

Discussing the various significations of the flower in Genet's writings, Derrida alludes to the argument de la gaine:

> Ainsi la fleur (qui égale castration, phallus, etc.) 'signifie' --encore!-- recoupe du moins la virginité en général, le vagin, le clitoris, la 'sexualité féminine,' la généalogie matrilinéaire, le seing de la mère, le seing intégral, soit l'Immaculée Conception.... Pour que la castration recoupe la virginité, le phallus se renverse en vagin, les opposées prétendus s'équivalent et se réflichissent, il faut que la fleur se retourne comme un gant, et son style comme une gaine (GL, 57-R).

This passage not only demonstrates the logic of fetishism in relation to one of the major motifs in Derrida's discussion of Genet, it also forms a link between the argument de la gaine and the logic of dreams. For the flower is one of the examples that Freud chooses to demonstrate the contradictory (sexual) meanings that a single dream symbol can bear. In fact, this example from The Interpretation of Dreams plays a prominent role in Derrida's article on metaphor, "La Mythologie Blanche" (1971). The example appears as an epigraph to a section of Derrida's essay called "Les Fleurs de la Rhétorique: l'Héliotrope"; as we shall see, the position of the example at the head of a section that treats the flower as the rhetorical figure par excellence, the figure for figuration generally, will be less and less indifferent. Here, then, is the passage quoted by Derrida:

> Le rêve ne saurait exprimer l'alternative 'ou bien, ou bien'... Il excelle à réunir les contraires ou à les représenter en un seul objet.... La même branche de fleurs ('la fleur de la vierge' dans la Trahison de la meunière de Goethe) représente donc l'innocence sexuelle et aussi son contraire... Une seule des relations logiques est favorisée par le mécanisme du rêve. C'est la relation de ressemblance (Ähnlichkeit) de correspondance (Übereinstimmung) de contact (Berührung), le 'de même que' ('Gleichwie'); le rêve dispose, pour les représenter, de moyens innombrables (...) Ici aussi 'expensive flowers, one has to pay for them' aurait une signification, et bien réelle, financière. La symbolique des fleurs dans le rêve contient donc le symbole de la jeune fille et de la femme (jungfraülichweibliche), le symbole de l'homme et une indication de défloration

> forcée... elle insiste d'autant plus sur le caractère précieux du 'centre' (elle le nomme à un autre moment <u>a centre piece of flowers</u>), de sa virginité (quoted in MP, 293,).

The resemblances between this passage and the passage in <u>Glas</u> are remarkable : both view the flower as a figure for innocence as well as sexuality, virginity and defloration, penis and vagina. In fact, the <u>Glas</u> passage is a virtual translation of the section from <u>The Interpretation of Dreams</u>, except that where Freud writes "dream symbolism," Derrida substitutes "fetishism." We might be tempted to conclude that <u>The Interpretation of Dreams</u> is the secret "intertext" of this passage or even of <u>Glas</u> as a whole: this is not altogether unwarranted but it suggests that there is a single text presumed to lie behind <u>Glas</u>. As it happens, the passage also "rewrites" or translates a section of Hegel's <u>Phenomenology of Spirit</u>, Genet's <u>Journal du Voleur</u> and other writings, and Derrida's own "Mythologie Blanche," to name only a few of the possible source texts.[3] Derrida describes <u>Glas</u> as the sewing together or grafting of many texts (GL, 190-R and passim): no doubt <u>The Interpretation of Dreams</u> is one of these grafted texts.

CHAPTER VI

THANATOPRAXIS

Le reste

In <u>Glas</u>, Derrida links this activity of grafting or glossing to an autobiographics:

> J'oublie, d'une certaine manière, tout ce que... je lis. Sauf telle ou telle phrase, tel morceau de phrase, apparemment secondaire, dont le peu d'importance apparente en tous cas ne justifie pas cette sorte de résonance, de retentissement obsédant qui se garde, détaché, si longtemps après l'engloutissement, de plus en plus rapide, de tout le reste. On doit toucher là... à la matrice compulsionelle de l'écriture, à son affect organisateur (GL, 218, 9-R).

This description brings to mind Freud's discussion of the "indifferent impressions" of the dream-day that serve as source material for the dream (IV, V: 65, 88). These impressions, of course, are charged with significance by unconscious thoughts and desires seeking to gain expression. The quotations in <u>Glas</u> function in a similar way: episodes from Genet's autobiographical writings, dialogue from his theater, images and arguments from Hegel's philosophical texts, and even the two-columned form of Genet's short essay "Ce qui est resté d'un Rembrandt déchiré en petits carrés bien réguliers et foutu aux chiottes" all serve to describe Derrida's textual activity in <u>Glas</u> and, in particular, his Oedipal relation to his philosophical forefather Hegel. <u>Glas</u> is a family romance (GL, 7-L), a "travail du deuil" or "thanatopraxie" (GL, 99-L), the story of Derrida's philosophical ancestry. Thus, his decision to focus on the question of the family in Hegel "est loin d'être innocent." As Derrida admits, it stems from "des motivations inconscientes qu'il faut mettre en jeu et au travail, sans qu'aucune théorisation préalable en soit possible" (GL, 11-L).

Glas stages the death and burial of the imposing philosopher Hegel: it works at Hegel's philosophy, transforming the monolith of his writings into a tomb. Yet Derrida realizes that a tomb does not simply bury the dead; it also commemorates, creates a lasting monument that grants the deceased, now merely human remains, a place within the human community. In a sense, then, the <u>glas</u> for

Hegel never stops tolling; the corpse continues to rattle about in its coffin.

The passage that describes the scraps of text that remain in one's mind as a "résonance" or "retentissement" suggests that the gloss is a kind of _glas_, a reverberation that outlives the reading of a text. Derrida describes this reading as consuming, incorporating by swallowing, and suggests that writing proceeds from the undigested bits of text that somehow impel the writer (Derrida will sometimes use the term _sfeinctor_ [GL, 280-R]) to produce a text of his own. Thus, the activities of reading and writing are seen as both the sounding of a death knell and the consuming of a dead body. Both metaphors invoke the notion of _Trauerarbeit_ and both figure prominently in Derrida's description of his textual practice in _Glas_.

Glas begins with a consideration of _le reste_. The term (though generally in the plural) means "remains" and designates what is left of a human body after death, the corpse. "Les restes d'un repas," further, are the scraps and crumbs left after a meal; the notion of cannibalism, of course, allows these two meanings to intersect. Derrida often uses the term, along with its variant "restance" to refer to a text, to the capacity of language to continue to function in the absence of the writer, the reader, the referent, and the writer's intentions. The _reste_ is the part of language that does not belong to anyone, that cannot be claimed by an author, nor fully appropriated by a reader. Thus, those persistent passages of a text that remain behind in the mind of the reader, that lead him to write as if from compulsion, are also _le reste_.

In the context of Derrida's reading of Hegel, moreover, the _reste_ is the negative moment of the dialectic before it has been reassimilated, sublated, _aufgehoben_; more radically, it is the moment in Hegel's dialectic that cannot be _aufgehoben_, that which remains behind after the _Aufhebung_ has taken place. But Genet also develops a notion of the _reste_: it is clear that "what has remained of a Rembrandt" is the essay "Ce qui est resté..." itself. Thus Genet offers Derrida a model of reading as _reste_, as the destruction of another work of art (for Genet, the paintings of Rembrandt) in order to produce a text. Derrida concludes that "il y a du reste, toujours, qui se recoupent, deux fonctions": the _reste_ "se divise en deux," may function in two ways: "L'une assure, garde, assimile, intériorise, idéalise, relève la chute dans le monument. La chute s'y maintient, embaume et momifie, monumémorise, s'y nomme--tombe. Donc, mais comme chute, s'y érige" (GL, 7-R). This is the Hegelian model of _reste_: the _chute_ is the negative moment of the dialectic and it is idealized, raised (_relevé_, Derrida's translation of _aufgehoben_), reassimilated into the system. The above passage is a description of the general operation of the Hegelian dialectic, but it is also, more particularly, a description of Hegel's concept of burial rites. Human remains, in a sense, remain human, because the family commemorates the death by building a tomb. The tomb commemorates the fall into death (thus the play on words with "tombe," which

112

functions as both noun and verb). The second function "laisse tomber le reste" (GL, 8-R). This is Genet's notion of reste, remains that are not recuperated, a body that is not resurrected: "Notre-Dame-des-Fleurs eut la tête coupée par un vrai couteau. Et rien ne se passa. A quoi bon? Il ne faut pas que le voile du temple se déchire de bas en haut parce qu'un dieu rend l'âme" (quoted in GL, 16-R).

But Derrida adds that these two functions intersect, the second "risquant de revenir au même" (GL, 8-R). If the reste is the quotation or passage that continues to obsess the reader, until he produces a text of his own, that text may come to function as a monument, an idealization of the reste. This is one of Derrida's major concerns or fears, especially in his discussion of Genet's texts: the right-hand column records Derrida's reluctance to interpret Genet, his hesitancy to idealize, totalize a literary text that he feels exceeds every such effort. Thus, as a tomb for Hegel and Genet, Glas put the two functions of the reste into play.

Cannibalism

We have already seen that Derrida characterizes reading as analogous to eating, the consuming of the dead body of the author who dwells in the tome. Explaining that Hegel, conforming to a "vieux thême humaniste et métaphysique," believed that "la sépulture est le propre de l'homme," Derrida describes the function of the tomb: "l'opération familiale... du deuil transforme le vivant en conscience et en arrache la singularité à la nature. Elle empêche le cadavre de retourner à la nature" (GL, 163-L). But this act of burial as commemoration does not simply struggle against nature, against the decomposition of the human body into inorganic matter. Hegel suggests that "la force contre laquelle travaille la pompe funèbre... réprime un désir inconscient. La famille veut empêcher que le mort ne soit 'detruit' et la sépulture violée par ce désir" (GL, 163, 4-L). Although Hegel does not name the unconscious desire that would lead the family to violate the tomb, Derrida suggests that his remark "forme l'ouverture systématique de cette analyse sur des problématiques ultérieures concernant le travail du deuil, l'anthropophagie, le cannibalisme, tous les processus d'incorporation et d'introjection" (GL, 164-L). In other words, the repressed desire is the desire to consume the corpse, to make one's own body into a sepulcher for the dead. The monument, then, substitutes for the repressed wish, takes the place of the body-monument.

Glas is a tomb of this sort, the product of a cannibalistic desire. But, in quotations and glosses, Derrida offers two models of cannibalism, the Hegelian and the Genetian. The first paradigm occurs in the discussion of the Last Supper where Jesus, soon to be crucified, offers bread and wine to his disciples and proclaims: "This is my body." This symbolic act, which announces Jesus' sacrifice of his body for the sins of mankind, is not at this point a "sacrifice utile": the act of eating and drinking together unites the disciples, not as the beneficiaries of a sacrifice but as a group that shares the same feeling of love.

Si ce qui les unit était un avantage, un bienfait découlant du sacrifice du corps et de l'effusion de sang, ils ne se trouveraient unis sous ce rapport que dans l'égalité d'un concept...; mais en tant qu'ils mangent le pain et boivent le vin, que son corps et son sang passent en eux, Jésus est en eux tous, et son essence... les a divinement pénétrés (durchdrungen) 'comme amour' (Hegel, quoted in GL, 81-L).

That love is objectified, represented as an object, the bread and the wine. "L'esprit de Jésus, en qui ses jeunes disciples... sont un ... est devenu, pour le sens externe, présent comme objet, quelque chose d'effectif" (GL, 82-L). In the act of eating the object, however, the bread and wine are "resubjectified"; the object disappears, the disciples are united, not by the physical object but by the spirit of love that penetrates them. "La consommation intériorise, idéalise, relève" (GL, 81-L). Hegel explains that "la Cène accomplit certes une consumation d'amour que la plastique grecque ne peut atteindre" (GL, 82-L) precisely because it involves an interiorization of the object that symbolizes love:

Quand les amants sacrifient sur l'autel de la déesse de l'amour et que l'effusion de leur sentiment dans la prière en anime [ou spiritualise, begeistert] au plus haut la flamme, la divinité elle-même est descendue dans leur coeur --mais l'image de pierre reste toujours devant eux...; par contre, dans le festin d'amour, le corporel s'efface et seul est présent (vorhanden) le sentiment vivant (Hegel quoted in GL, 83-L, Derrida's brackets).

The act of eating and drinking together at the Last Supper is superior to both of these Greek forms of worship because it combines the symbolization of love in an external object and the resubjectivization of that object in the act of eating:

La spiritualité de la Cène chrétienne consomme ses signes, ne les laisse pas tomber au dehors, aime sans reste.... L'amour devient visible en quelque chose, attache à quelque chose qui doit être anéanti" (GL, 83-L).

Yet this is not yet an "opération religieuse" because the internalized object does not simply disappear, leaving only the feeling of spiritual love; it is digested by the body.

Consommé sans reste, l'objet mystique redevient subjectif mais cesse par là même d'être objet d'adoration

114

> religieuse. Une fois dedans, le pain et le vin sont sans
> doute subjectives mais ils redeviennent aussitôt pain et
> vin, nourriture digérée, de nouveau naturalisée; ils
> perdent leur qualité divine. Ils la perdraient aussi
> bien, il est vrai, à n'être pas digérés. Leur divinité
> se tient, très précaire, entre l'engloutissement et le
> vomissement (GL, 83-84-L).

Before being consumed, the bread and wine are objects that
symbolize something divine; after they are swallowed and digested,
they are also material objects, food to be digested. But in that
moment of communion, as the symbol of love vanishes and before it
becomes again a morsel to be digested, the bread and wine attain
a certain "qualité divine." In what Derrida terms a "remarquable
réflexion," Hegel compares this act of communion, the act of eating
the signs of divine love, to the silent reading of a text.

> La voix tue, la voix absolument retenue anéantit
> l'extériorité objective du signifiant. La lettre et le
> mot disparaissent au moment où ils sont entendus
> au-dedans et d'abord tout simplement saisis, compris.
> Pourvu qu'il nomme, qu'il engage un discours, le
> mouvement de la langue est analogue à la copulation dans
> la Cène.... 'L'amour objectivé, ce subjectif devenu
> chose, retourne à sa nature, redevient subjectif dans
> l'acte de manger. Ce retour peut être comparé... à
> celui de la pensée devenue chose dans le mot écrit,
> retour qui d'un mort (aus einem Toten), d'un objet,
> recouvre dans l'acte de lire sa subjectivité' (GL,
> 81-2-L).

Just as Christ's divine love is given an objective form in the
bread and wine, then once more subjectivized by the act of eating
the object, the thought of an author is granted the form of the
written word, then returned to thought in the act of silent
reading. We notice that the written word is not only an object
but un mort, a dead man or corpse. The act of reading kills off
this corpse but also reanimates it, converts the material object
into an idealized form.

Hegel goes on to point out that his comparison between the
Last Supper and silent reading

> 'serait plus pertinente dans le cas où le mot écrit
> s'évanouirait comme chose dans la lecture silencieuse à
> travers la compréhension; de même... dans la jouis-
> sance... du pain et du vin, ces objets mystiques
> n'éveillent pas simplement le sentiment... l'esprit n'y
> devient pas simplement vivant, mais ils disparaissent
> eux-mêmes comme objets. Et ainsi l'opération paraît plus
> pure, plus conforme à sa fin, dans la mesure où elle
> produit seulement l'esprit, le sentiment et ravit à
> l'entendement son propre... anéantit la matière...

l'inanimé' (Hegel, quoted in GL, 82-L).

When one reads a text, the text remains behind; unlike the act of eating together at the Last Supper, the signs do not disappear after they have been transformed. Thus, the act of consuming bread and wine appears "plus conforme à sa fin": the telos in both cases is a consumption that leaves no _reste_, a telos that is only glimpsed in that moment that Derrida describes as "entre l'engloutissement et le vomissement."

We have, then, the first model of reading as cannibalism that Derrida puts forward in _Glas_. This Hegelian model seeks to reduce the materiality of the text, and insists on the transformation of the dead, written word into thought. The second model is offered by Genet: here, it becomes clear that a written text can give rise not only to comprehension, immaterial thought, but also to another text, that is, a _vomissement_ or excrement. After a long quotation from _Miracle de la Rose_, where Genet compares in vivid language the "rhythme rapide de ma pensée" to a ride on horseback, Derrida stops to reflect on the act of interpreting Genet and, alluding to certain motifs that he has pointed to in discussing Genet's texts, writes:

> Ne pas arrêter la course d'un Genet. C'est la première fois que j'ai peur, en écrivant, comme on dit, 'sur' quelqu'un, d'être lu par lui. Ne pas l'arrêter, le ramener en arrière, le brider.... Il n'écrit presque plus, il a enterré la littérature comme pas un, il saute partout où ça saute dans le monde... et ces histoires de glas, de seing, de fleur, de cheval doivent le faire chier (GL, 45-R).

A _genet_ is a type of horse native to Spain, and much of the right-hand column of _Glas_ is concerned with the ways that Genet undermines the legal status of a signature (as the guarantor of the author's status as creator or owner of the text) by playing with his proper name, making it a figure within the text, using the _genet_ and the _genêt_ (a type of flower called "broom") as motifs in his writings. At this point, however, Derrida feels a certain uneasiness or disgust at his interpretations, fearing that he has arrested the flow of Genet's writing by insisting on only a few of its themes, and further, that he has betrayed Genet by discussing his writings at all, since Genet has stopped writing and has become immersed in political activities.

Nevertheless, Derrida continues to interpret Genet:

> Si toute cette éloquence sur la signature en forme de cheval le fait chier, tant pis. Le seing tombe aussi comme un excrément sous scellé.... Reste --à savoir-- ce qui fait chier (GL, 46-R).

Derrida's use of the vulgar term "ça fait chier" to describe the reaction that _Glas_ might have on Genet reading it, introduces the excremental motif into the discussion. His expressed reluctance to interpret, far from bringing the interpretation to an end, introduces a further motif and prolongs the discussion. In fact, Derrida's reaction against interpretation actually becomes part of the interpretation: for if a signature truly guarantees that the text belongs to its author, how is it possible that the text continues to function even after the author has stopped writing? How is it possible to continue to give literary interpretations of a text whose author has buried literature like no one else? On the other hand, if the signature is completely without effect, how to account for the reaction of disgust one feels at having misrepresented the text or the author?

Derrida's answer to these questions is to examine Genet's description of the volcano-shaped hole that the prisoners in <u>Miracle de la Rose</u> use as a latrine. This description in <u>Glas</u> serves as a figure for the signature. Thus, the phrase "Reste --à savoir-- ce qui fait chier," which introduces this discussion, poses the question: "It remains to be seen what makes one shit." In other words, it asks: What can Genet's description of the prisoners' excremental habits tell us about the issues we have been discussing in relation to Genet's texts and, in particular, about the signature?

According to another reading of the phrase, however, it is already a partial answer to the question. We have seen that, in Derrida's idiolect, <u>reste</u> refers to the brief passages or scraps of dialogue that remain in the mind after one has read a text, the quotations that persist, obsess the reader, and lead him to produce a text of his own. Thus, the phrase might be translated, "<u>reste</u>: that is, what makes one shit," and would serve as a definition of the term "<u>reste</u>." This suggests that the two columns of <u>Glas</u> are fecal columns, the products of a reading of certain passages that, because they cannot be wholly incorporated, are expelled --as another text. In fact, Derrida describes his text as

> un discours dont les unités se moulent à la manière d'un excrément.... L'association est une sorte de contiguité gluante, jamais un raisonnement ou un appel symbolique; la glu de l'aléa fait sens, et le progrès se rythme par petites secousses" (GL, 161-R).

It is not only the materiality of his text that leads Derrida to compare it to an excrement: <u>Glas</u> proceeds by associations of contiguity which Derrida compares to the rhythmic movements of the bowels. For Hegel, reading is the consumption of a dead body (the written word) in order to make it alive again in the mind of the reader; for Derrida, that consumption leads to another text, a material excrement.

As the analysis of excrement in Genet's text continues, however, it becomes clear that this second aspect of the <u>reste</u> intersects, to a certain degree, the idealized, Hegelian <u>reste</u>. For the prisoners' excrement does not simply fall: the latrine is a tub (<u>tinette</u>) of about a meter in height and the prisoners are obliged to climb up onto the seat in order to defecate. Thus, the tinette is an "érection en abîme," a hole that rises up in the middle of the "ronde des punis." Furthermore, Genet describes the odor of the excrement as rising up from the hole. The excrement rises and falls at the same time. And of course, Genet's text glorifies and aesthetizes the scene of defecation, idealizes it in some sense; it becomes part of a literary text. Derrida concludes: "L'excrément solide... s'élève dans le chant incorporel de l'odeur alors que tout 'descend,' s'effondre, pend, provoquant le bâton liquide à gicler en hauteur" (GL, 48-R). In other words, Genet's project to "magnifier l'étron" (GL, 46-R) in some ways resembles Hegel's efforts to constantly recuperate the reste.

Phallic Columns

In the very first pages of Glas, Derrida records two restes, two passages from Hegel that, he claims, are the only part of Hegel's corpus that he plans to "donner à lire." In fact, he will not discuss the passages explicitly until the very end of the book, after a long detour that follows the question of the family in Hegel. In another sense, however, the passages are omnipresent, reappearing in various forms in both columns of Glas and finally functioning as figures for the operation of the text itself. They are, then, the sort of passages that Derrida sees as persisting in the mind because they form a link with unconscious desires.

The first of these passages, drawn from the Phenomenology of Spirit, concerns the change from the religion of flowers to the religion of animals; it alludes, in the context of Glas, to the way that Genet's proper name functions as both a flower and an animal (a horse). I shall discuss it in more detail at a later point. The second passage, from Hegel's Aesthetics, describes "la colonne phallique de l'Inde." Derrida explains that

> elle se serait propagée vers la Phrygie, la Syrie, la Grèce, où, au cours des fêtes dionysiaques, selon Hérodote cité par Hegel, les femmes tiraient le fil d'un phallus qui se dressait alors en l'air, 'presque aussi grand que le reste du corps' (GL, 8-L).

In India, writes Hegel, this veneration of the Zeugungskraft, virility or power of procreation, of the phallus took the form of large stone columns shaped like a phallus. At first, these columns

> étaient intactes, inentamées, lisses. Et c'est seulement plus tard (erst später) qu'on y pratique, dans le flanc, si l'on peut dire, des entailles, excavations, ouvertures (GL, 9-L).

These carvings or sculptures on the phallic column

> annonçaient les petits temples portatifs et hermétiques

des Grecs, commes elles entamaient le modèle de la pagode qui n'est pas encore tout à fait une habitation... Milieu à peine déterminable entre la colonne et la maison, la sculpture/ et l'architecture (GL, 9-L).[4]

Thus, the phallic columns are at first solid rock with a smooth surface, "apparemment introuables" (GL, 9-L); as time passes, however, they are carved, sculpted, and finally hollowed out, transformed into a pagoda which, not yet a dwelling, still announces the dwelling that is to follow.

Derrida concludes the paraphrase of Hegel's passage by asserting of the columns: "on ne peut donc y loger. Quoi que ce soit, mort ou vif. Ce n'est ni une maison ni une sépulture" (GL, 9-L). In this gloss of Hegel's text, Derrida introduces a number of figures that will come to describe _Glas_ and Derrida's activities of reading and writing: there is, first, the allusion to the women at the dionysiac rites who erect a false phallus, a fetish; second, the large phallic columns, at first smooth, then, bit by bit, carved with images; finally, the hollowed-out pillars that will serve as a dwelling or a sepulcher, a home for the living or for the dead (as we shall see, these two dwellings will become virtually indistinguishable in _Glas_). _Glas_ is written "au nom de Hegel," in Hegel's name and in his honor. As he develops the figures of reading and writing, Derrida asks: What does it mean to honor the dead? Can one erect a tomb without already desecrating it? Does the _glas_ that one tolls commemorate the dead body, or bury it, kill off the already dead?

Honoring the Dead

As the gloss of Hegel's discussion of the phallic columns proceeds on the left-hand side of the text, the right-hand column records a number of dictionary entries from _Littré_. The second of these is "catafalque," an "estrade elevée, par honneur, au milieu d'une église, pour recevoir le cerceuil ou la représentation d'un mort" (Quoted in GL, 8-R). Littré adds that "_catafalque_ est le même mot que _échafaud_" since both are combinations of "_cadare_," to look, and "_falco_," balcony. A catafalque is a space erected to hold and honor the dead; the "same word," "échafaud" is the platform erected to kill, to bring about a death. In addition, one of the variant etymological forms of "catafalque" is "cadaphallus," which suggests "cadat phallus," "let the phallus fall." Already we perceive an intimate link between the divine, the phallic, and the dead. The phallic columns of India were erected in honor of the phallus' _Zeugungskraft_ and were sculpted with _Götterbilder_, the images of gods; later, these columns became pagodas, then dwellings and sepulchers. Thus, the phallus, at first an object of worship, is eventually hollowed out, made into a tomb.

Beneath the dictionary entries, Derrida describes the passages as

ouvrant --ici-- dans la pierre de chaque colonne des

119

> sortes de judas incrustés, crénaux, jalousies, meur-
> trières pour voir à ne pas se laisser emprisonner dans
> le colosse, tatouages dans la peau plissée d'un corps
> phallique ne se donnant jamais à lire qu'à bander" (GL,
> 8-9-R).

The vocabulary suggests that Derrida's task in _Glas_ is to make of Hegel's inpenetrable corpus a habitation, by tatooing on the phallus, carving out keyholes, battlements, peep-holes. The terms "judas," "crénaux," "jalousies," and "meurtrières" are all architectural terms, but "jalousies, meurtrières" can also be read in this context as "murderous jealousies," as if Derrida's effort to make Hegel readable, to erect a column in honor of Hegel's phallic text, were also inspired by a desire to murder Hegel, to erect a tomb for Hegel's corpse. It is as if the insertion of _judas_, Derrida's name for the pockets of text that sometimes interrupt the main columns, were a betrayal (and Derrida will link the _judas_ to Judas, the man who betrays Jesus (GL, 40-41-L).

This train of thought continues in the Hegel column on the next page, where Derrida announces his intention to write an introduction to Hegel for whoever "n'a pas encore lu ou entendu Hegel, ce qui est peut-être la situation la plus générale, en tous cas la mienne ici maintenant" (GL, 10-L). Evoking the German term for "introduction," Derrida writes: "_Einführung_, comme disent les philosophes allemands, introduction _dans_ Hegel. _Einführung_ commande l'accusatif et indique le mouvement actif de pénétration" (GL, 10-L). This active penetration is not, in appearance, anal or vaginal, but a penetration into the phallus itself, the hollowing out of Hegel's phallic text, which begins with the carving or sculpting on the phallus, glossing the text, and ends with the erecting of another phallus, Derrida's phallic column.

In a quotation from Genet's _Pompes Funèbres_, Derrida suggests that the erection of a phallus is one means of honoring the dead. In the scene, Genet sees his dead friend Jean on a _catafalque_, his stiff corpse wrapped in _bandelettes_: "Devant les fleurs je bandai et j'en eus honte, mais je sentis qu'à la rigidité du cadavre je ne pouvais opposer que la rigidité de ma verge. Je bandais and ne désirais personne" (quoted in GL, 18-R). The association of the corpse with an erect penis is made possible not only through the shared characteristic of rigidity but also by a verbal bridge provided by "bander," both "to bind up" and "to get a hard-on." As a tribute to Hegel's dead corpus, Derrida erects his own phallic text.

But if Derrida's text penetrates into Hegel's phallus, and if _Glas_ is itself a phallus, then the penetration is that of one column into another. As it happens, "une colonne dans l'autre" is the phrase that Derrida uses to describe the union that takes place within marriage, according to one of Hegel's early formulations of the nature of the family. It is the union, not of husband and wife, but of father and son:

120

L'infinité du désir, du mariage et de la loi intérieure se tient entre le fils et le père. A un bref détour près, à l'exception insignifiante d'une inessentialité (la femme est ici comme la matière), l'essence du mariage spéculatif consacre, avec toutes les conséquences systématiques qu'on peut en induire, l'union du père et du fils. Une colonne dans l'autre (GL, 44-L).

The family is not a relationship of love or desire between two finite beings: marriage produces a son who, by leaving the family to be educated and entering the community, brings about the Aufhebung of the family unit. Thus, the important relationship for Hegel is not the one between husband and wife, but between father and son. The father lives on in the son, and the family is made infinite. Thus, Derrida's act of penetrating into Hegel's text is an act of filial piety, the son's commemoration of the father. Yet it is also, as we have seen, a commemoration in the sense of a death knell, the carrying out of funeral rites. Derrida hollows out the phallus in order that it may serve as Hegel's tomb.

Burial Rites

In Hegel's texts, however, it is not the son who buries the father; rather, it is the daughter, the wife, the sister, or the mother --woman in general-- who performs the rites of burial. As we shall see, Derrida is this woman also; or, at least, he dresses himself as a woman in order to achieve his goals, in order to bury Hegel, but also, in order to seduce, to play at and with philosophy.

Glas traces the passage in the Phenomenology of Spirit from the family to the state, that is, from the "singularity" of the family unit to the "universality" of the state. This passage is brought about through the son who, having been educated, leaves the family unit and becomes a citizen. Yet in this operation, this passage from singularity to universality, something or someone remains behind (reste): the mother, wife, or daughter, the woman who guards the hearth. Derrida explains that Hegel posits a tension between "la loi de la singularité" and "la loi de l'univer-salité." These two laws organize a series of oppositions: divine law/human law, family/city, woman/man, night/day, etc. Human law, produced and administered by men (males) is public, visible, and universal: it regulates the state rather than the family and is associated with daylight. Divine law is a hidden, nocturnal law; it governs the family and is proper to women. It is more natural than human law but it is also in conflict with it since it works against universality.

Naturel, divin, féminin, nocturne, familial, tel est le système prédicatif, la loi de la singularité.... Le but propre de la famille, de la femme qui la représente, strictement, c'est le singulier comme tel.

121

The problem is that "dans son essentialité, la singularité ne peut que disparaître" (GL, 161-L): according to the Hegelian dialectic, singularity must be overcome, sublated into universality. Yet woman remains in contradiction to this dialectical progression: as guardian of the hearth, she obeys a contradictory law, works against universalization, against the male law: "Le gouvernement --la tête-- autorise et organise [le] droit familial, élément et être-là naturel de la communauté, [mais] il est aussi menacé par lui. La famille met la tête en peril" (GL, 165-L). Hegel writes that the "objet essentiel" of the family is not the citizen, since he does not belong to the family but to the government, nor is it the individual who is not yet a citizen but will become one; if the goal of the family is "le singulier comme tel" (a goal in contradiction with the goals of the government), its proper object can only be "cet être singulier appartenant à la famille, mais pris comme une essence universelle, soustraite à son effectivité." That is, the family is not concerned with a living being but with

> le <u>mort</u>, celui qui hors de la longue succession... de son être-là dispersé se receuille... dans <u>une seule</u> figuration accomplie... et hors de l'inquiétude de la vie contingente s'est élevé à la quiétude de l'univer-salité simple. --Puisque c'est seulement comme citoyen qu'il est effectif et substantiel, l'être singulier, en tant qu'il n'est pas citoyen... et appartient à la famille, est seulement l'ombre sans force... et ineffective (Hegel, quoted in GL, 162-L).

The only moment when the individual belongs completely to the family, not as a contingent, empirical being but as "universalité simple" is when he is dead; otherwise, he belongs to the universality of the government, as a citizen. The activities proper to the family are, then,

> toilette du mort, institution de la mort, veillée, monumentalisation, archive, héritage, généalogie, classification des noms propres, gravure sur les tombes, ensevelissement, sépulture, chant funèbre, etc. (GL, 162-L).

The family perpetuates itself by remembering those who have died, by granting the human remains a place in the genealogy of the family, by engraving the proper name in the family archives. Thus, concludes Derrida, "la famille ne connaît pas encore le travail producteur d'universalité dans la cité, seulement le travail du deuil" (GL, 162-L).

As we have seen, it is women who guard the hearth, remaining behind after men have become citizens; thus, women are the representatives of the family. Derrida concludes that, since men only belong to the family in death,

> il revient à la féminité épousée de gérer, strictement,
> un cadavre. Quand un homme se lie à une femme..., il
> s'agit toujours de lui confier sa mort.... Confier la
> mort, la garde d'un corps sans moelle, a charge pour la
> femme d'ériger sa sépulture après avoir enseveli le
> cadavre rigide (onction, bandelettes, etc.), le
> maintenant ainsi dans une surrection vivante, monumen-
> tale, interminable (GL, 162-63-L).

When a man marries, what he offers his wife is not himself as a
living subject (since that still belongs to the government) but
his dead body, the only part of himself that belongs essentially
to the family. In some sense, the wedding night is already a wake;
the image of the rigid penis entering the woman's body blends with
that of the cadaver entering the earth since "la nuit du monde
souterrain est la femme, précise Hegel" (GL, 162). In addition,
the dwelling that the woman oversees is already in some sense a
sepulcher. Thus, if Derrida is burying Hegel, hollowing out the
phallic text so that it may serve as a dwelling or sepulcher for
Hegel's proper name, he is acting as (or like) a woman.

Women and Fetishism

Derrida suggests that Glas is a Trauerarbeit: we are, then,
justified in asking whether this mourning gives way to a phase of
triumph, whether, as in The Interpretation of Dreams and in Freud's
theory of mourning, there is not a moment when Derrida separates
himself completely from the dead father, and lays him to rest at
last. As it happens, there is a triumph of sorts, but it does not
lay Hegel to rest, nor does it consist in Derrida's becoming a
father: it is in becoming woman that Derrida escapes Hegel's
influence, or rather, in pretending to be a woman --who is
pretending to be a man.

We recall that in the passage from the Aesthetics that Derrida
quotes in the first pages of Glas, Hegel alludes to certain
dionysiac rites, where women adorn themselves with a false phallus,
and pull on a string in order to erect it "presque aussi grand que
le corps." Describing his own project in Glas, Derrida writes:
"Pour travailler au nom de Hegel, pour l'ériger, le temps d'une
cérémonie, j'ai choisi de tirer sur un fil.... C'est la loi de la
famille" (GL, 10-L). Thus, Derrida disguises himself as woman,
adorned with a fetish object, in order to erect the false phallus
in the name of Hegel.

The image suggests Derrida's later discussion of Kant and the
problem of sexual difference. For Kant, Derrida begins: "La femme
veut être un homme, l'homme ne veut jamais être une femme.... Kant
ne s'étend pas sur cette dernière proposition, en chute de
paragraphe" (GL, 148-L). This leads Derrida to speculate:

> Que voudrait dire, pour un homme, vouloir être une femme,
> dès lors que la femme veut être un homme à mesure qu'elle
> se cultive? Cela voudrait donc dire, à l'apparence d'un

> détour près, vouloir être un homme, vouloir être --c'est
> à dire rester-- un homme (GL, 148-L).

For Kant, man is the goal toward which woman strives; limited in her powers, she wishes to become a man "pour pouvoir donner à ses inclinations un espace de jeu (_Spielraum_) plus grand et plus libre" (Kant, quoted in GL, 148-L). Thus, the man who wants to be a woman, would, like every woman, want to be a man; the desire to be a woman would simply be a detour on the way to becoming what both sexes want to be --male. In the next paragraph, Derrida revises and complicates this first paradigm:

> Est-ce si simple? Kant dit-il que la femme veut être un
> homme? Il dit plus précisément qu'elle voudrait, dans
> certaines situations, se parer des attributs de l'homne
> pour réaliser ses desseins de femme: être mieux en mesure
> d'avoir tous les hommes. Elle fait semblant de vouloir
> être un homme ou d'être un homme pour 'étendre l'espace
> de jeu' de ses inclinations (GL, 148-L).

Woman does not really want to be a man; she only wants to appropriate a certain "maleness," male power or prowess, in order to achieve her female aims. What, then, would a man who wants to be a woman desire?

> Tout se renverse: ou bien l'homme qui ne veut être
> qu'homme veut être femme en tant que la femme veut être
> homme; il veut donc être femme pour rester ce qu'il est.
> Ou bien l'homme qui veut être femme ne veut être que
> femme puisque la femme ne veut être homme que pour
> parvenir à ses desseins de femme. A savoir l'homme.
> Etc. (GL, 148-L).

The first instance is simply the logical consequence of Derrida's _first_ paradigm: the man who wants to remain a man shares with woman his desire, since she too wants to be a man. His desire to be a man puts him in the same position as woman, who also wants to be male.

This is not entirely accurate, however, since, for Kant, woman does not really want to be a man, but merely to simulate maleness in order to better accomplish her designs, in order to seduce men. A man who wanted to be a woman would thus want to be a woman who merely _simulates_ maleness. That, of course, is precisely how Derrida characterizes himself in the passage cited earlier: he has become a woman, but a woman adorned with a false phallus. The possibility that Derrida does not consider in his discussion of Kant (or that he merely subsumes under an "etc.") is that of a man who wants to be a woman (simulating maleness) in order to achieve his _male_ designs, whatever those might be.

Continuing to paraphrase Kant, Derrida links this transvestism of women to both fetishism and to reading:

En fait, même si elle le voulait vraiment, ce qui n'est pas le cas, la femme ne pourrait jamais être homme. Les attributs masculins dont elle se pare ne sont jamais que du toc, des signifiants sans signification, des fétiches. De la montre. Mal réglée sur le mouvement du soleil. Pour illustrer le fait que la femme ne peut en aucun cas s'approprier l'attribut masculin, par exemple ou substitution la science, la culture, le livre, Kant dénonce une sorte de travestissement: 'En ce qui concerne les femmes savantes: elles en usent avec leurs livres comme avec leur montre; elles la portent pour montrer qu'elles en ont une, bien qu'à l'ordinaire elle soit arrêtée ou ne soit pas réglée sur le soleil' (GL, 149-L).

By writing "attribut masculin" in the singular form, and suggesting that science, culture, and books are <u>substitutions</u> for that attribute, Derrida is hinting that what women lack is a phallus, and that their attempts to appropriate male power amount to fetishism, the merely ornamental use of a false penis. In the same way, a woman wears a watch simply as an ornament, not attending to its true function of telling time. The equivalent of displaying a watch that is not set to follow the movement of the sun would be treating books only as ornaments, or attending only to the ornaments of the book --the images, metaphors, figures, or verbal expressions-- without looking past the words for the ultimate meaning or truth of the book that is presumed to lie outside language. A reading "réglée sur le mouvement du soleil" is a reading that recaptures the author's intentions, that considers the author to be the father or source (as the sun is the source of light) of his writings, a reading that believes that the author's intentions "center" the text.[5]

It is not difficult to read Kant's comments about women readers as a characterization of Derrida, since he has long mounted an assault on the notion that the author's intentions govern or control the text and, as a reader, has often stressed the decentering effect of language. We begin to suspect that Derrida takes on the role of woman in order to escape the pervasive influence of the father Hegel, developing a method of reading that does not inherit the father's name and that does not simply replicate the father's text.

In his essay on Nietzsche, <u>Eperons</u>, Derrida addresses the question of woman, linking the notion of truth as unveiling (<u>aletheia</u>) to the Freudian notion of the castration complex. According to Freud, the boy child recognizes the threat of castration when he sees the female genitals and concludes that girls have been castrated. Derrida explains "la vérité-castration, c'est justement l'<u>affaire</u> de l'homme, l'<u>affairement</u> masculin" (EP, 47) and that woman believes neither in castration, nor in truth. He adds that

la femme... ne croit pas davantage à l'envers franc de

125

> la castration, à l'anti-castration. Elle est trop rusée
> pour cela et elle sait... qu'un tel renversement lui
> ôterait toute possibilité de simulacre, reviendrait en
> vérité au même....
> Or la 'femme' a besoin de l'effet de castration,
> sans lequel elle ne saurait séduire ni ouvrir le désir
> --mais évidemment elle n'y croit pas. Est 'femme' ce
> qui n'y croit pas et qui en joue. En joue: d'un nouveau
> concept et d'une nouvelle structure de la croyance visant
> à rire (EP, 48).

Here again, woman adorns herself with a phallus, knowing that it is false, in order to produce desire and to seduce. She manipulates an "effet de vérité" without believing in truth. Unlike the male fetishist, for whom the fetish commemorates his belief in the mother's phallus, a belief he cannot bring himself to give up entirely, woman knows that the fetish stands for no lost object, no ultimate signified.[6]

In characterizing himself as a woman who erects Hegel's name "le temps d'une cérémonie," Derrida suggests that his object is to seduce, to feign a philosophical discourse, a discourse on truth, in order to produce desire. Genet once more provides a quotation to serve Derrida as a description of his fetishistic writing. In the right-hand column, Derrida quotes Genet's question to his friend Stilitano: "Tu voudrais que je m'habille en femme?" (GL, 249-R). The question appears in Le Journal du Voleur: Stilitano has proposed that Genet earn money for them by working as a prostitute out of a nearby bar. Whereas in Kant's paradigm, it is women who take on male attributes in order to be better able to seduce men, here it is a man who dresses as a woman in order, once more, to seduce men. The possibility that is left out of Derrida's consideration of Kant, the very figure that describes Derrida's activity of fetishism, is provided by Genet.

The quotation from Le Journal du Voleur appears in Glas at the moment that Derrida turns to Freud's essay on fetishism. The question at hand is whether Freud's theory of fetishism is sufficient as a mode of interpreting the sexual fantasies that Genet records in his writings. In another passage from Le Journal du Voleur, much quoted by Derrida, Genet describes how he became emotionally attached to Stilitano:

> D'un geste de sa main vivante il me fit signe qu'il
> voulait se déshabiller. Comme les autres soirs je
> m'agenouillai pour décrocher la grappe de raisin. A
> l'intérieur de son pantalon il avait épinglé une de ces
> grappes postiches dont les grains, de mince cellulose,
> sont bourrés de ouate.... Chaque fois, à la Criolla,
> troublé par la boursouflure, qu'un pédé lui mettait la
> main à la braguette, ses doigts horrifiés rencontraient
> cet objet qu'ils redoutaient être une grappe de son
> véritable trésor, la branche où comiquement, s'ac-
> crochaient trop de fruits....

> Durant le temps qu'il l'avait portée cette grappe n'avait pas nui à sa beauté. Au contraire, le soir, en les encombrant un peu, elle avait donné à ses jambes une légère incurvation, à son pas une douce gêne un peu arrondie et quand il marchait près de moi, devant ou derrière, je connaissais un trouble délicieux puisque mes mains l'avaient préparé. C'est par l'insidieux pouvoir de cette grappe, crois-je encore, que je m'attachais à Stilitano.

Derrida poses the hermeneutic question: "Le style en question, le postiche retenu par l'épingle à nourrice, est-ce un fétiche" (GL, 249-50-R), adding that this form of question assumes "qu'on sache au moins du fétiche que c'est quelque chose." At first glance, the grappe de raisin appears to function as a fetish:

> substitut du pénis adoré par l'enfant qui ne veut pas rénoncer au phallus de la mère, érection monumentale du triomphe sur la menace de castration, déni, compromis, etc. Tout cela n'est-il pas très reconnaissable?" (GL, 250-R).

Things are not so simple, however; for Freud, the fetish "saves the fetishist from becoming a homosexual, by endowing women with the characteristic which makes them tolerable as sexual objects" (XXI, 154). Genet is a homosexual and Stilitano already has the penis that the fetish is supposed to substitute for. The fetish is, then, a supplementary penis, as well as a "plaie postiche" (Genet, quoted in GL, 251). This supplementary castration also serves to "re-marquer-compenser un autre substitut de castration," Stilitano's missing right hand. As both a supplementary penis and a supplementary wound, the grappe de raisin compensates for the lost hand and, at the same time, symbolizes it. But, in order for the grappe de raisin to symbolize the lost hand, it must act as supplement of a supplement, since for Freud, "castration" is the ultimate meaning that mutilated members, missing eyes and teeth, and decapitation signify.

"Castration" is the signified that is not itself a signifier, that which cannot represent something else.[8] Derrida shows, however, that the phallus and castration can be brought into the play of signification. Stilitano's grappe de raisin does not signify simply an absent phallus, and his missing arm actually seems to make him more virile. In fact, Genet writes that "quand un membre est enlevé, m'apprend-on, celui qui reste devient plus fort. Dans le sexe de Stilitano, j'espérais que la vigueur de son bras coupé s'était ramassé" (quoted in GL, 156-R). Thus, the penis itself seems to compensate, supplement the lost member. But if the penis functions as a supplement, it is in the position of the fetish. Derrida concludes that

> dès lors que la chose même, en sa vérité dévoilée, se trouve déjà engagée... dans le jeu de la différence

127

> supplémentaire, le fétiche n'a plus de statut rigour-
> eusement décidable. Glas du phallogocentrisme....
> L'économie du fétiche est plus puissante que celle de la
> vérité --décidable-- de la chose même ou qu'un discours
> décidant de la castration (pro aut contra). Le fétiche
> n'est pas opposable (GL, 252-54-R).

The grappe de raisin signifies both castration and non-castration: by adorning himself with it, "Stilitano semble s'affirmer aussi bien comme femme pudique ou comme 'pédé qui se hait'" (GL, 252-R). Adorned with the grappe de raisin, Stilitano has, as it were, a supplementary phallus, like the man disguised as a woman adorned with a false phallus or like the double-columned Glas. This fetishism is undecidable: Stilitano is both male and female; the fetish object both represents and guards against castration; the "thing itself," the penis, may also function as a fetish; and "phallogocentrism," which posits that the phallus and its absence, castration, are the ultimate signified of fetishism, is called into question, decentered by that very fetishism.

A fetishistic reading, then, would escape the author's influence, would decenter the reading that tries to recuperate intentions or locate an extratextual truth. "Si j'écris deux textes à la fois," writes Derrida, "vous ne pourrez pas me châtrer" (GL, 77-R).

> Si je délinéarise, j'érige. Mais en même temps, je
> divise mon acte et mon désir. Je --marque la division
> et vous échappant toujours, je simule sans cesse et ne
> jouis nulle part. Je me châtre moi-même --je me reste
> ainsi-- et je 'joue à jouir.'
> Enfin presque.
> (Ah!) tu es imprenable (eh bien) reste (GL, 77-R).

This passage alludes to Freud's claim that the multiplication of phallic symbols in dreams is a device that the unconscious uses to guard against the threat of castration. But the multiplication also reveals the underlying fear of castration that it guards against: thus, it both protects against and represents that threat.

In this case, the threat of castration is the fear of having one's discourse "cut off," reduced to a single, ultimate signified. As we recall, this is Hegel's model of reading: the signs ought to disappear, consumed altogether by the reader. It is the father Hegel's law that poses the threat of castration, and it is his law that Derrida tries to escape. His means of escape: the fetishism or transvestism that consists in adorning himself with a sup-plementary phallus. As we have seen, this fetishism is associated with both male homosexuals and women: in fact, the phrase "joue à jouir" is used by Genet to describe one of his lovers (quoted in GL, 32-R), but it also suggests the women in Eperons who "'se donnent pour,' même quand elles --se donnent.... [DaB sie 'sich geben,' selbst noch, wenn sie --sich geben]." (Nietzsche, quoted in EP, 56). Thus, Derrida's means of escaping Hegel's influence, of escaping the law of reading that would castrate his text, is to engage in a textual fetishism, to pervert Hegel's phallocentric law by becoming a woman or a homosexual. The form of the text is thus a triumph of sorts, but a triumph caught up in the double bind or undecidability of fetishism itself: the text remains "imprenable"; it is not, as Hegel would have it, consumed without _reste_, but at the same time, Derrida writes, "je simule sans cesse et ne jouis nulle part." Unlike Freud, whose _Trauerarbeit_ culminates in his becoming a father and taking the father's place, Derrida can only mock the father Hegel by practicing a textual perversion.

The very first page of _Glas_ conveys the weight of Hegel's influence and, in the facing column, offers the strategy for escaping it. The text begins:

> quoi du reste aujourd'hui, pour nous, ici, maintenant, d'un Hegel? Pour nous, ici, maintenant: voilà ce qu'on n'aura pu désormais penser sans lui.... Sa signature, comme la pensée du reste, enveloppera ce corpus mais n'y sera sans doute pas comprise (GL, 7-L).

Faced with the task of writing on Hegel, Derrida must admit that perhaps Hegel has already foreseen all that there is to say, has already programmed him with his ideas, thoughts, and methods, has already signed his name to _Glas_. How to escape such an all-pervasive influence? The answer appears in the right-hand column: "'ce qui est resté d'un Rembrandt déchiré en petits carrés bien réguliers, et foutu aux chiottes' se divise en deux" (GL, 7-R). Genet's short essay, whose title refers to a destruction or fragmentation of the works of a great artist, also takes the form of two columns. In a description of that essay, Derrida records his own strategy for the two columns of _Glas_:

> Deux colonnes inégales, disent-ils, dont chaque-- enveloppe ou gaine, incalculablement renverse, retourne, remplace, remarque, recoupe l'autre. L'incalculable de _ce qui est resté_ se calcule, élabore tous les coups, les tord ou les échafaude en silence, vous vous épuiseriez plus vite à les compter. Chaque petit carré se délimite, chaque colonne s'enlève avec un impassible suffisance et pourtant l'élément de la contagion, la circulation infinie de l'équivalence générale rapporte chaque phrase, chaque mot, chaque moignon d'écriture... à chaque autre, dans chaque colonne et d'une colonne à l'autre de _ce qui est resté_ infiniment calculable.
> A peu près (GL, 7-R).

We have seen only a very few instances of this contagion effect: by writing two texts in one, two columns whose only relation to each other is a set of common concerns, Derrida produces an infinitely tolling _Glas_ that allows the play of signification to continue through the juxtaposition of passages and quotations in endless combinations. In this way, the language never comes to rest, never points to a single, ultimate signified: Hegel is never laid to rest, but he is never totally idealized either. The _glas_ never stops tolling for Hegel and something of his text remains behind, _reste_.

CHAPTER VII

SIGNATURES

Literary Discourse and the Case of the Signature

The first example that Derrida chooses to illustrate the double function of the _reste_ is the signature and from the beginning, the status of this example is at issue. He suggests that the case (_cas_, _Fall_) of the signature may also be a trap (_Falle_) and later criticizes Jean-Paul Sartre for making of Genet's texts "le cas d'une structure universelle" (GL, 37-R). Nevertheless, Derrida suggests at other times that the signature and Genet's use of it are of paradigmatic importance in the study of literary discourse. Furthermore, Derrida's comments on Genet's use of the signature describe his own practice in _Glas_; the definition of literature that Derrida develops on the basis of this issue identifies _Glas_ as a literary text. As we shall see, it is largely Genet's autobiographical writings that come to stand as paradigmatic of literary discourse generally, and it is the autobiographical moments in Derrida's text that conform to his theory of literary discourse.

Having outlined the two intersecting functions of the _reste_, Derrida, by way of example, suggests that this is "peut-être le cas (_Fall_) du seing" (GL, 8-R). Playing on the etymology of both the French and German word for "case," he introduces the notion of falling into the discussion of the signature. Thus, he writes, "le seing tombe" (GL, 8-R). The syntax of the phrase (the fact that "tombe" can function as both a verb and a noun) allows it to express both functions of the signature at once: the signature erects itself into a monument or tomb, and the signature falls. On the next page, Derrida suggests that the issue of the signature is a

> préliminaire indispensable à l'explication de la formalité (par exemple 'littéraire') avec tous les juges musclés qui l'interrogent depuis des instances apparemment extrinsèques (question du sujet --biographique, historique, économique, politique, etc.-- classé). Quant à la textualité générale, le seing représente peut-être le cas, le lieu de recoupement (topique et tropique) de l'intrinsèque et de l'extrinsèque (GL, 9-10-R).

131

Even a formal explication of a text, an explication of its intrinsic properties, must come to terms with the question of the signature, since every interpretation or judgment makes certain assumptions about the text's "outside," its author, history, and position in literary discourse. The signature, as the articulation between the inside and the outside, is thus the privileged locus of a discourse that seeks to investigate the relationship between the text and what lies beyond it.

Derrida suggests that the role of the signature is at issue in any sort of discourse; nevertheless, he takes literary discourse as a privileged example. The question of narrative voice and of fictionality complicates, or at least foregrounds, the signature's relation to the text, and in particular, the relation of the "I" in the text to the name that signs it. This is _a fortiori_ the case of autobiography, where the fundamental issue in defining the genre involves the relation between the author and the subject of the text. And, just as the signature lies at the margin of the text, autobiography appears marginal to literature; for this very reason, all the issues regarding the definition of literature, the notion of fictionality, and the relation of literature to non-literature are concentrated in autobiography.

Derrida offers two alternative ways of looking at the signature's position in relation to the text it signs: either the signature is within the text, or it lies outside it. In the first case, the signature "ne signe plus, elle opère comme un effet à l'intérieur de l'objet, joue comme une pièce dans ce qu'elle prétend s'approprier ou reconduire à l'origine. La filiation se perd. Le seing se défalque" (GL, 10-R). If the signature is inside the text, it is not a signature at all. It is simply a name, a word, one of the elements in the play of signification. It cannot guarantee an ultimate signified, cannot function as the expression of an author's intentions or as the source of the text. It cannot refer to the text's "father" (i.e. author), cannot watch over the text and guarantee its legitimacy. If, on the other hand, the signature is outside the text, "elle émancipe aussi bien le produit qui se passe d'elle, du nom du père ou de la mère dont il n'a besoin pour fonctionner. La filiation se dénonce encore, elle est toujours trahie par ce qui la remarque" (GL, 10-R). If the signature is simply outside the text, then, by definition, the text does not depend on it and is already complete without it. The text can operate without the presence of the author or even the author's name.

Drawing on a persistent metaphor that he analyzed with acuity in "La Pharmacie de Platon," Derrida describes the relation of author to text as one of filiation. Throughout _Glas_, he uses and distorts Plato's metaphor: whereas for Plato, the parent in question is always the father, Derrida suggests here that the author is alternatively the father and the mother of the text. Furthermore, since, as we saw in the last chapter, the signature does not simply refer to an already-existing subject, but constitutes it as a legal entity, the signature is not just a representative of the author, but its producer, that is, its father or mother.

These distortions of Plato's model allow Derrida to assimilate his discussion of the family, and in particular, of Genet's family, to the question of the signature. For, as it happens, "Genet," the author's nom de plume, is also the name of the mother: illegitimate and abandoned by his parents at birth, all he knows of his genealogy is the name "Gabrielle Genet" that appears on his birth certificate. Derrida studies the relationship between this abandoned, bastard child and his mother's name as characteristic of the text/signature relationship.

Having established the two possible functions of the signature, Derrida adds that, whether the signature lies within or outside the text, "la perte sécrétée du reste" is recuperated by the signature. The text is somehow reappropriated by the name that signs it. In fact, "tout le texte... se rassemblerait dans tel 'cerceuil vertical'... Comme l'érection d'un seing" (GL, 10-R). The cerceuil vertical, an allusion to Genet's Miracle de la Rose, is a prison: the signature, then, would imprison the text, enclose it in a tomb. And, Derrida writes, "le texte r(est)e--tombe, la signature r(est)e--tombe--le texte" (GL, 11-R). The syntax, the play of dashes and of parentheses allow for multiple readings. The text is, remains, falls, and falls again; the text is, remains, a tomb; the signature is, remains, falls, falls again, and even "kills off" the text; the signature is, remains, a text. Both the text and the signature erect themselves even as they fall, erect themselves in falling.

We already perceive a certain conflict between the text and the signature: the text seems to be able to function on its own; it seems to kill off the father or mother that produces it, to function without a proper name. Nevertheless, the signature tries to imprison the text, to make it a tomb or a dwelling for the signature. Derrida compares this conflict to a reciprocal work of mourning: "La signature reste demeure et tombe. Le texte travaille à en faire son deuil. Et réciproquement" (GL, 11-R). The text tries to liberate itself from the signature, to engage in a play of signification without being encumbered by the signature which, in turn, works to reduce the play of signification by returning the text to its source, reducing the effects of language by centering the meaning of the text in the author's intentions. Signature and text work against each other, each trying to consume or bury the other.

In the next paragraph, Derrida offers a definitiom of literary discourse: although it at first seems to have little to do with the question of the signature, the discussion that follows makes the connection clear. Derrida writes:

> Le grand enjeu du discours --je dis bien discours-- littéraire: la transformation patiente, rusée, quasi animale ou végétale, monumentale, dérisoire aussi mais se tournant plutôt en dérision, de son nom propre, rebus, en choses, en nom de choses (GL, 11-R).

133

The passage presents itself as a general formulation of the nature of literature, or rather, of literary _discourse_. The term suggests that like other discourses (psychoanalytic, philosophical, scientific), literature orders, organizes, and even constitutes its object and, in so doing, exerts a force on the world.[1] Derrida does not indicate specifically what the _object_ of literary discourse might be but, since what is at stake is the transformation of its proper name into a thing or common noun, it is reasonable to assume that its object is language itself, or rather, the materiality of language. If literature is conceived as a set of norms, themes, practices, and _topoi_, then literary discourse would reflect or comment on those _topoi_ by converting them into figures in the text. Derrida describes Genet's _Journal du Voleur_ as a text that "_se présente_ comme le métalangage du langage qui ne se présente pas" (GL, 148-R). This again suggests that literary discourse would be a constant effort to create figures, things, in order to demonstrate how language operates. For this reason, literary discourse is essentially subversive: it is ridiculous, but in its foolishness it mocks; the ridiculous appearance conceals a craftiness. Literary discourse undermines language, in particular, metalanguage, by constantly turning against itself.

The phrase "quasi animale ou végétale" unquestionably refers to the meanings of Jean Genet's proper name, the two things or common nouns (plant and animal) that his name can be transformed into. It thus suggests that one of the _topoi_ that literary discourse reflects upon or puts into play is precisely the question of the signature: the transformation in question is also that of the author's proper name into a thing.

In fact, this passage immediately precedes the first use of Genet's name in _Glas_ and announces the discussion of the act of naming (others and himself) in Genet's texts. This nomination is precisely of the kind that Derrida describes in relation to literary discourse: it consists of transforming proper names into names of things or using common nouns to refer to individuals. Derrida examines this practice of nomination in relation to the question of the signature, of the signature's function in relation to the (literary) text.

Flowers and Figuration

The phrase "quasi animale ou végétale," in addition to alluding to Genet's proper name, also echoes the first of two passages from Hegel that Derrida offers in the first pages of _Glas_. We have already seen how the passage concerning the phallic columns of India is intimately linked to Derrida's autobiographics. We were led to conclude that the two passages are the sort of obsessive _restes_ that Derrida sees as pointing to the unconscious structure of writing: the passages persist in Derrida's mind and organize his text. In fact, the first passage takes up the issues that will surface in tbe discussion of Genet's signature and provides a link between Genet's autobiographics and Derrida's. For the issues raised are also put into play in relation to Derrida's

134

signature; <u>Glas</u> also records the transformation of "Derrida" into words and things.

The passage in question occurs in Hegel's discussion of religion in the <u>Phenomenology of Spirit</u>. Natural religion is the first phase of the development toward absolute religion and the religion of plants and animals is the second moment in the syllogism of natural religion. Derrida focuses on the religion of <u>flowers</u>, which is not even a moment in the syllogism, but only part of the religion of plants and animals. The religion of flowers "s'épuise presque dans un passage" and the passage from flowers to animals is a movement from innocence to culpability. The religion of flowers is innocent, whereas the religion of animals is guilty (<u>coupable</u>). In fact, the religion of flowers "procède à sa propre mise en culpabilité, à sa propre animalisation" (GL, 8-L). This is because the flower, not yet a self, a subject, an "être-pour-soi destructeur" nevertheless is the representation (<u>Vorstellung</u>) of such a self:

> 'L'innocence de la religion des fleurs, qui est seulement représentation de soi-même sans le soi-même (<u>die nur selbstlose Vorstellung des Selbsts</u>) passe dans le sérieux de la vie agonistique, dans la culpabilité de la religion des animaux; la quiétude de l'impuissance de l'individualité contemplative passe dans l'être-pour-soi destructeur' (Hegel, quoted in GL, 8-L).

The passage from the religion of flowers to the religion of animals corresponds to the passage from <u>genêt</u> to <u>genet</u>, plant to animal. That is in fact the order that Derrida follows in discussing Genet's signature in the first pages of <u>Glas</u>. At this point, however, we have no indication of the importance of the Hegelian passage to Derrida's discussion; after quoting it in both French and German, he moves on immediately to the phallic columns of India. It is only 250 pages later that he deals with the passage in detail.

As it turns out, the Hegelian passage that Derrida leaves out at this point, the moment that immediately precedes the religion of plants and animals (the first moment of the syllogism) corresponds to the transformation of Genet into <u>genêt</u>, of the signature as origin or source of the text to the name as a figure within the text. For the first moment of natural religion is the religion of the sun, and the characteristic feature of this religion is that it does not involve representation or figuration: "Cette première figure de la religion naturelle figure l'absence de figure, un soleil purement visible" (GL, 265-L). The movement from the religion of the sun to the religion of plants and animals is the passage from the realm of pure phenomenality, of a light as source without <u>reste</u>, a light that therefore consumes itself, to the realm of figuration. The development of religion, in fact, proceeds as a development of the figure, as representation, work of art, language, and so forth. Moreover, the stage that follows the last phase of religion (i.e. absolute religion) is absolute

135

knowing and it, too, is characterized by the absence of figure:

> Le Sa [savoir absolu] n'a pas de figure, n'est pas une figure, alors que la religion absolue est encore figure (vraie) et représentation. D'où le cercle de cet enchaînement syllogistique.... Le premier moment du premier moment est aussi, comme le Sa, à l'autre bout, absence de figure, moment irreprésentable. La figure se dérobe à l'origine et à la fin de la religion avant et après la religion; dont le devenir décrit littéralement une consumation de la figure, entre deux soleils (GL, 264-L).

The stage of absolute knowing that follows absolute religion, which is also the last section of Hegel's text, brings an end to figuration, representation, destroys or consumes the reste. If the development of religion is assimilated to the operation of reading (of reading the Phenomenology, for example, we find that Hegel's ideal text is made up of figures or symbols that, like the bread and wine of the Last Supper, are consumed as they are apprehended; it is the model of a text that always returns to its source, consumed by the light of the sun.

Tracing the passage from the religion of the sun to the religion of flowers, Derrida offers an alternative to this apocalyptic mode of reading: "Alors au lieu de tout brûler on commence à aimer les fleurs. La religion des fleurs suit la religion du soleil" (GL, 268-L). This, then, is the model of reading that Genet's texts institute: they transform the signature as source, sun, non-figure, into the proper name as flower, that is, the proper name as comon noun.

Genet's signature becomes a flower in two senses. First, the word genêt refers to a type of flower in his texts and the proliferation of flowers can be taken as so many signatures. Secondly, the transformation of proper name into common noun is itself a rhetorical figure, that is, a flower of rhetoric, namely an antonomasia, a type of synecdoche that consists in taking a proper name for a common noun, or the reverse (GL, 294-R). As a result, genêt is not only a figure for Genet's signature but a figure for figuration in general. The flower genêt names at once Genet's signature and the operation that allows the signature to be transformed into a thing. Furthermore, since the flower is "l'objet poétique par excellence" (Sartre, quoted in GL, 21-R), it can also stand as a figure for poetry or poetic language.

Derrida writes:

> En apparence, cédant à la Passion de l'Ecriture, Genet s'est fait une fleur. Et il a mis en terre, en très grande pompe, mais aussi comme une fleur, en sonnant le glas, son nom propre, les noms de droit commun, le langage, la vérité, le sens, la littérature, la rhétorique et, si possible, le reste.
>
> C'est du moins l'apparence. Et cela aurait commencé

> par empoisonner les fleurs de la rhétorique ou de la
> poétique. Celles-ci, parodiées, altérées, transplantées,
> commencent très vite à pourrir.... Ces fleurs ne sont
> ni artificielles ni tout à fait naturelles. Pourquoi
> dit-on les 'fleurs de rhétorique'? Et que serait la
> fleur quand elle devient l'une seulement des 'fleurs de
> rhétorique'? (GL, 19-20-R)

Derrida is claiming, first, that Genet's use of antonomasia is a
subversive activity: by figuring his signature as a thing in the
text, he undermines the function of the signature which guarantees
truth and meaning. Second, since the flower of rhetoric, the
antonomasia, is itself a flower (a genêt), it turns the expression
"flowers of rhetoric" into a pun and so parodies rhetoric and
poetry. No doubt Derrida is also alluding to other aspects of
Genet's texts, for example, his use of mythological topoi and of
sophisticated literary devices in order to render the life of the
criminal-homosexual. That is why, in Derrida's formulation of what
is at stake in literary discourse, the phrase "la transformation...
quasi animale ou végétale... de son nom propre" can refer just as
well to Genet's proper name as to the proper name of literature.
The use of antonomasia is only one example of Genet's practice of
commenting on and undermining literature by parodying it.

On two occasions in the passage cited above, Derrida qualifies
his appraisal of Genet's use of the signature, suggesting that the
subversive aspect is only an appearance. If we take Derrida's
discussion of Hegel as a commentary on Genet's practice of
antonomasia, we discover the reason for this qualification. Hegel
writes that the religion of flowers is innocent and the religion
of animals guilty. As we have seen, the guilt is assumed with the
passage to subjectivity, to an être-pour-soi inaugurated by a
self-representation. The flower is innocent, but it is not
entirely outside the opposition innocent/guilty: "On ne déclare son
innocence (ce qu'on ne ferait pas du soleil ou de la plante) que
dans la mesure où elle est susceptible de culpabilité, coupable de
pouvoir devenir coupable" (GL, 274-L). This is because the flower,
though not yet a subject, incapable of the division or separation
that constitutes the self, nevertheless is a representation (or
pre-sentation, Vorstellung) of the être-pour-soi that is realized
in the animal. Derrida explains (glossing Hegel) that the plant
is torn away from itself but only by an external force rather than
by an internal, subjective act: "La plante est arrachée à
elle-même, vers l'extérieur, par la lumière," that is, by the sun.
The plant's flower, however, "libère un progrès dans le mouvement
de réappropriation et de subjectivation" (GL, 273-L). The flower
is not only acted upon, altered, made exterior by light, it also
produces its own light as color: "La lumière ne vient plus
provoquer ou arracher du dehors, elle s'engendre au contraire
spontanément, depuis le dedans de la plante" (GL, 273-L).

The flower does not possess true subjectivity; it does not
represent itself as an other. The flower's color is only a figure,
a Vorstellung, of self-representation, a selfless representation

of the self (_selbstlose Vorstellung des Selbsts_). Nevertheless, it is the first step toward subjectivity in the form of a self--representation or self-figuration. This selffiguration, as we have seen, involves guilt and reappropriation, in particular, the reappropriation of the sun. This raises the question: if Genet's use of antonomasia is a self-figuration of this kind, is it also a reappropriation? Does the transformation of the signature as sun into a flower involve the reappropriation of the sun _into_ the text? Are Genet's flowers also little suns?

Antonomasia

In fact, this is one of the major issues that Derrida addresses in his discussion of Genet's use of antonomasia. Genet's self-figuration is only one case of his use of antonomasia. In general, Genet's literary texts glorify thievery, cowardice, betrayal, prostitution, poverty, homosexuality, all negative values of what Genet calls "votre monde."[2] Derrida explains that Genet often defines this "opération 'magnifiante'" as an act of naming (GL, 11-R). This leads Derrida to examine the function that Genet's naming of his characters plays in his writing. As it happens, this naming is also an antonomasia, since Genet often converts common nouns into proper names, calling his characters, for example, "Mimosa, Querelle, Divine, Yeux-Verts, Culafroy, Notre-Dame-des-Fleurs, Divers, etc" (GL, 13-14-R). Derrida asks what function this act of nomination plays:

> Quand Genet donne à ses personnages des noms propres, des espèces de singularités qui sont des noms communs majusculés, que fait-il? .... Arrache-t-il violemment une identité sociale, un droit de propriété absolue? Est-ce là l'opération politique la plus effective, la pratique révolutionnaire la plus signifiante? Ou bien, mais voici la rengaine des contraires qui se recoupent sans cesse, les baptise-t-il avec la pompe et le sacré --la gloire/ est son mot--qu'il confère toujours à la nomination? (GL, 14-15-R).

It is not a question of deciding between these two possibilities. Genet's use of antonomasia, like his glorification and aesthetization of the underworld in general, is both an expropriation and a reappropriation, a decapitation and a "recapitation," a dissemination and a recapitalization (GL, 19-R).

"Quand Genet donne des noms, il baptise et dénonce à la fois" (GL, 12-R). The use of antonomasia simply foregrounds what is true of naming in general: no name is absolutely proper to the person it designates; it operates within a system, classifies the individual, grants him a place within language and within the state.[3] Further, the proper name can always be used to refer to someone else, can be repeated, expropriated and reappropriated. In this sense, antonomasia uncovers the lie of the proper name, which, like private property, is presumed to belong properly to someone. Antonomasia is, then, a kind of theft, but one that reveals the original thievery involved in the accumulation of private property in the first place. As such, the use of antonomasia is subversive, even revolutionary: it uncovers the institutional (i.e. merely conventional) status of the proper name.

On the other hand, antonomasia is quite literally an appropriation, the making proper of a common noun. By adorning the word with a capital letter, one attempts to take it out of circulation, out of the system of language, and make it one's own. From this point of view, antonomasia is a kind of theft, but, like the orphan Genet who steals, not because he scorns private property but because he wishes to possess something that is truly his,[4] the use of the rhetorical figure simply reaffirms the institutional status of the proper name. The use of autonomasia, then, like the "opération 'magnifiante'" in general, is a double gesture that both calls into question the institution (of literature or of the proper name) and reaffirms it.

> Le (sur)nom propre donné relève la tête qui tombe sur l'échafaud mais simultanément redouble l'arbitraire de la sentence par la décision nominante, consacre et glorifie la chute, coupe une fois de plus, et grave-- sur un monument littéraire (GL, 15-16-R).

Or again: "Qui donne le nom et le seing approche sa lame de votre cou. Pour vous diviser. Et du même geste, vous transforme en dieu" (GL, 19-R). Thus, like the <u>reste</u> in general, the name as antonomasia at once falls and is recuperated, idealized.

Having concluded the discussion of Genet's use of antonomasia in naming others, Derrida adds that "la division se complique à peine quand le dénominateur... s'institue ou s'érige lui-même dans sa propre signature. Habitat colossal: le chef-d'oeuvre" (GL, 17-R). In other words, Genet's transformation of his signature into a thing, a plant or an animal, functions in the same (double) way as his naming of others. The major example of this antonomasia is drawn from <u>Le Journal du Voleur</u>. Genet writes:

> Je suis né à Paris le 19 décembre 1910. Pupille de l'Assistance Publique, il me fut impossible de connaître autre chose de mon état civil. Quand j'eus vingt et un ans, j'obtins un acte de naissance. Ma mère s'appelait Gabrielle Genet. Mon père reste inconnu.... Quand je rencontre dans la lande... des fleurs de genêt, j'éprouve à leur égard une sympathie profonde.... Je suis seul au monde, et je ne suis pas sûr de n'être pas le roi —peut-être la fée de ses fleurs.... Elles savent que je suis leur représentant vivant.... Elles sont mon emblème naturel...
> Par [cette fleur] dont je porte le nom le monde végétal m'est familier. Je peux sans pitié considérer toutes les fleurs, elles sont de ma famille.[5]

As Derrida points out, the passage begins with an account of Genet's civil and legal status, enumerating the facts found on a birth certificate: name, date and place of birth, mother's name, father's name (unknown). It thus establishes Genet's place in a genealogy and in an institution (the state). In the lines that follow, however, Genet denies that genealogy: "Je suis seul au monde." Taking on his mother's name and adorning it with a circumflex accent, Genet, rather than recognizing his heritage, instead establishes his own natural genealogy. The antonomasia serves to extract the proper name from its civil status and places it in the natural world; as a result, Genet becomes, if not the mother of flowers, at least their king or fairy. He scatters his name over the field of flowers and makes those flowers his family.

The Name of the Mother

Derrida characterizes the operation whereby Genet takes on his mother's name in the following manner:

> Je... me surnomme fleur (le baptême est une seconde naissance), je nais une fois de plus, je m'accouche comme une fleur. La race étant condamnée, l'accent circonflexe se sacre en ouvrant la bouche et tirant la langue... s'élève et se place lui-même en tête couronnée (GL, 203-04-R).

Thus, Genet becomes a mother, the mother of his own life, in taking on the name of his mother. "L'accent circonflexe" is Derrida's nickname for the "narrator" (as opposed to the author) of the Journal du Voleur; the passage, then, also points to Genet's activity as a writer, his act of making himself into a rhetorical or poetic "flower" in his texts. Genet is both his own mother and the mother of his text.

In one of the passages leading up to the "hymne au nom propre" (GL, 193-R) cited above, Genet compares his activities to that of a mother of a monstrous child. Having described the baseness and poverty of his life of crime, he explains: "Mon talent se développait de donner un sens sublime à une apparence aussi pauvre. (Je ne parle pas encore de talent littéraire.)"[6] This talent consists in creating a religion of abjection, a new, mythical world out of the criminal underworld he is thrown into. This talent for transforming his life anticipates his literary talent, since Genet's texts involve precisely a transformation of this sort. In the next paragraph, he adds:

> Je me voulus semblable à cette femme qui, à l'abri des gens, chez elle conserva sa fille, une sorte de monstre hideux, difforme, grognant et marchant à quatre pattes, stupide et blanc. En accouchant, son désespoir fut tel sans doute qu'il devint l'essence même de sa vie. Elle

décida d'aimer ce monstre, d'aimer la laideur sortie de son ventre où elle s'était élaborée, et de l'ériger dévotieusement.... Avec des soins dévots, des mains douces malgré le cal des besognes quotidiennes, avec l'acharnement volontaire des désespérés elle s'opposa au monde, au monde elle opposa le monstre qui prit les proportions du monde et sa puissance.'

In a footnote, Genet adds that

par les journaux j'appris qu'après quarante ans de dévouement cette mère arrosa d'essence --ou de pétrole-- sa fille endormie, puis toute la maison et mit le feu. Le monstre (la fille) succomba. Des flammes on retira la vieille (75 ans) et elle fut sauvée, c'est-à-dire qu'elle comparut en Cour d'assises.[8]

Derrida takes this scene as a description of Genet's relation to his text. Taking on his mother's name, the name that he uses to sign his texts, Genet becomes the mother of his text and, by dispersing his name throughout it (through antonomasia), keeps it to himself, devotes himself to it, and finally, kills it off, keeps it away from "the world," from the reader:

Rêvant visiblement de devenir, à resonner, son propre (glas), d'assister à <u>son propre</u> enterrement après avoir accouché de lui-même ou opéré sa propre décollation, il aurait veillé à bloquer tout ce qu'il écrit dans la forme d'une tombe. D'une tombe qui se résume à son nom, dont la masse pierreuse ne déborde même plus les lettres, jaunes comme l'or ou comme la trahison, comme le genêt (GL, 52-R).

In this view, Genet's practice of antonomasia would stem from the desire for the proper, the wish to erect his signature into a tomb or dwelling or to shape his entire corpus into the tomb of his proper name. As his own mother, he would give birth to himself as a flower (a name or figure in a text) only to keep the text for himself. He would have written nothing but his own signature:

Genet... aurait, le sachant ou non... silencieusement, laborieusement, minutieusement, obsessionellement, compulsivement, avec les gestes d'un voleur dans la nuit, disposé ses signatures à la place de tous les objets manquants. Le matin, vous attendant à reconnaître les choses familières, vous retrouvez son nom partout, en grosses lettres, en petites lettres, en entier ou en morceaux, déformé ou recomposé. Il n'est plus là mais vous habitez son mausolée ou ses chiottes. Vous croyiez déchiffrer, dépister, poursuivre, vous êtes compris. Il a tout affecté de sa signature (GL, 51-R).

Just as Genet scatters his name over a field of flowers by transforming it into _genêt_, he disseminates his signature throughout the text through the operation of antonomasia. He does not sign once, but an infinite number of times; he does nothing but sign; his corpus is a sepulcher for the signature.

The question remains, however: does Genet succeed in signing his text? Can any text, even a text littered with signatures, be ultimately governed, regulated by a signature? Summarizing his argument that the flowers in Genet's texts are anagrams or figures for the proper name, Derrida writes:

> Genet anagrammatise son propre, sème plus que tout autre et glane son nom sur quoi qu'il tombe. Glaner égale lire.... Mais si cette (double) opération... était possible, absolument praticable ou centrale, si s'effectuait l'irrépressible désir qui l'agit (de mort ou de vie, cela revient ici au même), il n'y aurait ni texte ni reste. Encore moins celui-ci. Le résumé serait absolu, il s'emporterait, s'enlèverait lui-même d'un coup d'aile (GL, 55-56-R).

Genet's desire to gather his dispersed signature back to himself, to reclaim his text, cannot but fail. The text falls; it escapes the prison of the signature. Derrida reads it and writes another text. No doubt "glaner" is a pun on "glas" and thus refers to the operation of Derrida's text. Derrida gleans and glosses Genet's text, reads it; in so doing, he steals it away from its author.

Chiasmus: Derrida and Genet

A text, like a name (common or proper), can always be appropriated. One can always use another's text to describe oneself, or name oneself in feigning to name another. If Genet does not succeed entirely in signing his text, it is partly because Derrida also signs it, in an autobiographics that appropriates the other into the self. Following the preliminary discussion of the signature, he returns to the essay "Ce qui est resté..." which, as we saw, serves as a model of sorts for _Glas_. Describing the form of Genet's short essay, Derrida writes: "X, chiasme presque parfait, plus que parfait, de deux textes mis en regard l'un de l'autre" (GL, 53-R). The chiasmus in question is, in the first place, the effect produced by placing two texts on the same page so that they exchange gazes, gloss each other.

As Derrida realizes, however, the form of Genet's text stages the experience that the narrator relates in the left-hand column. The event in question takes place in a train: seated in his compartment, the narrator happens to look up and catches the gaze of the stranger sitting across from him. He has the overwhelming experience of looking, not into the eyes of another, but into his own eyes. He relates the "desagréable expérience" in these terms:

142

> Ce que j'éprouvais je ne pus le traduire que sous cette forme: je m'écoulais de mon corps, et par les yeux, dans celui du voyageur en même temps que le voyageur s'écoulait dans le mien.... Qu'est-ce donc qui s'était écoulé de mon corps--je m'ec...,-- et qu'est-ce qui de ce voyageur s'écoulait de son corps?[9]

Thus, the autobiographical essay relates an exchange of identities, the reversal of position between self and other. Derrida associates Genet's "je m'ec" with, among other things, "je m'écrivais," suggesting that the activity of writing (oneself) involves such an exchange of identity.

This exchange is quite common in _Glas_: the gloss that describes Genet's writing turns back upon itself and comments on Derrida's textual practice. There are, for example, numerous instances of antonomasia in _Glas_, the transformation of Derrida's signature into a common noun: most appear in the _judas_ of the Genet column and involve a chiasmic movement between Genet and Derrida. For instance, Derrida takes up the specific details of Genet's life and shapes them into his theory about the signature, then staging this theory in the play of his own proper name.

One of the first of these moments appears as a _judas_ that runs alongside Derrida's discussion of naming in Genet's texts. He first quotes a passage from _Le Journal du Voleur_ where the narrator, discussing the name of another, then turns to consider his own name:

> Armand était en voyage. Encore que j'entendisse parfois qu'on l'appelât de noms différents, nous garderons celui-ci. Moi-même n'en suis-je pas, avec celui de Jean Gallien que je porte aujourd'hui, à mon quinze ou seizième nom? (quoted in GL, 12-R).

In his gloss, Derrida suggests that he will remotivate the apparent arbitrariness of the proper name "Gallien" and of the initials "J.G." This comment anticipates the discussion of the subjective remotivation of the sign and its relation to the unconscious and to mental illness, notably schizophrenia (see GL, 110-R sq and passim). In the next phrase, Derrida adds that in Genet's _Pompes Funèbres_, the initials are not "J.G." but "J.D." Thus, in a move that parallels Genet's shift from Armand's name to his own, Derrida introduces _his_ initials into the discussion and, in so doing, remotivates an apparently arbitrary signifier that figures prominently in Genet's novel.

In the following paragraph, still ostensibly discussing Genet, Derrida raises a number of issues about the signature, the text, and their relation to death and genealogy. As he proceeds, he insinuates his name and his text into the analysis:

> Quant au sigle, dans _Pompes funèbres_, c'est J.D., Jean D.... Le D majuscule à qui il échoit de représenter le

143

nom de famille ne revient pas forcément au père. Il intéresse en tous cas la mère et c'est elle qui bénéficie de son titre. 'La mère était anoblie par cet écusson portant le D majuscule brodé d'argent' (GL, 12-R).

Pompes Funèbres is a study in mourning: the book is dedicated to one of Genet's lovers, Jean Decarnin, and the entire novel is organized around his funeral and the period of mourning that follows. The coat of arms with the capital D appears on the hearse that bears the corpse to the place of burial. It thus names and envelopes a corpse, but also brings prestige to the mother who presides at the burial. But the initials of the dead man are also Derrida's initials, and he exploits this ambiguity in order to further develop his theory of signatures in figuring his own name. Derrida continues:

> Quant à celui qui organise les Pompes funèbres --c'est-à-dire littéraires-- de J.D., dira-t-on que c'est l'auteur, le narrateur, le narrataire, le lecteur, mais de quoi? Il est à la fois le double du mort (colossos), qui reste vivant après lui, son fils, mais aussi son père et sa mère (GL, 12-R)

On the one hand, ths passage is simply a further discussion of Pompes Funèbres: Genet does characterize himself as both Jean D.'s son and his mother and father. In fact, the novel enacts the sort of chiasmic movement, the exchange of identities that we noted earlier. Aided no doubt by the shared first name of the lovers, but due primarily to the operation of mourning itself, Jean Genet becomes Jean Decarnin: "Aujourd'hui je me fais horreur de contenir, l'ayant dévoré, le plus cher, le seul amant qui m'aimât. Je suis son tombeau"; "Mais Jean vivra par moi, je lui prêterai mon corps. Par moi, il agira, pensera."[16] In the next lines, Genet even compares this lending of his body to a dead man to an actor's performance of a role on stage: "J'assume un rôle très grave.... Avec la même émotion le comédien aborde le personnage qu'il rendra visible." This links mourning as incorporation and reactivation to the performance, the quoting, of a work of art.

But the doubt that Derrida attaches to the source of the text's meaning or "organization" tends to bring the qestion around to this use of quotation in Derrida's autobiographics. That is, he characterizes his own activity in Glas as the reactivating, the taking on the role of a dead man. Genet's notion of mourning as the performance of the dead man's role is extended to the activity of reading. As in Pompes Funèbres, where Genet exploits the similarity of names, Derrida allows the ambiguity of the initials "J.D." to effect a blurring of identities. In fact, since a "glas" is obviously associated with a funeral rite, the phrase "les Pompes Funèbres de J.D." can be taken as a reference to Derrida's work as well as to Genet's. Derrida, as well as Genet, is "le double du mort": in rewriting Genet's texts, he imitates them, doubles them, claims them as an ancestor; at the same time, he also (re)produces

144

them, stitching together a tissue of quotations or an anthology of Genet's writings. He is, then, Genet's son as well as his father and mother.

In the last section of the judas, Derrida speaks of Genet's fear that someone will steal his death from him and claims that to guard against such an expropriation "il a d'avance occupé tous les lieux où ça meurt. Bien joué? Qui fait mieux, qui dit mieux, le mort" (GL, 12-R) This issue is also related to the signature and the text: the signature, writes Derrida, is a kind of death and one way of guarding against this death is to multiply it, to multiply the signatures throughout the text. Thus, Genet tries to occupy his tomb by scattering his signature throughout the text. But what of Derrida, who not only appropriates Genet's text, but also steals his initials, his signature, making his antonomasia coincide with Genet's? If it is the reading of a text that prevents it from being proper to its author, then it is Derrida who is stealing away Genet's death and his text, stealing it in order to stage his own death.

Déjà and Derrière

Since the name "Derrida" does not have any semantic value in French, Derrida's use of antonomasia involves a number of mutations of his name: the two most common are "Derrière" and "Déjà." As for Genet, the figure of antonomasia stands not only for Derrida's signature, but also for the operation of figuration, of antonomasia itself. And, as for Genet, the signature carries with it a certain relation to death and to his ancestry. Thus, he writes in a judas:

> Derrière: chaque fois que le mot vient en premier, s'il s'écrit donc après un point, avec une majuscule, quelque chose en moi se mettait à y reconnaître le nom de mon père, en lettres dorées sur sa tombe, avant même qu'il y fût. A fortiori quand je lis Derrière le rideau (GL, 80-R).

At the beginning, the term "Derrière" seems to involve a simple, largely unmotivated referentiality: its similarity to "Derrida" leads him to recognize, not his own name, but that of his father. But the word quickly takes on its semantic value as well. The word "Derrière" points to something behind, specifically, to the corpse that lies behind the tombstone. The word "derrière" is not itself behind; it is the name engraved on the outside of the tombstone; it stands in the place of the father, and it points to the father presumed to lie behind it.

Oddly, this reading of "Derrière" as the father's name on a tombstone occurs even before the father's death; the tombstone points to something behind itself, but the grave is empty. This undermines the simple reference of the proper name. Not only does the word refer to nothing behind it, it appears to bring about the illusion of reference. "Quelque chose en moi se mettait à y reconnaître...": it is as if the word itself, or the meaning of the word, invoked the image of a tomb, and of the father within.

Of course, Derrida describes the functioning of the signature or of the proper name on the cover of a book in precisely the same terms. The signature is not simply an outward mark of a private intention; it is the mark that produces the intentional subject. Or, to take up the metaphor that Derrida plays with persistently: the name of the book's "father" appears on the cover of the book, but its very appearance <u>outside</u> the text announces the death of the father and makes of the book a tomb for its author.

In the next paragraph, the link between "Derrière" as the proper name of Derrida's father, and "Derrière" as figure for the signature in general, is made explicit: "Derrière n'est-ce pas toujours déjà derrière un rideau, un voile, un tissage. Un texte toisonnant..." (GL, 80-R). Whereas in the first instance, the word "derrière" was visible on the outside of the tombstone and only indicated something else presumed to lie <u>derrière</u>, it now appears that the signature "Derrière" is <u>itself</u> behind a text, and a text "toisonnant." The term alludes to Derrida's discussion of the notion of text as a textile, a garment woven of various threads. He cites Freud's belief that women invented weaving out of the desire to weave their pubic hair into a penis or, at least, to cover their lack with the braided pubic hair (GL, 79-R). Thus, if the text is a <u>toison</u>, what it conceals is precisely a lack: if the signature lies behind the text, the signature is simply an empty space, like the father's empty tomb. The text and signature have exchanged places: in the first formulation, the signature was on the outside; the text was a tomb; and the grave was empty. In the second example, the text is the covering or veil; the signature is within, but void. Thus, in these few lines, Derrida stages the two functions of the signature that he posits at the beginning of <u>Glas</u>. In the first case, the signature is a tombstone, a <u>cerceuil vertical</u> that stands before an empty grave; the signature is erected as a monument and the text disappears behind it. In the second case, the text works to hide the signature; the signature itself is void and disappears behind the weave of the text. Derrida thus stages the reciprocal work of mourning between text and signature in relation to his own (and his father's) name.

Following the allusion to the "texte toisonnant," Derrida quotes Genet:

> Un autre de mes amants orne de rubans sa toison intime. Un autre a tressé pour la tête de noeud de son ami, miniscule, une couronne de pâquerettes. Avec ferveur un culte phallique se célèbre en chambre, derrière le rideau des braguettes boutonnées (quoted GL, 80-R).

This quotation continues Derrida's train of thought, which follows the <u>argument de la gaine</u>. Whereas the "texte toisonnant" alludes to castration and the means of disguising or compensating for it, this passage deals with another kind of fetishism; the ribbons and crown of daisies do not substitute for an absent phallus, but adorn

146

an existing member. If the signature is seen as a phallus that can be cut off from the body of the text, this fetishism involves a multiplication of the signature, a staging of the signature in the text.

Like the scene of Genet's tribute to his dead friend lying rigid on the catafalque, the above passage moves by association from the "derrière le rideau" that points to a corpse, the father's dead body, to a "derrière le rideau" that refers to the phallus behind the buttoned fly. This association of the corpse with the erect penis, and the benefit Derrida derives from the association, is developed when he turns to speak of the signature as his own death. Instructing us to "lire le déjà comme sigle," he explains:

> Quand je signe, je suis déjà mort. J'ai à peine le temps de signer que je suis déjà mort. Je dois abréger l'écriture, d'où le sigle, parce que la structure de l'événement 'signature' porte ma mort en lui-même. En quoi il n'est pas un 'événement' et ne signifie peut-être rien, écrit depuis un passé qui n'a jamais été présent et depuis la mort de qui n'a jamais été vivant.... Le passé n'est plus un présent passé, ni le futur un présent à venir. Et toutes les valeurs qui dépendent de cet axiome, le sigle les enraye. Elle ne fonctionnent déjà plus, elles sont d'avance défuntes. Ici même (GL, 26-R).

"Déja," a shorthand form for "derrida jacques" (FH, 482), illustrates the function of the signature that we have already examined in the context of La Voix et le Phénomène and "Signature Evénement Contexte." The signature, which is supposed to guarantee the identity of the subject or author, also puts him in peril since the signature can function independently of the author's intention. Thus, it kills off the "father" of the discourse and takes his place even as it establishes the link between author and discourse. Furthermore, since the signature is never an event in the sense of a unique, non-repeated, non-divisible act, but rather a repetition of another signature, it undermines the very notion of event, of the here and now. Since the signature brings the legal subject into being retroactively, the subject is already dead when the signature announces its birth. The signature announces the absence of the signer as well as his presence, both links and separates the text and the author.

Being dead, however, has certain advantages, especially when, as we have seen, the corpse is consistently associated with an erection. Derrida writes:

> déjà. La mort a déjà eu lieu, avant tout. Comment déchiffrer cette étrange antériorité d'un déjà qui vous met toujours un cadavre sur les bras? .... Il veut que vous ne puissiez jamais vous défaire du corps très raide que sa littérature, sa pompe funèbre, aura bandé pour

> vous. Comment séduire, comment se faire aimer sans vous
> dire <u>je suis mort</u>?.... Qui fait mieux? Qui dit mieux?
> ... Le <u>déjà</u> que je suis sonne son propre glas, signe
> lui-même son arrêt de mort, vous regarde d'avance, vous
> voit avancer sans rien comprendre à ce que vous aurez
> aimé, suivant, en colonne, la marche funèbre d'une
> érection dont tout le monde entendra désormais disposer
> (GL, 92-R).

The expression "Qui fait mieux? Qui dit mieux?" echoes Derrida's comments about Genet's desire to die his own death and his efforts to guard against the theft of his death. Derrida is expressing the same desire. By pronouncing himself dead on arrival, he manages to seduce the reader with a monument erected to his death: he delivers his text, his cadaver, to the reader who cannot be rid of it. The text remains proper to him; the reader can do nothing but bear the text or pay tribute to it in a eulogy, knell, or funeral march.

We are already approaching the figure of the mother who bears a child only to keep it to herself, then finally, to kill it, take it back into herself. Derrida develops this train of thought in another use of antonomasia:

> Je suis <u>déjà</u> (mort) signifie que je suis <u>derrière</u>.
> Absolument derrière, le <u>Derrière</u> qui n'aura jamais été
> vu de face, le <u>Déjà</u> que rien n'aura précédé, qui s'est
> donc conçu et enfanté lui-même, mais comme cadavre ou
> corps glorieux (GL, 97-R).

"Derrière," earlier associated with the name of the father, now clearly represents the mother, the signature as mother who gives birth to a child already dead, a child who will never belong to anyone besides herself, who will never venture out of the home. In another passage, this is developed even further:

> Je suis la mère. Le texte. La mère est derrière-- tout
> ce que je suis, fais, parais-- la mere suit. Comme elle
> suit absolument, elle survit toujours... à ce qu'elle
> aura engendré, assistant... à la mise en terre de ce dont
> elle a prévu la mort.... Ah! Si ma mère pouvait
> m'assister à mon enterrement (GL, 134-R).

We begin to see why the signature of preference is that of the mother, and why Derrida chooses to dress himself as a woman: in so doing, he can give birth to himself, kill himself, bury himself, and thus remain absolutely proper to himself. Nevertheless, Derrida recognizes the impossibility of this desire. Alluding once more to the details of Genet's genealogy, he writes:

> On sait que la paternité s'attribue toujours au terme
> d'un procès, dans la forme d'un jugement. Donc d'une
> généralité. Mais la mère? Surtout celle qui se passe

de père? Ne peut-on espérer une généalogie pure, purement singulière...? Le propre n'est-il pas finalement de la mère? (GL, 170-R)

That, in any case, is the hope or desire. But in the next paragraph, alluding to Genet's encounter with a thief or beggarwoman whom he imagines to be his mother, Derrida concedes: "Pas plus que le glas qu'elle met en branle. La mère est une voleuse et une mendiante. Elle s'approprie tout mais parce qu'elle n'a rien en propre" (GL, 170-R). The mother is a thief: the signature as mother steals its status from the state and from language. To appropriate and reappropriate the signature is to admit that nothing is proper, not even one's own death. Thus, explaining that through his use of antonomasia, he has given birth to himself as a corpse, Derrida adds:

Le Derrière et le Déjà me protègent, me rendent illisible.... Toutes les fleurs de rhétorique dans lesquelles je disperse ma signature, dans lesquelles je m'apostrophe et m'apotrope, lisez-les aussi comme des formes de refoulement. Il s'agit de repousser la pire menace (GL, 97-R).

What is repressed in the recourse to antonomasia, in the effort to sign and resign the text, to place the signature _en abyme_ in the text so as to remain unreadable, is precisely the possibility of being read. Derrida has said that Genet's text is only readable because, at some point, he has failed in keeping it to himself, subsumed under his signature. Derrida admits the same thing in reference to his own text:

Vous ne pouvez vous intéresser à ce que je fais ici que dans la mesure où vous auriez raison de croire que --quelque part-- je ne sais pas ce que je fais... ni ce qui s'agit ici.... Il ne suffit pas d'être rusé, il faut disposer d'une théorie générale de la ruse qui en fasse partie. Ce qui revient à passer aux aveux, inconscients bien sûr. L'inconscient est quelque chose de très théorique (GL, 76-77-R).

Glas is a general theory of the ruse: it analyzes Genet's desire for the proper, and his various tricks and acts of thievery that this desire leads him to commit. But _Glas_ also repeats and appropriates Genet's ruse, and the theory that it develops is itself part of that ruse. When Derrida makes his confessions, reveals his obsessions, he too is trying to trick, steal, and seduce. The unconscious is not only theoretical, not only capable of building a theoretical system, it is also _rusé_. But the ruse fails to the extent that the unconscious is not proper to the self. At some point, Derrida does not know what he is doing; the confessions stem from an unconscious that speaks through him but is not controlled by him. After all the tricks, conscious and unconscious, there is

149

a _reste_, a text to be read, and the reader's interest in it lies precisely in those moments in _Glas_ that reveal "un 'je m'écarte,' ou 'je m'écrase'" (GL, 76-R). Derrida locates the interest of his autobiographics in the revelations he makes in spite of himself, those that stem from the unconscious and point to what he calls, in reference to Freud's autobiographics, "l'inanalysé."

Glas and the Question of Genre

Glas is certainly not what one normally thinks of as "autobiography." It is not a narrative; it does not fulfill an autobiographical pact; and it reveals very little about Derrida's personal life. We have seen how quickly an apparent reference to something outside the text, to the father, for instance, is incorporated into the play of signification in the text. In fact, Derrida has said that "il y a beaucoup d'événements 'réels,' comme on dit 'autobiographiques,' cryptés, réinvestis par la logique de la scène dans _Glas_, mais ils ne sont là que dans la mesure de cette logique interne" (JA, 113). In other words, _Glas_ constantly subordinates reference to rhetoric or to the play of language. But _Glas_ is autobiographical in the sense that it reflects upon the unstated assumptions of autobiography --the relation of self to other, of self to language, and of signature to text-- by placing _en abyme_ the figure of the writer. In a text that deals theoretically with the family, the subject, and the signature, Derrida incorporates the figure of a son, a mother, a father, a subject, and a signature; _Glas_ reveals the obsessions of the writer and describes the writer's activity as he writes. And, although _Glas_ may not correspond to our genre definitions,[11] it corresponds almost exactly to the structure that Derrida traces in Freud's _Beyond the Pleasure Principle_, a structure he calls "l'autobiographie de l'écriture." Developing a theory of the institutional status of autobiography, he turns once more to Freud; the theory cannot fail to turn back on him.

PART FIVE

THE FORT/DA OF AUTOBIOGRAPHY

PSYCHOANALYSIS AND THE POSTAL SERVICE

La Carte Postale de Socrate à Freud et Au-delà (1980) takes as its point of departure

ce qui va des postes, des postes en tous genres, à la psychanalyse... pour renvoyer d'un singulier événement, la psychanalyse freudienne, à une histoire et à une technologie du courrier, à quelque théorie générale de l'envoi et de tout ce qui par quelque télécommunication prétend se destiner (CP, 7).

Derrida raises the question of how a philosophical or literary heritage, for example, is transmitted to Freud (and beyond), and how psychoanalysis is transmitted or willed to those presumed to be its heirs. What are the conditions for Freud's message arriving intact? Can Freud decide who shall receive the message? Can he limit his heirs? What sorts of detours and delays must occur for the message to arrive at all? And if Freud's designated heirs or addressees are not there to receive it, what shall happen to the message? Shall it remain in poste restante (general delivery) or be returned to sender? These are questions of la poste.

But Derrida writes that he is concerned with "postes en tous genres," that is, with both la poste and le poste. The masculine noun designates not only another form of telecommunication (radio and television sets) but also a military watchpost, that is, the point that marks the boundary between enemy territory and an "inside" that needs to be guarded against foreign invasion. Derrida characterizes the institution of psychoanalysis as an outpost of this kind, determined to guard against any intrusion of foreign ideas or disciplines. Finally, un poste is also a political or academic post, that is, a position of power within an institutional structure. It thus points to the power exercised by the institution of psychoanalysis and by those who fill posts in that structure.

The two central essays of La Carte Postale use the figure of the postal service to bring together a number of issues relating to psychoanalysis as an institution. "Spéculer--sur 'Freud,'" a reading of Beyond the Pleasure Principle, unites three aspects of Freud's essay under the question of the poste: first, the relation Freud develops between a dominant pleasure principle and a supposedly subservient reality principle that, however, may deflect the organism from its goal of pleasure, is viewed by Derrida as a postal system of relay and deferral; second, the example that Freud

152

records of a child at play who, under the dominance of the pleasure principle, manipulates a spool attached to a string, sending and receiving his own "message," also offers certain clues about the nature of the _envoi_; third, this general structure serves to describe Freud's position as the _Urvater_ of psychoanalysis, author of a testament, a letter to his heirs, which must submit to the "postal principle" in order to arrive. "Le Facteur de la Vérité" also deals with the question of the heritage of psychoanalysis by focusing on an essay by Jacques Lacan, the self-declared heir to Freud and, in particular, by countering Lacan's claim (in reference to Poe's "The Purloined Letter") that "la lettre arrive toujours à sa destination." This also affords Derrida the opportunity to examine the relation of psychoanalysis to literature and to question Lacan's use of Poe's short story as a simple illustration of his theory of the signifier.

These two essays are framed by texts of a more personal sort: the last portion of the book is a curious interview between Derrida and members of the Parisian community of psychoanalysts regarding his theories and writings on Freud. In the opening pages of "Du tout," Derrida registers his uneasiness at having been invited to a place "jusqu'à ce soir réservé au dedans, au prétendu dedans de l'enclos analytique auquel je suis censé être étranger" (CP, 533) and even refers to the situation as "ce saloon surchargé de toute sorte de bandes plus ou moins fastes, plus ou moins prêtes à la détente, qui guettent du coin de l'oeil depuis leur comptoir" (CP, 529). It is thus as an outsider that Derrida approaches the problems of psychoanalysis, and one of the crucial problems is precisely the division between an inside and an outside.

The first portion of _La Carte Postale_, a lengthy preface of sorts, presents itself as the remains of a correspondence spanning two years, between "Jacques Derrida" (who signs the first letter, which is addressed to the reader) and an unnamed or multinamed lover. It is thus both an enactment and a further discussion of the structure, history, and technology of the postal system: the letters or _envois_ not only discuss such matters as the authenticity of Plato's extant letters, the relation between public and private writings, and the past and future of the postal service but, in their form and fate, demonstrate all that can happen to letters en route.

In this analysis of the history or transmission of a science, of the legacy Freud leaves to his heirs, autobiographics is a central concern. Psychoanalysis is peculiar in that it is a "science qui pour une fois est essentiellement inséparable, en tant que science, de quelque chose comme un nom propre, comme un effet de nom propre" (CP, 353). Founded by a single individual, a Robinson Crusoe working in isolation, and founded on that individual's self-analysis, psychoanalysis owes its greatest discoveries to Freud's insights into himself. But Freud's autobiographics is not merely the record of his self-analysis: his writings inscribe as well what he could not analyze, and it is to this _inanalysé_ that Derrida directs his attention. In "Du Tout," he explains the necessity of this strategy:

153

> Ce reste d'inanalysé qui... rapporte [la psychanalyse] en dernière instance au dehors absolu du milieu analytique ne jouera pas la forme d'une limite autour du psychanalytique, ce à quoi le psychanalytique comme théorie et comme pratique n'aurait hélas pas eu accès, comme s'il lui restait du terrain à gagner. Pas du tout. Ce sera, cet inanalysé, cela aura été ce sur quoi et autour de quoi se sera construit et mobilisé le mouvement analytique: tout aurait été construit et calculé pour que cet inanalysé soit hérité, protégé, transmis intact, convenablement légué, consolidé, enkysté, encrypté (CP, 547).

In other words, what Freud could not see, but which nevertheless found its way into his texts, does not simply function as a gap in psychoanalytic knowledge or as a limit beyond which psychoanalysis cannot progress: that blind spot actually constitutes the condition for psychoanalytic knowledge in the first place. Thus, it cannot simply be eliminated by the supplementary work of later generations. The blind spot is part of the very structure of the science, the condition for its transmission, and to eliminate it would radically alter psychoanalysis as an institution.

For this reason, Derrida explains, the analysis or "décryptage" of the inanalysé de Freud "ne peut plus venir du simple et prétendu dedans de... la psychanalyse. Et il n'aura pas un effet partiel d'aménagement ou de réforme" (CP, 547). Nevertheless, this critique does not come simply from outside psychoanalysis, either: Derrida locates the strategic position of the critic, his own position, on the margins of the institution, both within and outside it. And, as in Glas and Eperons, this position is that of women in a genealogy presumed to pass from father to son. Thus, Derrida places himself in Freud's female line, among the daughters or the daughter's sons. In his autobiographics, begun in "Envois" but continued through the other essays of La Carte Postale, he analyzes that position and even hints at the blindness involved in this strategy of becoming woman. For, in effect, Derrida comes to occupy and to replicate Freud's blind spot: Freud excludes women as other and neglects the specificity of female sexuality; Derrida appropriates it and this appropriation is strategically necessary for his project of deconstruction.

It is clear that, for Derrida, autobiographics is not simply the record of a life, or of a relation between self and self: it involves necessarily the other, and in particular, the legacy which the self inherits from his ancestry. If the subject is not a discrete individual, but a construct formed through a relation with the déjà-là, then autobiography can only be genealogical in nature, the record of a struggle between the self and those who precede it. Furthermore, autobiography is testamentary in two senses : not only because the writing of the self is a relation of one's own death, but also because it takes the form of a legacy that is passed on from one generation to the next. Finding himself heir to Freud's legacy, and, increasingly, the influential father in a deconstructive "movement," Derrida puts into practice the theory of autobiography developed in his essays on Freud, and places _en abyme_ his own position in the genealogy of psychoanalysis.

CHAPTER VIII

THE LEGACY OF BEYOND THE PLEASURE PRINCIPLE

Structure

In Beyond the Pleasure Principle, Freud attempts to posit a drive more primitive and more fundamental than the pleasure principle (the tendency of an organism to keep the level of excitation as low as possible in order to avoid unpleasure). This primitive drive, manifested in a compulsion to repeat, would stem from the organism's desire to return to an earlier, inorganic state, that is, to "die its own death." The search for the evidence of such a death drive (Todestrieb) leads Freud toward philosophical speculation and biological determinism.

In the second chapter of Beyond, having underlined the necessity for new avenues of research concerning these fundamental drives, Freud takes up the example of the so-called "war neuroses." The dreams of patients who have suffered a severe trauma and who have fallen ill of neuroses as a result "have the characteristic of repeatedly bringing the patient back into the situation of his accident, a situation from which he wakes in another fright" (XVIII, 13). This tendency is a challenge to Freud's theory that dreams are without exception "wish fulfillments" and it is also the first challenge to the presumed dominance of the pleasure principle. The repetition of an unpleasurable, traumatic experience goes against the assumption that the organism seeks to avoid unpleasure. It thus points to a compulsion to repeat (in essence, a compulsion for autobiography since it is life experiences that are repeated) that is independent of the pleasure principle.

Freud will take up the subject of war neuroses in the third chapter of his essay and will link the repetition of unpleasurable experiences in dreams to the repetition of childhood traumas that occurs in the analytic session. Only at this point will he finally advance a tentative hypothesis concerning a compulsion to repeat. In this second chapter, however, Freud only slightly hints at the problem raised by war neuroses and, just when one would expect him to draw the consequences or advance a claim, he abruptly breaks off:

> At this point I propose to leave the dark and dismal subject of the traumatic neuroses and pass on to examine

156

the method of working employed by the mental apparatus in one of its earliest normal activities--I mean in children's play (XVIII, 14).

What Freud inserts at this point is an autobiographical incident, a personal observation of a child with whom Freud lived for several weeks. What he does not indicate is that the child in question is his grandson Ernst, the elder son of his daughter Sophie. In any case, Freud interrupts his thesis regarding a compulsion to repeat experiences from one's life in order to repeat an experience from his life. That is, the anecdote is an example of the tendency Freud describes in reference to his neurotic patients.

Derrida comments:

> Il est donc pressé d'en venir là, au risque d'abandonner un problème non réglé qu'il devra retrouver plus tard, et surtout au risque de ne faire avancer en rien (ce qui sera en effet le cas) la démonstration d'un au-delà du PP [principe du plaisir]. L'enjeu d'un tel empressement serait donc autre, d'un autre ordre. L'urgence ne se laisse pas déchiffrer sur la portée de la déclaration démonstrative, de l'argumentation manifeste (CP, 318-19).

From the point of view of a reader who expects a logical development that moves step by step toward its conclusion, the intervention of the autobiographical anecdote does not make sense. For Derrida, this is not simply a clumsiness of exposition on Freud's part; the form of the text is motivated by other considerations.

Derrida aims to show that the interest of the example does not lie, as the "canonical" reading would have it, at the level of the demonstration. The "argument de la bobine," as he calls it, cannot answer the question that psychoanalysts have asked it, namely: "Avons-nous raison, nous psychanalystes, de croire à la domination absolue du PP?" (CP, 315). In fact, writes Derrida, Freud "ne retient rien de cette histoire du fort/da, du moins dans sa démonstration en vue d'un au-delà du PP" (CP, 315). Derrida looks for the significance of the chapter in the relation between Freud's reporting of the scene (le rapportant) and the scene reported (le rapporté):

> On constate que quelque chose se répète. Et (l'a-t-on jamais fait?) il faut identifier le procès répétitif non seulement dans le contenu, les exemples, le matériau décrits et analysés par Freud mais déjà, ou encore, dans l'écriture de Freud, dans la démarche de son texte, dans ce qu'il fait autant que dans ce qu'il dit (CP, 315-16).

We may distinguish three types of repetition in this chapter. In the first place, Ernst repeats his game with the toy spool; the

157

spool returns to his hand only to leave again, disappears only to reappear. Second, Freud observes Ernst's game repeatedly not, as he says, over a period of weeks, but over a span of years. He reports five different games, each leading to a slightly different interpretation, of which the spool game is only the paradigm, the "complete game." Third, Freud makes repeated attempts in this chapter to draw a theoretical conclusion from the observation he has made. What Ernst does repeatedly with his toy, Freud does with the thesis of a death drive: every time he seems about to catch hold of it, to conclude that it exists, he defers that conclusion, sends it away once more.

Since Freud's writing mimes the grandson's game which it reports, it appears that Freud is in a state of identification with Ernst: something in the scene so captivates him that he feels compelled to repeat it. Since, as we shall see, Freud interprets Ernst's game as the enactment of a certain relation to his family (his mother especially, but also his father and younger brother), Freud's interest in the scene and his miming of it at the level of writing has to do with his own relationship to the same individuals (his daughter, son-in-law, and grandsons) and to the family of psychoanalysis that they come to represent. Derrida writes:

> Je parie que ce double _fort/da_ coopère, que cette coopération coopère à initier la cause psychanalytique, à mettre en mouvement le 'mouvement' psychanalytique, à l'être même, à l'_être_ même, à son être _même_, autrement dit à la structure singulière de sa tradition, je dirai au nom propre de cette 'science'... qui garde à son histoire un rapport à nul autre semblable.... Si, dans l'événement inouï de cette coopération, le reste inanalysé d'un inconscient demeure, si ce reste travaille et construit de son altérité l'autobiographie de cette écriture testamentaire, alors je gage qu'il sera transmis les yeux fermés par tout le mouvement du retour à Freud. Le reste qui travaille en silence la scène de cette coopération est sans doute illisible (maintenant ou à jamais, telle est une restance au sens où je l'entends) mais il définit la seule urgence de ce qui reste à faire, à vrai dire son seul intérêt. Intérêt d'une répétition supplémentaire? ou intérêt d'une transformation génétique, d'un renouvellement déplaçant effectivement l'essentiel? Cette alternative est infirme, elle est d'avance rendue boiteuse par la démarche qu'on peut lire ici, dans le document bizarre qui nous occupe (CP, 324-25).

Thus, Derrida takes Freud's reporting of the scene as a moment in his self-analysis, one that marks an important point in the psychoanalytic movement. In the scene that Freud sees played out before him, he finds something that responds to his desire for a science that retains its identity, its identity with the proper name of Freud. We shall later examine certain events that took place in the psychoanalytic movement at the time Freud was writing <u>Beyond</u>; such events give Derrida's interpretation a certain plausibility. We note, however, that that interpretation is taken on as a <u>wager</u>, and as an impossible task to make readable what is perhaps destined to remain unread. And Derrida suggests that his reading may be simply a "répétition supplémentaire," that is, an interpretation that compulsively repeats, at the third degree, Freud's repetition of Ernst's repetition. In fact, Derrida's interpretation of the scene often appear fanciful, speculative, or exorbitant,[1] but it is in this exorbitance that the theory of interpretation as autobiography is played out. We shall return to this question later.

By analyzing Freud's report of Ernst's game, Derrida seeks to uncover "le reste inanalysé d'un inconscient" that has been passed on to Freud's successors, who have received the legacy without investigating the conditions and limits of a science based on a self-analysis. He locates the evidence of this <u>reste</u> in the scene of writing that mimes and repeats the game it describes. It is in Freud's identification with his grandson that <u>Beyond</u> turns back upon itself: since he and Ernst are playing the same game, any comment about the child or the game can also be taken as a statement about himself. Furthermore, since Freud's writing is an <u>example</u> of the repetition compulsion that is posited in <u>Beyond</u>, whatever conclusions Freud draws about the relation of this compulsion to the pleasure principle or the death drive refer to his writing as well. In the description of Ernst's games, Freud describes himself and his writing.

The <u>Fort/Da</u> Games.

The game with the spool as object is the second in a series of games. In the first scene that Freud observes, Ernst throws "any small objects he could get hold of" (XVIII, 14) away from him, under the bed or into a corner, and it is the family's task to collect his toys. Freud and Ernst's mother Sophie watch this game and take part in it, not only by bringing the child's toys back to him, but by interpreting the "long-drawn-out 'o-o-o-o'" as the German word <u>fort</u> ("gone").

In the second game, then, Ernst holds his toy spool by a string, throws it behind the curtain or skirt of his bed and pulls it back to him, uttering in turn "o-o-o-o" and "da" ("here").[2] Freud takes this as a confirmation that his interpretation is correct; he also believes that this is the "complete game," that the first observation did not include the dénouement and that "there is no doubt that the greater pleasure was attached to the second act" (XVIII, 15). Freud concludes that the child, who did not cry during his mother's periodic absences, was compensating himself for his good behavior, by representing his mother's departures and returns in a game, and thus mastering them.

In a footnote appended immediately to this observation, Freud adds a third instance of the <u>fort</u> game. This time, there is no toy or object involved, only the child himself. When the mother returns after several hours, Ernst announces "bebi o-o-o-o" and it is soon discovered that he "had found a method of making __himself__ disappear" (XVIII, 15n) by crouching beneath a full-length mirror in which he had discovered his reflection.   nC the next page, Freud adds yet another supplementary observation, this one taking place a year later. At this time, the child was in the habit of "punishing" his toys by throwing them to the ground and exclaiming: "Go to the front!"

> He had heard... that his absent father was 'at the front,' and was far from regretting his absence; on the contrary, he made it quite clear that he had no desire to be disturbed in his sole possession of his mother (XVIII, 16).

In this case, then, the __fort__ game is not aimed at mastering an undesirable absence but at prolonging a desirable one. Freud adds that even Ernst's game with the spool may have involved an impulse of revenge, a way of saying to the mother: "All right then, go away! I don't need you. I'm sending you away myself" (XVIII, 16).

In a final footnote, Freud reports the fifth episode, where the child no longer plays __fort__ but experiences the definitive loss of his mother:

> When this child was five and three-quarters, his mother died. Now that she was really 'gone' ('o-o-o'), the little boy showed no signs of grief. It is true that in the interval a second child had been born and had roused him to violent jealousy (XVIII, 16n).

These, then, are the __fort/(da)__ games that Ernst plays and that Freud observes and reports. In the second chapter of __Beyond__ and, in fact, throughout the essay, they are supplemented by Freud's game: on four separate occasions during the development of the chapter, he avoids taking the step beyond the pleasure principle, sends his thesis __fort__. We have already seen the first instance: he interrupts the discussion of war neuroses, breaks off, and turns to the question of child's play. But having reported Ernst's games, he explains that "no certain decision can be reached from the analysis of a single case like this" (XVIII, 16). This statement is followed by two tentative interpretations: the child is attempting to master an experience to which he submitted passively by assuming an active role or he is sending his toys away in an act of revenge against the mother. But once more and for the third time, Freud finds himself unable to advance and is forced to conclude: "Nor shall we be helped in our hesitation between these two views by further considering children's play" (XVIII, 16). There follows a discussion of artistic imitation and a call for a study of aesthetics from an economic point of view. But, since he has asserted the dominance of the pleasure principle even in the case of the work of art, Freud must conclude that such avenues of study would be "of no use for __our__ purposes, since they presuppose the existence and dominance of the pleasure principle; they give no evidence of the operation of tendencies beyond the pleasure principle" (XVIII, 17).

Having pointed out these four interruptions or renvois in Freud's essay, Derrida notes:

> Nous n'avons pas avancé d'un pas, seulement des pas pour rien dans la voie de la recherche manifeste. Ça se répète sur place. Et pourtant, dans ce piétinement, la répétition insiste et si ces répétitions déterminées, ces contenus, espèces, exemples de répétition ne suffisent pas à détrôner le PP, du moins la forme répétitive, la reproduction du répétitif, la reproductivité même aura-t-elle commencé à travailler sans rien dire, sans rien dire d'autre qu'elle-même se taisant, un peu comme à la dernière page il est dit que les pulsions de mort ne disent rien (CP, 317).

The last page of Beyond says not only that the death drive does its work silently or unobtrusively (unauffällig) but that "the pleasure principle seems actually to serve the death instincts" (XVIII, 63). Thus, even if Freud does not succeed, at the level of the demonstration, in positing a drive beyond the pleasure principle, even if his repeated and repetitive examples do not argue conclusively for a compulsion to repeat, the repetitive, inconclusive, unobtrusive form of the essay functions in precisely the same way as the death drive it posits. The repetitions in the chapter silently confirm what Freud cannot quite bring himself to say.

Derrida links this structure of a pleasure principle, a reality principle, and a death drive that seems to work silently from within the structure to the genealogical movement (continuation or extinction) of his family and of the family of psychoanalysis. That is, he associates the pleasure principle (PP) with the grandfather (pépé) and finds in Freud's reaction to his daughter's (and later, to his younger grandson's) death an indication of a death drive that touches the psychoanalytic movement. The point of articulation between the structure of the pleasure principle and that of the psychoanalytic movement lies in the identification of Freud with Ernst in the fort/da scene.

The Freud Family

Derrida thus superimposes Freud's reaction to the death of his daughter onto Ernst's response to the periodic absences of his mother and, in so doing, opens the text to a reading that records certain events in the psychoanalytic movement. The story of Ernst as Freud tells it exhibits all the features of a classic "family romance": Ernst yearns for exclusive possession of his mother; he is jealous of his father and of his younger brother. Nevertheless, he is capable of a "great cultural achievement --the instinctual renunciation (that is, the renunciation of instinctual satisfaction)" which consists of "allowing his mother to go away without protesting" (XVIII, 15). He achieves this by representing his mother's departure in a game. Sophie, of course, provides the intermediate link between Freud and Ernst: she is the one whose absence they both regret and whose presence they both desire. They are not, however, for this reason rivals: the rivals (son-in--law/father and grandson/younger brother) are excluded from the scene. Thus, the generation that intervenes between Freud and his grandson allows the identification to take place; Sophie serves as a kind of partition through which the reversal of roles can occur. Thus, Derrida writes, "un supplément de génération y trouve toujours à employer ou déployer son désir" (CP, 321).

But what is the nature of Freud's desire? When Sophie dies, he refers repeatedly in his letters to a "blessure irréparable comme offense narcissique" (CP, 350). This not only echoes Ernst's feelings toward his mother's absence (at least as Freud interprets them), it also repeats one of the central theoretical questions of Beyond. For one of the enigmas about analysis is that the patient compulsively repeats a life experience that cannot have produced pleasure: namely, the severe blow to narcissism that results when the child attempts to investigate the mystery of sexuality. Freud explains that

> the child's sexual researches, on which limits are imposed by his physical development, lead to no satisfactory conclusion.... The tie of affection, which binds the child as a rule to the parent of the opposite sex, succumbs to disappointment, to a vain expectation of satisfaction or to jealousy over the birth of a new baby --unmistakable proof of the infidelity of the object of the child's affections. His own attempt to make a baby, carried out with tragic seriousness, fails shamefully (XVIII, 21).

The birth of Ernst's younger brother, then, brings about a separation from the mother, inflicts a narcissistic scar and a sense of inferiority. This accounts for Ernst's indifference following the death of his mother: in effect, the work of mourning, the separation from the mother, had already taken place.

A remnant of this first disappointment or failure survives into adulthood. Freud writes that his neurotic patients characteristically complain, "I can't accomplish anything; I can't succeed in anything," as if they were constantly reliving that first narcissistic wound. And this sense of inferiority, grounded in the child's failed attempts to understand sexuality, also applies to Freud and links him to his grandson Ernst. Both perform a work of mourning (Ernst in the fort/da game, Freud in Beyond). Freud also finds himself unable to accomplish anything, unable to advance in his "researches" concerning the nature of pleasure. He too is unable to bear a "child," a thesis that is not aborted.

And of course, the pain Freud feels at the loss of his daughter is that of a break in the lineage. He writes to his friend Binswanger immediately after Sophie's death: "Nous n'avons pas surmonté cette monstruosité: que des enfants puissent mourir avant les parents" (quoted in CP, 352). It is as if, in dying, Sophie had failed to provide a sufficient "return" (in the form of children) on Freud's investment in a lineage; the man to whom he entrusted his daughter would have failed to make good on the investment.

As we saw in our discussion of "Mourning and Melancholia," the goal of mourning is to separate oneself from the lost object, to distance oneself from that absence in order to avoid death oneself. When Ernst vengefully sends his mother away ("All right then, go away! I don't need you"), he is performing a work of this kind. And Freud, too, sends his daughter away:

> Une fois _fort_, Sophie peut bien rester où elle est. C'est 'une perte qu'il faut oublier' (à Jones le 8 février). Elle est morte 'comme si elle n'avait jamais existé' (le 27 janvier, à Pfister, moins d'une semaine après la mort de Sophie) (CP, 350).

Derrida also points to the division of _Beyond_ into seven chapters, which recalls both the seven-day period of mourning in the Jewish tradition (CP, 129) and the seven days that passed between the first news of Sophie's illness and her death (CP, 350-51).

If Freud seems to accomplish his work of mourning with relative ease, continuing to write and declaring "la séance continue" after Sophie's death, it is because he, like Ernst, has already suffered an earlier separation --seven years before, when he married his daughter to another man. Ernst and his grandfather are also joined in their ambivalence toward Sophie's husband. For Ernst, the father interferes with his desire for "exclusive possession" of the mother. For Freud, the son-in-law represents the other family name, the loss of his proper name that the lineage through the daughter brings about. After Sophie's death, "la lutte pour la 'possession exclusive' de la file [sic] (mère) morte fait rage de tous côtés" (CP, 351). Unable to attend his daughter's funeral and cremation, Freud arranges for his two sons and daughter to be there. "Le gendre... ne sera pas resté seul avec la morte. Freud est représenté par les siens, malgré la suspension du train, par une autre fille et deux fils, porteurs du nom" (CP, 352).

Freud cannot attend the funeral because there are no trains running at the time of his daughter's death. This provides yet another link with the _fort/da_ anecdote. Ernst expresses his desire for his father to stay away from his mother by throwing down his toys, by sending them "to the front." But Freud imagines another game. In reporting the _fort/da_ scene, he says that Ernst might have found another use for his spool: "It never occurred to him to pull it along the floor behind him, for instance, and play at its being a carriage (_Wagen_)" (XVIII, 15). Derrida comments:

> Il a l'air de s'étonner, y mettant un regret certain, que le brave enfant n'ait jamais eu l'idée de traîner la bobine derrière lui et de jouer à la voiture: au wagon

plutôt (<u>Wagen</u>), au train. C'est comme si l'on pouvait parier (<u>wagen</u> encore) que le spéculateur (dont le goût inverse, disons la phobie pour le chemin de fer, <u>Eisenbahn</u>, est assez connu pour nous mettre sur la voie) aurait joué, lui, au petit train (CP, 335).

If Freud has a phobia about trains, it is natural that he should try to master it in a game (or in a self-analysis, as was in fact the case)[3] just as Ernst masters his mother's absence. Furthermore, Freud must passively submit to the trains that remain at a distance and that keep him from traveling to his daughter's funeral: all the more reason to control the toy train, to hold the string that keeps the train at a distance, or to wish that his grandson would do it for him.

The last link of identification between Ernst and Freud is the feeling of jealousy towards a younger brother, Ernst's brother Heinerle, who stands in the same relation to Ernst as Freud's younger brother Julius to him. As it happens, both younger brothers die at an early age. The death of Julius, corresponding to Freud's wish, "suscita en lui un sentiment de culpabilité, tendance qui ne l'abandonna jamais" (Jones, quoted in CP, 356). When Heinerle dies, following a tonsillectomy that coincides with Freud's first operation for the throat cancer that would eventually kill him, Freud becomes profoundly depressed. He considered Heinerle the most intelligent child he had ever known and the grandson who stood for all filiation. Thus, he experiences the death of Heinerle as his own death, the extinction of his lineage. But his identification with Ernst would lead him to desire this death, the death of the rival. This desire would, in turn, elicit a feeling of guilt when it is realized. Derrida writes:

> Si la culpabilité se rapporte sur celui dont il vécut la mort comme sa propre mort, à savoir celle de l'autre, du petit frère d'Ernst comme celle de son petit frère, Julius, on tient quelques fils (seulement) dans le lacet d'identification meurtrières, endeuillées, jalouses et coupables, infiniment, qui prend la spéculation au piège (CP, 357).

In other words, Freud experiences another's death as his own, and his own death as that of another (a rival); in these multiple identifications, Freud's relation to his lineage (and to himself) can only be highly ambivalent.

To put it simply: Freud both desires and fears a lineage, both desires and fears his own death, desires to die his own death when, in fact, that death is always experienced as another's. It is no wonder that the essay <u>Beyond</u> stalls or becomes paralyzed just when it is about to posit a death drive: Freud's complex feelings of guilt, rivalry, and identification toward his own descendants make it impossible for him to advance. And Derrida underlines another example of the limits of a science based on a self-analysis: less complex than the structure of identification, it too involves

Julius and takes the form of a simple denegation. Having written Fliess in 1897 confessing his intense jealousv toward his brother "l'on a peine à comprendre que Freud ait écrit, vingt ans plus tard, que lorsque 'l'enfant n'a que quinze mois à l'époque de la naissance d'un cadet, il lui est à peu près impossible d'être jaloux'" (Jones, quoted in CP, 356-57).

The Family Romance of Psychoanalysis

A number of the incidents recorded or alluded to in the second chapter of Beyond, incidents relating to Freud's family, have a correlative in the genealogy of the psychoanalytic movement and thus allow for an interpretation of wider scope concerning Freud's grief over his daughter, his grandson and the Trauerarbeit in the form of a fort/da of the essay. For example, Anton von Freund, one of the original members of the psycho- analytic Committee, died only a few days before Sophie. The ring that Freud had given him, which should have been passed on to von Freund's successor, was instead claimed by his widow. Thus, just as Sophie interrupts the genealogy of the proper name, von Freund's widow establishes a break in the "alliance de Freud." Heinerle's death in 1923 is also associated in time with further breaks in the psychoanalytic movement; in fact, Ernest Jones titles his account of the years 1921-26, "Disunion." These fissures in the movement eventually lead to the dissolution of the Committee. Less than a year after Heinerle's death, Freud writes to Ferenczi:

> J'ai survécu au Comité qui aurait dû être mon successeur. Peut-être survivrai-je à l'Association internationale. Il est à espérer que la psychanalyse me survivra. Mais tout ceci constitue une sombre fin pour la vie d'un homme (quoted in CP, 355).

A year and a half later, Freud explains to Marie Bonaparte that, since the death of his young grandson, he feels unable to become attached to anyone; only the old attachments are maintained (CP, 355). This regression to an earlier state, the incapacity to move forward is characteristic of the death drive: in this instance, it is also associated with the psychoanalytic movement or rather, with an arrest of that movement, Freud's feeling that he has survived his own heirs and his inability to form a new alliance.

In more general terms, the question of the proper name and its relation to Freud's genealogy is pertinent to the history of the psychoanalytic movement as well, since both the science and the family are associated with the name "Freud." This points to the peculiar position of women within this movement, to the question of female sexuality and of female psychoanalysts within this science of the proper name. The question of the proper name is also that of the legitimacy of Freud's heirs, their right to bear his name, and the testament that the name carries with it.

Derrida follows the genealogical line that leads from Freud to the French branch of psychoanalysis by focusing on Marie

165

Bonaparte. She is, at the time of Heinerle's death, Freud's confidante, part of the old alliance; it is to Bonaparte that Freud writes of his depression and indifference. Derrida explains:

> Si j'insiste sur l'aveu à Marie Bonaparte, c'est pour faire suivre. Par le facteur de la vérité jusqu'à la scène de famille du côté de la branche française, au moment où on croit décacheter un testament.... Un des éléments du drame: plusieurs familles portent le même nom sans toujours le savoir. Et il y a d'autres noms dans la même famille. (J'interromps ici ce développement. Si on veut bien en lire la conséquence, jusqu'à son appendice dans Le Facteur de la Vérité, on y percevra peut-être une contribution à tel décryptage encore à venir du mouvement analytique français.) (CP, 355)

This passage, which links "Spéculer" to "Le Facteur de la Vérité," Freud's generation to Lacan's (and Derrida's), treats the psychoanalytic heritage as a problem involving the proper name, its transmission, and of women's relation to that name. It concerns a certain male prejudice passed on from father to son, Freud to Lacan, that not only distorts the theory of psychoanalysis but actually determines the structure of the heritage and the institution. It concerns, that is, the "phallo- centrism" of Freud's theory.

The Heritage of Phallocentrism

In "Le Facteur de la Vérité," Derrida argues that Lacan, in his reading of Poe as an illustration of his own theory of language has, like Freud, adopted a specifically male point of view even while claiming to occupy a privileged position outside or beyond any interested viewpoint. This leads Lacan: first, to practice a "mauvais formalisme" in reading Poe's story and to overlook the interested positions of the narrators in the story they are telling; second, to ignore or deny knowledge of Marie Bonaparte's psychobiographical reading of the same short story even while borrowing heavily from her; and third, to thereby deny Marie Bonaparte's prior claim to Freud's legacy and to claim for himself the direct and legitimate lineage with Freud, and the access to psychoanalytic truth.

To follow Derrida's critique more closely: he claims that Lacan, like Freud, views female sexuality as simply lack, female genitals as castration. Lacan would view woman as "figure de la castration et de la vérité" (CP, 469).

> Le lien de la Féminité et de la vérité... est selon Lacan l'ultime signifié de la 'Lettre Volée'.... Lacan insiste surtout sur ce lien et sur ce sens. Il y met à la Femme ou à la Féminité une majuscule qu'il réserve ailleurs, très souvent, à la Vérité (CP, 470).

And, writes Derrida, this determination of truth as (women's) castration, allows Lacan to grant both truth and the phallus a central, privileged position in his discourse:

> La castration-vérité, c'est... ce qui se contracte... pour faire revenir le phallus, le signifiant, la lettre ou le fétiche en leur _oikos_, en leur demeure familière, en leur lieu propre. En ce sens la castration-vérité est le contraire du morcellement, son antidote même: ce qui y manque à sa place a sa place fixe, centrale, soustraite à toute substitution. Quelque chose manque à sa place, mais le manque n'y manque jamais. Le phallus, grâce à la castration, reste toujours à sa place (CP, 469).

Determining truth as absence rather than presence does not displace the fundamental system of a privileged, transcendental term that organizes and centers discourse. Truth and the phallus still have a "lieu propre" even if it is a gap always to be filled.

The link between truth, castration, and woman depends, however, on a certain point of view and on a certain interpretation: those of the male child who perceives the female genitals not as a sexual difference but as a lack, a lost penis.

> Auparavant, en tout cas, il a bien été là et par la suite il a été enlevé. Le manque de pénis est conçu comme le résultat d'une castration.... Au stade [...] de l'organisation génitale infantile, il y a bien un _masculin_, mais pas de féminin; l'opposition s'énonce ainsi: _organe génital masculin ou châtré_ (Freud, quoted in CP, 509n., ellipses in brackets are Derrida's).

It has been shown that Freud's entire theory of sexuality (the structure of the Oedipal complex and the symmetry between the male castration complex and female penis envy depends on his adopting the male child's point of view.[4]

Derrida writes that

> le point de vue de l'homme n'est pas le même que celui de la femne, donnant ainsi à penser que la Féminité voilée/dévoilée/chatrée n'est figure de la Vérité que pour l'homne. Celui-ci ne serait maître de la vérité que de ce point de vue (CP, 487).

It is not simply that Lacan has inherited unquestioningly the male prejudices of Freud, has perpetuated Freud's blindness in equating woman and castration, in seeing women as merely castrated men; the critique is of greater scope. In a lengthy footnote, Derrida explains that it might be possible to describe the phallocentrism of children's sexual lives and of society in general without necessarily ascribing to that view, but that "cette hypothèse... rencontre... une limite très strictement déterminable."

> La description est 'partie prenante' quand elle induit
> une pratique, une éthique et une institution, donc une
> politique assurant la tradition de sa vérité.... Le
> propos éthico-institutionnel est déclaré par Lacan: le
> motif de l'authenticité, de la parole pleine, de la foi
> jurée et de la 'convention signifiante' le montrait
> assez. Il se règle systématiquement sur une doctrine
> phallogocentrique du signifiant (CP, 509n.).

In other words, when Lacan identifies women-as-castration with truth, that view of sexuality becomes the paradigm for his position as "maître de vérité"; it allows him a privileged position from which to speak and consolidates the power he wields within the institution of psychoanalysis.

That the female child might have a different point of view with regard to the female genitals is an insight that Derrida finds in Marie Bonaparte's reading of "The Purloined Letter." He notes, however, that Bonaparte does not escape entirely from this male point of view and that she "s'y reporte avec reconnaissance à la lettre de certains éclaircissements que Freud lui confia" (CP, 487n.). In fact, she and Lacan reach virtually the same conclusion about the meaning of Poe's story: the letter that the inspector Dupin finds hanging in a letter-holder between the "cheeks" (jambages) of the fireplace represents the "rephallization" of the mother. We shall return later to Bonaparte's position as a woman psychoanalyst and her ambiguous relation to Freud. For the moment, however, we need to examine Lacan's ambivalent relation to this female heir to Freud.

Derrida points to evidence that Lacan had read Bonaparte's interpretation even though he does not acknowledge it explicitly. Bonaparte had noted an error in Baudelaire's translation of Poe: the translator places the letter-holder <u>above</u> the mantel-piece whereas in the original English, it rests beneath the mantel, between the cheeks of the fireplace. In an apparent allusion to Bonaparte's correction, Lacan writes:

> La question de savoir s'il le saisit sur le manteau,
> comme Baudelaire le traduit, ou sous le manteau de la
> cheminée comme le porte le texte original, peut être
> abandonnée sans dommage aux inférences de la cuisine.15
> [Ici, donc, une note de Lacan: "15. Et même de la
> cuisinière"] (quoted in CP, 474, Derrida's brackets).

Derrida comments :

> Sans dommage? Le dégât serait au contraire irréparable,
> à l'intérieur même du Séminaire: <u>sur</u> le manteau de la
> cheminée la lettre n'aurait pu être 'entre les jambages
> de la cheminée,' 'entre les jambes de sa cheminée.'
> L'enjeu est donc de taille, même si on laissait de
> côté... la nervosité méprisante à l'endroit d'une psych-

analyste et de son legs. Pourquoi reléguer la question à la cuisine, comme à la dépendance, et celle qui y répond au rang de la cuisinière?   (CP, 474-75).

In relegating Bonaparte to the kitchen, Lacan denies her claim to Freud's legacy and attempts to make himself sole and legitimate heir. The play on the English word "leg," within the context of the interpretation of Poe's story about women's castration, also suggests that Lacan's uneasiness has to do with the fact that Bonaparte is a woman. The specter of a woman psychoanalyst might endanger the male prejudices (woman as figure of truth-as-castration) upon which Lacan builds his system.

Derrida points to Lacan's repeated efforts to claim for himself the entire Freudian legacy and. especially, his repeated attacks on Bonaparte qui

s'est cru(e) en France, pendant longtemps, le dépositaire le plus autorisé, la légataire de l'autorité de Freud, entretenant avec lui une correspondance, des liens personnels de confidence, le représentant même dans notre pays comme une sorte de ministre dont l'auteur du séminaire connaît à la fois la trahison et l'aveuglement (CP, 484).

In a sense, Bonaparte is the mother that Lacan refuses to recognize, the female heir in a genealogy that ought to have passed from father to son. She is that break in the genealogy that is represented in the daughter's loss of the family name.

The Fort/Da Game as a Scene of Heritage

Derrida's analysis of how a blind spot (in this case, Freud's prejudice concerning female sexuality) can be passed from one generation to the next and can even become part of the very structure of an institution underlines the necessity of returning to Freud's texts, not in order to reestablish an orthodoxy, but to examine the condition for the science in the first place. It underlines, then, the importance of analyzing the "reste inanalysé d'un inconscient" in Freud's writings. Derrida takes on this task in his interpretation of the second chapter of Beyond, that is, in one of the texts and one of the moments privileged by Lacan.

The fort/da scene, of course, is also a scene of interpretation: the grandfather and the mother of a child interpret his game and the sounds that he utters. The mother stands silently beside her father, assenting to and guaranteeing what he says. Derrida writes: "Il y a une fille muette. Plus qu'une autre, qui aura usé du crédit paternel dans un abondant discours d'héritage, elle aura peut-être dit voilà pourquoi votre père a la parole. Non seulement mon père, mais votre père. C'est Sophie" (CP, 327). The other daughter, whether one takes that to be Anna Freud or Marie Bonaparte, inherits, with the discourse, the phallocentric system.   Thus, although Bonaparte is able to point to the

169

specifically male point of view of Poe's Dupin, she ends up adopting it in her own interpretation, even paying homage to Freud's comments on the subject.

In appearance, Sophie's position is not very different from Bonaparte's: she, too, shares Freud's point of view, agrees with his interpretation. But Derrida locates her contribution in her silence; in keeping silent, Sophie has said how it is possible for her father and for the father of psychoanalysis to speak. It is as if a certain silence about women and even, on the part of women, provided the condition for Freud's discourse on truth. We have already suggested why this might be the case: the identification of women with truth-as-castration, which effaces the female point of view on sexuality, grounds Freud's discourse in a privileged, transcendental term, the phallus. Sophie, who represents Freud's silence about women, thus reveals the very condition for his discourse.

Sophie's silence in this family scene also suggests that she is the <u>death drive</u> of the family or that women are the death drive in the psychoanalytic movement. For, as we recall, it is the death drive that works in silence, silently working against the pleasure principle (PP). A number of indications in "Spéculer" point to this interpretation. Throughout <u>Beyond</u>, Freud searches for a drive that is beyond the pleasure principle or independent of it: but Derrida aims to show that this drive is already inscribed within the structure of the pleasure principle. Pointing out that there is no opposition between the pleasure principle and the reality principle since "le principe de réalité n'impose aucune inhibition définitive, aucun renoncement au plaisir, seulement un détour pour différer la jouissance, le relais d'une différance" (CP, 301). Derrida adds:

> Mais la structure de différance peut alors ouvrir à une altérité plus irréductible encore que celle qu'on prête à l'opposition. Parce que le principe de plaisir... ne passe de contrat qu'avec lui-même... et ne rencontre en somme aucune opposition, il <u>déchaîne</u> en lui l'autre <u>absolu</u> (CP, 302).

That "absolute other" is the death drive and it is at work in the difference between the pleasure principle and the reality principle, in the detour that the pleasure principle submits to in order to finally attain pleasure. For the structure of the detour implies that one can always <u>not arrive</u>, that the drive can be definitively derouted, can die en route, and that the pleasure principle will never return to itself.

Derrida explicitly compares this structure to that of the psychoanalytic movement that Freud initiates:

> [C'est] comme si [le PP] produisait un socius, mettait en 'mouvement' une institution en signant un contrat avec la 'discipline,' avec le sous-maître ou le contre-maître qui pourtant ne fait que le représenter. Faux contrat,

pure spéculation, simulacre d'engagement qui ne lie le seigneur qu'à lui-même, à sa propre modifi- cation, à lui-même modifié.... Il s'écrit, il s'envoie: mais si la longueur du détour n'est plus maîtrisable, et plutôt que la longueur sa structure, alors le retour à soi n'est jamais assuré (CP, 301-02).

As we saw in "On the History of the Psycho-Analytic Movement," Freud assumes that, since he initiated the psychoanalytic movement, he should remain the ultimate judge of its orthodoxy; the contract should always return to him. But Derrida argues that nothing is less assured.

One finds the same general structure within the Freud family, between the grandfather (PP), his male heir (the PR or père, Ernst's father, Freud's son-in-law), and the detour in this male genealogy, the daughter Sophie. It is through this lineage that Freud hopes to return to himself, in the form of a grandson identical to him. But Sophie dies, as does her son, and with them, it appears, Freud's hope for a lineage.

Science of the Proper Name

Derrida poses the problem of the interrupted lineage as a question of the proper name. Sophie is the daughter "qui ne perpétue la race qu'en risquant le nom" (CP, 322) and, Derrida adds : "(je vous laisse suivre ce facteur jusqu'à toutes celles dont il est difficile de savoir si elles ont gardé le mouvement sans le nom ou perdu le mouvement pour garder, pour avoir gardé, le nom...)" (CP, 322-23). It is once more the question of female heirs (psychoanalysts) and their relation to Freud. We can again distinguish between two sorts of daughters: those who accept Freud's name, his legacy, his discourse, and the male point of view that goes with them; and those who continue the "movement" (which depends on a detour and on difference) that extends beyond the "PP" Freud or that returns to the conditions that make possible Freud's lineage.

Quoting Freud's remark to Havelock Ellis that his name will be forgotten in a few generations but that his discoveries will survive, Derrida writes:

Ce nom de Freud, l'institution classique d'une science aurait dû pouvoir s'en passer. Du moins faire de son oubli la condition et la preuve de sa transmission, de son propre héritage. C'est ce que Freud croyait ou affectait de croire.... Le grand spéculateur s'y dit en somme prêt à payer la science de son propre nom, à payer de son nom la prime d'assurance (CP, 352-53).

Freud stands to gain a great deal from the "speculation" with his proper name. For the loss of the name would insure that psychoanalysis had become an ideal object: Freud's discoveries would live on, would retain their identity and their identity with him, across time. But that speculation involves a risk: "C'est comme s'il ne savait pas, déjà, qu'en payant la science de son propre nom, c'est aussi la science de son propre nom qu'il paie" (CP, 353). Once the science is detached from its origin, from Freud's name, it may become associated with other names, appropriated by other psychoanalysts, and altered in the process.

Alluding to his own project of uncovering the conditions for Freud's founding of psychoanalysis, Derrida explains: "Mais la science de son propre nom, c'est aussi ce qui reste à faire, comme le retour nécessaire sur l'origine et la condition d'une telle science" (CP, 353). That is precisely what Freud tries to avoid when he offers to give up the name that would link psychoanalysis to an individual. His

> spéculation aura consisté --peut-être-- à prétendre payer d'avance, aussi cher qu'il faudra, les charges d'un tel retour à l'envoyeur.... Il doit y avoir eu... une manière de spéculer sur la ruine de son nom (nouvelle vie, nouvelle science) qui garde ce qu'elle perd (CP, 353).

The forgetting of Freud's proper name would have made it possible for Freud to avoid, or to control, the investigation into the status of psychoanalysis in relation to him.

Fort/Da as Self-Analysis

Freud, of course, cannot insure that the message he sends to himself will not be intercepted by the other names within his family, whose interest may lie in the envelope or material support of the letter rather than in its message. The letter can always be derouted and Freud's secrets uncovered. Among the daughters and sons-in-law who are both within and outside the family is Derrida, who finds in the fort/da scene a self-analysis, Freud's as well as Ernst's.

It is clear that Ernst's game is therapeutic: the child copes with his mother's absences by representing them in a game, that is, by manipulating signs (both the spool that represents the absent mother and the "o-o-o-o" that signifies the absence of the spool) in a kind of "talking cure." Nevertheless, the analysis never comes to term: it is compulsively repeated, apparently independent of the pleasure principle. The grandfather, looking on, repeats Ernst's game in the writing of Beyond. He finds in the scene played out before him a figure for one of the conflicts that is troubling him: his relation to the psychoanalytic movement, which he initiates, founding a lineage, but always in the hope that it will return to him. The indecisiveness of Beyond, then, represents Freud's attempt to keep his science out of someone else's hands, to make sure that the theses he puts forward never quite get out of hand but always return to him.

In this double self-analysis, it is important to note that Freud is not quite satisfied with the way Ernst plays his game,

172

that he seems to regret that the child did not put the spool on the floor behind him and play at its being a train. The game that Freud would have liked to play differs from the _fort/da_ game in several respects. First, he would deny himself the "supplément du plaisir" that is attached to the second part of the game, to the return of the spool. "Il s'en prive pour s'en épargner la peine ou le risque du pari" (CP, 335). Playing at train is a game without risks, since the object stays safely on the ground, does not disappear but remains "à même distance, la longueur du fil restant invariable"; if it moves at all, it is "au même rythme que soi" (CP, 336). Second, when Ernst plays his game, he flings the spool over the rim of the bed where it disappears behind the curtain or skirt of his cot. Pulling the object behind one would thus be an effort to "ne pas mettre en jeu le lit désiré" (CP, 336). The bed represents not only sexual desire (Ernst's Oedipal desire), but also the desire for offspring, a lineage, and the psychoanalyst's couch. Freud wants to keep desire out of the game; if the game is a self-analysis, he does not want the self to disappear from view in its pursuit of desire. Freud wants to be able to keep himself in view, to not leave anything unanalyzed, to turn away from the desired object and remain firmly planted on the ground:

> Jouer au wagon, ce serait aussi bien 'tirer derrière soi' l'objet investi, tenir la locomotive bien en main et ne voir la chose qu'en se retournant. On ne l'a pas devant soi.... Le spéculateur (l'analyste) est évidemment le premier analysant. L'analysant-locomotive pour qui la loi de l'écoute se substitue à celle du regard (CP, 336-37).

In this ideal self-analysis, the "patient" should always be within hearing range, capable of being scrutinized and no hindrance to the development of an objective science.

But, as Derrida points out, the self does disappear out of sight, behind the curtain. And what is the nature of the curtain behind which Freud sees himself disappear? "Le voile de ce 'jupon' est l'intérêt du lit et le _fort:da_ de toutes ces générations. Je ne me risquerai pas à dire: c'est Sophie" (CP, 337). Once again, women appear as the blind spot of Freud's self-analysis, and the moment of risk in the game: the spool can always get caught in the curtain; it can always not return to Freud's hand. Once out of sight, Freud cannot guarantee its return.

The Debt to Philosophy

Until now, we have dealt with only one side of the genealogy of psychoanalysis: Freud's position of _Urvater_ and the ambivalence he feels toward his descendants. That is perhaps as Freud would like it, that we forget his parentage and only see the genealogy that he initiates. In the _fort/da_ scene, which functions as his autobiography, he calls Ernst's activity "the first game played by a little boy... and invented by himself" (das erste selbst-geschaffene Spiel), and indeed, the game appears to be a solitary activity, a relation of self to self. Even so, it is important to remember that it articulates a relation between the child and his parents, both his father whom he wants to stay away, and his mother whom the father possesses. Ernst throws away the toys his parents have given him and they, in turn, bring them back to him. Derrida sees this scene, and Freud's relation to his philosophical ancestry.

In the first chapter of Beyond, Derrida locates a number of "positions," irreconcilable with one another, that Freud adopts toward philosophy:

> Si on l'en croit, il faut donc admettre 1. Une 'incapacité constitutionnelle' à philosopher. Langage occulte, voire obscurantiste: qu'est-ce que c'est, en termes psychanalytiques, une 'incapacité constitution-nelle' à philosopher? 2. Une 'tendance' --néanmoins-- à la speculation. 3. Un évitement délibéré de la philo-sophie, un rejet de la dette, de la généalogie ou de la descendance philosophiques. 4. Un non-évitement de ce que Freud appelle donc la 'speculation' et qui ne doit être, stricto sensu, ni la philosophie, ni l'ex-périmentation scientifique ou clinique dans ses modes traditionnels (CP, 290).

In these "conduites d'évitement ou de dénégation" (CP, 290), we recognize the familiar movement of a fort:da. What is the danger, and the attraction, of philosophy that leads Freud to react in this way?

Derrida describes the lure of philosophy in terms of a debt that must not be assumed, both because it is another's debt and because "l'autre s'est endetté de façon insolvable (impardonnable) en émettant des simulacres de concepts" (CP, 284). In order to pay off a debt of meaning, philosophers have minted counterfeit money, words or concepts with no "contenu propre à la psychanalyse qui seule peut en garantir la valeur, l'usage, et l'échange" (CP, 284). For this reason, precisely because of the similarity between the counterfeit bills and the "guaranteed" psychoanalytic concepts, Freud must avoid philosophy, refuse its legacy: "Qu'il l'analyse ou non, Freud se soumet à un impératif qui lui prescrit d'inter-rompre la chaîne et de refuser l'héritage" (CP, 284).

Derrida races Freud's attraction to and avoidance of philosophy in his use of two terms: "pleasure" and "speculation." Beyond the Pleasure Principle begins with the words: "In the theory of psycho-analysis we have no hesitation in assuming (nehmen wir unbedenklich an) that the course taken by mental events is automatically regulated by the pleasure principle" (XVIII, 7). Derrida claims that this statement is "ni une confirmation, ni une mise en question du bien-fondé" and that it will never become one or the other in the course of Beyond. Nevertheless, the term "unbedenklich" seems to indicate that the assumption is

174

trop assurée, trop autoritaire.... Quand Freud dit 'réglé par le principe de plaisir, c'est-à-dire..., ' il ajoute 'croyons-nous' : cette croyance peut être l'effet d'une crédulité et ce soupçon la suspend aussitôt (CP, 294).

The first sentence is at once overly self-assured and doubtful of its own self-assurance. One reason for this position (or non-position) is the nature of the object involved. For to say that one recognizes the authority of the "pleasure principle" is to assume, at least implicitly, what the term "pleasure" means. But Freud admits he does not know the nature of pleasure, its qualitative essence. "C'est à ce sujet que tout à l'heure, avec l'ironie requise, on feindra d'interroger le philosophe" (CP, 294).

In these first pages of Beyond, Freud claims that it is a matter of indifference to him "how far, with this hypothesis of the pleasure principle, we have approached or adopted any particular, historically established, philosophical system" since "we have arrived at these speculative assumptions in an attempt to describe and to account for the facts of daily observation in our field of study." On the other hand, he adds, "we would readily express our gratitude to any philosophical or psychological theory which was able to inform us of the meaning of the feelings of pleasure and unpleasure which act so imperatively on us" (XVIII, 7). But finding no illumination for this "most obscure and inaccessible region of the mind," Freud decides to adopt "the least rigid hypothesis" possible (XVIII, 7). Thus, Freud "laisse entendre ironiquement que même quand il parle du plaisir --et quel philosophe aura manqué?-- il ne sait pas et ne dit pas de quoi il parle" (CP, 295).

Rather than carefully defining his terms or depending on philosophical concepts, Freud leaves his speculation open and flexible. Of course, he relies to a certain extent on "l'expérience commune" to make his use of the term "pleasure" comprehensible, but this is not conclusive since Freud is led to posit a kind of pleasure "qui se donne à l'expérience commune, communément déterminée, à la conscience ou à la perception comme déplaisir" (CP, 295). The desires that have been repressed in the process of the ego's formation, should they achieve satisfaction, are experienced by the ego as unpleasure. So that the notion of pleasure, which appears "irréductiblement phénoménal" is complicated by the existence of the unconscious.

Derrida claims that, as a result,

cette spéculation serait donc étrangère à la philosophie et à la métaphysique. Plus précisément, elle représenterait cela même dont la philosophie ou la métaphysique se gardent, consistent à se garder, entretenant avec elle un rapport sans rapport, un rapport d'exclusion (CP, 296).

If philosophy has always labored to uphold the law of non-contradiction and has awarded a central place to the phenomenality of experience, then Freud's "speculation" on pleasure, no matter how distant from the "observations" he seeks to oppose to it, is in its essence non-philosophical. That is not to say, however, that it lies completely or simply outside philosophy: it is rather what philosophy guards against, tries to exclude without ever fully succeeding. It is, in other words, "l'autre de l'autre en l'habitant, en se laissant exclure sans cesser de le travailler de la façon la plus domestique" (CP, 296). Freud's speculation represents the repressed of metaphysics, the forces that work silently from within it.

Nor can Freud simply avoid the debt of philosophy, since the currency he uses (his words and concepts) is borrowed from or borrowed against the counterfeit bills of metaphysics. Derrida shows Freud's considerable debt to Plato, to Schopenhauer, and especially to Nietzsche. In his fort/da with philosophy, Freud contracts and annuls the debt in the same gesture, repeats and displaces philosophy, sounds its glas, but nevertheless enters into the game.

Thus, when Freud modifies his early remark that Ernst's game was invented by him by saying, "it is of course a matter of indifference from the point of view of judging the effective nature of the game whether the child invented it himself or took it over on some outside suggestion" (XVIII, 15), Derrida responds:

> Ah bon? Pourquoi? Naturellement indifférent? Tiens[1] Pourquoi? Qu'est-ce qu'une instigation dans ce cas? Par où passe-t-elle? D'où serait-elle venue? Que l'enfant se soit 'approprié' (zu eigen gemacht) le désir d'un autre ou d'une autre, ou de deux autres conjoints... cela serait 'naturellement indifférent'? .... Toutes ces questions auront été renvoyées éloignées, dissociées, voilà l'incontestable (CP, 347).

Freud's feigned "indifference" about the relation of his theories to philosophy, and his indifference regarding the source of the child's game both avoid the crucial question of the debt owed to past generations in the formation of one's own ideas. And it is that question that Derrida will take up in relation to his own philosophical heritage.

Derrida's Fort/Da

There are numerous indications in "Spéculer" that Derrida's reading of Freud stands in the same relation to Beyond the Pleasure Principle as Freud's text stands to Ernst's fort/da game: it mimes the movement of that essay and repeats again Ernst's fort/da, this time as a disguised autobiography of Derrida. The title of the essay makes of Derrida a third "speculator" and its structure confirms a close parallel between the two texts. My reading, with its concern for clear exposition, has minimized the fragmented, "non-positional" character of "Spéculer." I have considerably simplified the shifting, multiple meanings and relations between the various elements; I have juxtaposed passages and drawn analogies (between Ernst and Freud, for example) that are not explicitly stated in the text. Further, I have truncated quotations from "Spéculer" to make them appear simple assertions when, in fact, they are oddly suspended between assertion and denial.

For example, when Derrida draws a parallel between Ernst's bed and the analyst's couch, it takes this form: "Car enfin ce lit au bord si nécessaire et si indécidable, était-ce un divan? Pas encore, malgré tout l'orphisme d'une spéculation. Et pourtant" (CP, 338). The connection is made in the form of a question; it is then negated; and finally, it is _almost_ affirmed.

Again, the first time Derrida alludes to a relationship of identification between Freud and his grandson, he merely hints: "(Si Freud était son petit-fils, il faudrait être attentif à la répétition du côté du geste et non seulement du côté du _fort/da_ de la bobine, de l'objet. Mais ne brouillons pas les cartes; qui a dit que Freud était son propre petit-fils?)" (CP, 316) Once more, the assertion is suspended, the question left unanswered. O n e further example. At one point, Derrida suggests that, since the sounds "o-o-o-o" and "a-a-a-a," the opposition o/a, cannot be translated into just any language and still retain their value,

> il y a du nom propre là-dessous, qu'on l'entende au sens figuré (tout signifié dont le signifiant ne peut pas varier ni se laisser traduire dans un autre signifiant sans perte de signification induit un effet de nom propre) ou au sens dit 'propre' (CP, 333).

Without elaborating any further on what importance this might have and on what connection there may be between this and his other comments on the question of the proper name, Derrida concludes: "Je laisse ces hypothèses ouvertes, mais ce qui me paraît assuré, c'est la nécessité de former des hypothèses sur le conjoint des interprétations de o-o-o-o, voire o/a" (CP, 333).[5] Statements of this sort are numerous in "Spéculer": Derrida often suggests without affirming, or affirms and denies in the same breath, or leaves a question open, as if the important thing were not to come to a conclusion but rather to speculate on the possible conclusions one might draw. This speculation, of course, links "Spéculer" with the text it is describing.

A second link lies in the selectivity of the interpreters, Freud and Derrida, with regard to the object they describe. Derrida points out that when Freud reports his observation of the _fort/da_ game, "ce qui est rendu est d'abord criblé, sélectionné, activement délimité" (CP, 320). Derrida compares Freud to a director who plays a part in his own play and who is thus in a hurry to put everything in order so that he can prepare to appear on stage. "Cela se traduit par un autoritarisme tranchant, des décisions qu'on n'explique pas, des paroles qu'on coupe, des questions auxquelles on ne répond pas" (CP, 329). All of these attributes belong to "Spéculer" as well as to <u>Beyond</u>. Derrida writes, in effect: "<u>Au-delà du principe du plaisir</u>: j'en proposerai une lecture séléctive, criblante, discriminante" (CP, 279). Like Freud, Derrida actively selects the details he reports; he leaves questions unanswered, arbitrarily dismisses issues ("Laissons arbitrairement de côté tous les problèmes posés par..." CP, 299); and, as we shall see, he too has a role in the play he is staging.

We recall that in <u>Beyond</u>, the <u>fort/da</u> episode interrupts the flow of the argument and delays Freud's discussion of the war neuroses until the next chapter. The episode at first appears as a mere detour, but, in fact, it is an example of the compulsion to repeat (the compulsion for autobiography) and thus anticipates the theoretical discussion. The first chapter of Derrida's "Spéculer" has a similar structure. Derrida analyzes Freud's desire for originality, his need to found a science that is truly his own, and his unrecognized debt to philosophy. This discussion will eventually lead to the question of the word and the concept, in particular, the difficulties that arise when Freud must use the terms "pleasure" and "speculation" even as he tries to strip them of their philosophical connotations. Derrida describes this relation between an etymological use and a more "subversive" one as that of translation "à l'intérieur du 'même' mot."

> La traduction devrait trouver son lieu, entre le concept philosophique... dans sa détermination dominante, apparente, légitime, accordée au consensus élémentaire de la tradition philosophique, et celui qui s'annonce ici (that is, in Freud's <u>Beyond</u>) (CP, 296).

Thus, the practice of using the same word to designate something altogether different from its usual referent (Derrida elsewhere calls this practice "paléonymie") is a problem of translation.

Now, in the middle of the discussion of Freud's debt to philosophy, Derrida interrupts the argument and inserts an autobiographical comment of his own. He has just asserted that "la reconnaissance de dette est annulée, ou, si vous préférez, déniée, confirmée, au centre de <u>Au-delà...</u>" (CP, 284) and he goes on to demonstrate this debt, in this case, to Hering, from whom Freud borrows the notion of a "dualisme de la vie pulsionelle" (CP, 284). Two drives would continually be at work in the living organism: one drive would tend to assimilate, bring together, the other to disassimilate or break down. Thus, the first drive functions "en construisant (<u>aufbauend</u>), le second en dé-truisant (<u>abbauend</u>)" (CP, 285). At this point in the argument, Derrida breaks off his discussion of Freud's debt to Hering, a discussion that will culminate in the question of translation, in order to insert a comment about two translations involving the word most associated with Derrida, "deconstruction." "<u>Abbauen</u>: c'est le mot que certains heideggeriens français ont récemment traduit par 'déconstruire,' comme si tout était dans tout et toujours devant

178

la caravane" (CP, 285). This statement asserts Derrida's own desire for priority and for originality, denies his debt to Heidegger and suggests that "deconstruction," like Freud's "psychoanalysis" is a term that ought to retain its proximity to the object it names.

Derrida adds that the translation is not in itself illegitimate but that it makes it possible to manipulate "l'après-coup pour assimiler, précisément, et reconstruire ce qui se laisse mal assimiler" (CP, 285). Derrida is thus arguing that the drive to translate Heidegger's "abbauen" by Derrida's "deconstruct" is part of the assimilating drive that Hering and Freud posit, the drive to organize and appropriate that which, precisely, strives to avoid such assimilation.

In the next sentence, Derrida introduces the notion of debt into this context:

> Il est vrai aussi qu'en ce domaine la concurrence se fait
> d'autant plus âpre qu'on peut toujours faire passer le
> déjà-là d'un mot pour l'antériorité d'un concept dont on
> prétend alors endetter, voire ensemencer tout le monde
> (CP, 285).

The French term "concurrence" means "concurrence" or "coincidence" (as in a coincidence of opposites or of events) and may, in this context, simply refer to the manufactured appearance of the same word ("déconstruire") in the writings of both Heidegger and Derrida. Thus, the sentence would mean: the fact that "déconstruire" now occurs in Heidegger's texts could lead one to believe that I, Derrida, have inherited it from him, that I am indebted to him for the concept, that I am his heir. Concurrence, however, also means "competition" or "rivalry." One might then translate the passage as: the rivalry between myself (Derrida) and Heidegger is made all the more bitter by the fact that one can always attribute to Heidegger a concept that is in fact mine. Such a translation is by no means out of place: Derrida is claiming in this passage that Heidegger has not invented deconstruction and that the translation of "abbauen" by "déconstruire" reverses the genealogy, places Derrida in Heidegger's debt when in fact, Derrida is the rightful father of deconstruction. We begin to see that the issues of genalogy, rivalry, possession, etc. that Derrida analyzes in Beyond are by no means foreign to Derrida's own position as the originator of deconstruction.

The passage goes on to consider another instance of translation, this time, of Marx's German Ideology: "Jusqu'ici 'aufgelöst' était fidèlement traduit par 'résolu' ou 'dissous.' Une traduction récente de l'Idéologie allemande dit 'peuvent être déconstruites' pour 'aufgelöst werden können,' sans autre forme de procès et sans la moindre explication" (CP, 285). Once more, Derrida explains that the translation is not invalid in itself, but that, in the context of the passage, it tends to "égarer le lecteur." The translated passage runs as follows:

179

> Elle [cette nouvelle conception matérialiste de l'histoire] n'explique pas la praxis d'après l'idée, elle explique la formation des idées d'après la praxis matérielle et parvient en conséquence à ce resultat que ce n'est pas par la critique intellectuelle, par la réduction à la 'conscience de soi' ou par la transmutation en 'revenants,' en 'fantômes,' en 'obsessions' etc., que peuvent être déconstruites (<u>aufgelöst werden können</u>) toutes les formes et les productions de la conscience, mais seulement par la subversion pratique... des rapports sociaux réels, d'où sont sorties ces fariboles idéalistes (quoted in CP, 285-86, Derrida's brackets).

Marx is criticizing the idealist position that claims that a critique of consciousness can by itself alter the forms of consciousness, without a corresponding change in economic structures. The use of the term "déconstruit," which is associated with Derrida, suggests that Derrida's project is an idealism of this kind and that Marx provides a critique of Derrida in advance. "On veut donner à croire que la 'déconstruction' est d'essence 'théoricienne,' voire théoriciste, ce par quoi on fait une... économie... de la lecture" (CP, 286). Derrida suggests that any careful reading of his texts would reveal that his critique of philosophy does not limit itself to a deconstruction of superstructures or to strictly "theoretical" matters, but that, despite the clever translation of Marx that accuses Derrida, Derrida's critique also functions at the level of praxis.[6] Nevertheless, the critique is a common one among Marxists and rather than answering it here, Derrida goes on to criticize Marx: "On aura remarqué au passage, c'est la destination essentielle à mes yeux de cette citation d'apparence philologique, le bon marché que Marx fait des 'fantômes' et des 'revenants.' C'est notre problème" (CP, 286). In effect, Marx speaks disparagingly of those philosophers who believe that, by way of intellectual critique, they can reduce all the belief systems or ideas into mere ghosts or specters. In "Spéculer," Derrida treats these specters not as the result of such a reduction, not as the imperceptible, fuzzy remains of a belief system that has been deconstructed, but as a haunting presence that continues to be at work even in the "demythified" philosopher. If, as Marx claims, idealist philosophers reduce the products of the mind to "mere ghosts," believing that they thereby achieve a transformation of consciousness, then Derrida is not an idealist, since he analyzes the <u>persistence</u> of such ghosts even after they are believed to have been surmounted by the intellect. And yet, as he analyzes this persistence, Derrida also illustrates it, by expressing his own desire to cling to "deconstruction" as his word, to keep it in his exclusive possession, to deny a debt and an ancestry.

In the next paragraph, Derrida alludes to a self-critique of deconstruction:

> Si maintenant on traduisait abbauen par 'déconstruire'

dans <u>Au-delà</u>..., on entreverrait peut-être un lieu d'articulation nécessaire entre ce qui s'engage là sous la forme d'une écriture athétique et ce qui m'a jusqu'ici intéressé au titre de la déconstruction (CP, 286).

In <u>Beyond</u>, Freud distinguishes two drives: the drive to construct and the drive to "deconstruct." Derrida applies this drive to writing, and links the deconstructive drive to Freud's compulsive <u>fort!</u> gesture in <u>Beyond</u>, his "athetical" writing that takes apart the thesis every time it is about to be posited. And Derrida also suggests that his own operation of deconstruction may be a compulsive drive as well.

In the next paragraph, Derrida adds:

> Freud voit un rapport d'opposition (<u>Entgegensetzung</u>), du moins dans la doctrine d'Hering, entre le processus d'assimilation constructrice et le processus de dissimilation déconstructrice. Voilà qui imposerait une limite à la traduction si l'on acceptait de considérer que la déconstruction ne s'oppose pas seulement mais travaille autrement (et sans travailler si le travail est déterminé comme opposition). Je laisse cette question opérer en silence, elle nous attend ailleurs (CP, 286).

The vocabulary here is highly suggestive. For what subverts without opposing, what operates in silence is, of course, the death drive. In the analogy with Hering's psychic processes, the project of deconstruction generally, and not just Derrida's approach in this one essay, is charactecized as a drive or a compulsion. "La répétition se lègue, le legs se répète" (CP, 357); in analyzing Freud's legacy, Derrida becomes part of it; he too contracts a debt. The question that remains is how his autobiographics (in "Envois" as well as "Spéculer") functions to reveal and/or dissimilate his position in the heritage and how his writing, indefinitely suspended between mastery and compulsion, mimes and becomes part of the object it seeks to describe. It is at this point that the question of literature reasserts itself.

CHAPTER IX

THE LITERARY FRAMEWORK

Fort/Da as Autobiography

Derrida claims that

> Au-delà... n'est... pas un exemple de ce qu'on croit déjà
> connaître sous le nom d'autobiographie....
> L'autobiographique n'est... pas un espace préalablement
> ouvert dans lequel le grand-père spéculateur raconte une
> histoire, telle histoire de ce qui lui est advenu dans
> sa vie. Ce qu'il raconte, c'est l'autobiographie. Le
> fort:da ici en cause, comme histoire particulière, c'est
> une autobiographie qui enseigne: toute autobiographie est
> l'aller-revenir d'un fort/da, par exemple celui-ci (CP,
> 344).

There are a number of reasons for taking the fort/da anecdote as
a paradigm of autobiography in general. In the first place,
Ernst's game is a means of making sense of his life, mastering an
experience by representing it with signs. This manipulation of
signs involves the recognition that language can function in the
absence of a referent: by pronouncing the sound "o-o-o-o" even when
he cannot see the spool, the child recognizes this capacity of
language. And the sequel to this game extends this recognition to
include the absence of the self. As he makes his own reflection
disappear, he announces "bebi o-o-o-o"; that is, he names himself
as one who is or may be absent (i.e. dead). In short, the game
is a form of auto-affection that, Derrida claims, constitutes the
subject.

This auto-affection, as we have seen, involves a relation to
death and to otherness: it is only through difference that
something like identity comes into being:

> Il se rappelle.... Mais on ne peut savoir si ce 'lui'
> peut dire 'moi'; et, même s'il disait 'moi,' quel moi
> prendrait alors la parole.... L'autobiographique...
> oblige à reconsidérer toute la topique de l'autos (CP,
> 343).

Thus, autobiographics is a means of constituting the self but it
involves, at the same time, otherness and others. Watching the

child's solitary game, Freud is so captivated that he goes on to repeat it in Beyond, as his own autobiography. Referring to the first game where Ernst throws away all his toys (his collection of toys, Spielzeug), Derrida writes:

> S'il se sépare de son Spielzeug comme de lui-même et en vue de se laisser rassembler, c'est qu'il est aussi lui-même un collectif dont le réajointement peut donner lieu à toute une combinatoire des ensembles. Tous ceux qui jouent ou travaillent à rassembler en sont parties prenantes (CP, 331).

The dispersal of his toys (of himself) is made possible by the fact that the self is already a "collective," like the Spielzeug that "rassemble dans un mot" the various toys that Ernst is intent on dispersing. This auto-affection that passes through the other makes it possible for the grandfather to become part of Ernst's "self" and vice versa. The operation of fort/da, then, in whatever form, is the formation of a self that is haunted by its other: it is an autobiographics that is always heterographic, always a relation to a genealogy. The self-appropriation involved in coming to consciousness also entails an expropriation.

Repetition and Aesthetics

A further link between the fort/da game (Ernst's and Freud's) lies in the question of the aesthetic or literary. For Freud explicitly links aesthetics to repetition and to autobiographics as repetition. After discussing Ernst's game and children's play generally, Freud adds that

> the artistic play and artistic imitation carried out by adults, which, unlike children's, are aimed at an audience, do not spare the spectators (for instance, in tragedy) the most painful experiences and can yet be felt by them as highly enjoyable. This is convincing proof that, even under the dominance of the pleasure principle, there are ways and means enough of making what is in itself unpleasurable into a subject to be recollected and worked over in the mind (XVIII, 17).

Thus, for Freud, what is unusual about the literary work is its capacity to produce a yield of pleasure by repeating or reproducing unpleasurable experiences. Repetition seems to produce pleasure in and of itself, despite the unpleasure associated with the experience repeated. This repetition is not exactly opposed to the pleasure principle, since it too involves a yield of pleasure, but it seems to be independent of the principle, operating without regard for the unpleasure encountered along the way. Artistic imitation or repetition seems to slip away from the dominance of the pleasure principle.

In "The 'Uncanny,'" a companion essay to Beyond, Freud

explains that "the uncanny as it is depicted in <u>literature</u>, in stories and imaginative productions, merits in truth a separate discussion" because "there are many more means of creating uncanny effects in fiction than there are in real life" (XVII, 249). Derrida suggests that literature's capacity to produce such effects is not simply a matter of accumulating unlikely coincidences or disturbing situations, but is a function of the literary form itself. What is most uncanny and most moving in such cases is the literary repetition (a term Derrida prefers to the more conventional "imitation" or "mimesis") of repetition. This capacity also extends to the pleasurable effects produced by the literary work: "L'élément de ce qui fait-oeuvre," that is, the literary form,

> saisit l'esthétique dominée par le PP... sans se laisser par elle ressaisir. Il est plus 'originaire' qu'elle, il en est 'indépendant': on peut le décrire dans les termes mêmes par lesquels Freud ailleurs décrit l'au-delà du PP (CP, 364-65).

Linking this definition of the aesthetic to the anecdote Freud tells in the second chapter, Derrida argues that the <u>fait-oeuvre</u> is not only the source of pleasure for Ernst in his playful repetition of his mother's departure and return, but that

> il constitue l'élément de la scène d'écriture, de 'l'oeuvre' intitulée <u>Au-delà du principe du plaisir</u>, dans ce qu'elle a de plus saisissant et de plus insaisissable (CP, 365).

That is why, when Freud includes, among a number of cases where a subject repeatedly finds himself in the same situation at several points in his life, the example of Tasso's <u>Gerusalemme Liberata</u>, Derrida can write: "Le recours à 'l'exemple' littéraire ne saurait être simplement illustratif dans <u>Au-delà...</u>" (CP, 364). For what strikes Freud about the story is precisely the repetition of a repetition, that is, the practice that he himself employs in telling the <u>fort/da</u> story:

> Ce qu'il y a de 'plus saisissant' dans ce que Freud appelle un 'epos romantique,' ce n'est pas seulement le meurtre inconscient, par deux fois, de la bien-aimée dissimulée sous un homme... ce n'est pas seulement le retour de la voix fantômique de Clorinde; ce n'est pas seulement la répétition <u>unheimliche</u>, au-delà du PP, du meurtre de l'aimée. Non, ce qu'il y a de '<u>plus</u> saisissant'(<u>ergreifendste</u>), quoi que déclare Freud... c'est la répétition (dites si vous voulez 'littéraire'...) de ces répétitions de répétitions <u>unheimlich</u> (CP, 364).

The structure of this "literary" text is also the structure of <u>Beyond</u> and, notably, of the autobiographical anecdote Freud records in the second chapter. Like the artists he alludes to and like Ernst, Freud is putting on a play, for his readers but also for himself. And, like the hero of <u>Gerusalemme Liberata</u>, who seems "pursued by a malignant fate or possessed by some 'daemonic'power" (XVIII, 21), Freud submits to his writing as to a force beyond himself. Derrida continually refers to the "ventriloquy" of Freud's writing, its ghostly and demonic character. He thus links the autobiographical aspect of Freud's writing to both the literary or aesthetic and to the repetition compulsion: Freud's autobio- graphics would be an attempt to master a conflict through repetition as well as a repetition without mastery.

Such a hypothesis links the particularly literary nature of autobiography to the various psychic phenomena we have been dealing with throughout this study. The repetition of life experiences in analysis, for instance, is an aesthetic creation to the extent that the <u>fait-oeuvre</u> produces a yield of pleasure regardless of the unpleasure of the original experience; conversely, the artistic creation is compulsive inasmuch as it repeats without fully mastering the experience or the repetition. Autobiography is located at the undecidable limit between compulsion and mastery.

Derrida's Autobiographics

In the theory of an aesthetic/compulsive repetition characteristic of autobiography, we find a point of entry into Derrida's "Envois." For the <u>fort/da</u> of "Spéculer," the repetition of Freud's gesture in <u>Beyond</u> (itself a repetition of Ernst's game), is only one instance of repetition in a book filled with effects of doubling, echoes, and parallels. Each of the four parts of <u>La Carte Postale</u>, in fact, repeats not only the text or texts that it discusses but also the other essays in the collection. As we have seen, the relation between Freud and Marie Bonaparte, explicated in "Spéculer," is repeated and reversed in "Le Facteur" as a relation between Lacan and Bonaparte. This, in turn, repeats the situation of the <u>fort/da</u> scene, where Freud's relation to his daughter Sophie reverses into its mirror image, Ernst's relation to his mother.

Such effects of repetition and reversal are too numerous and too complex to deal with adequately here. I shall limit myself to one such effect: the repetition in "Envois" of the autobiographi- cal situation recorded in "Spéculer" and its relation to the theory of autobiography developed there, in both its institutional and literary aspects. If Derrida is repeating Freud repeating Ernst, how does that repetition reflect upon his philosophical project? What links the father of psychoanalysis to the philosopher of deconstruction? What does "Envois" reveal about Derrida's heritage and lineage?

There is no question that what corresponds to the game that so captivates Freud and that Derrida interprets as a scene of heritage is the post card that Derrida happens upon in the Bodleian Library at Oxford. The card, a reproduction of a work by Matthew

185

Paris, depicts the two progenitors of Western philosophy, Socrates and Plato. In what appears to be a reversal of roles, Socrates is seated at a writing desk, a writing instrument in each hand, while a diminutive Plato stands behind him, his body pressed against the high back of Socrates' chair, watching and gesturing as Socrates prepares to write. In a spectacular example of overinterpretation, Derrida explicates this curious scene through the nearly 300 pages and two years of "Envois." In fact, most of the correspondence with the lover is written on the back of copies of this post card.

Derrida encounters the post card with the same fascination and puzzlement that Freud shows when he comes across his grandson's odd behavior:

> Tu as vu cette carte, l'image au dos de cette carte? Je suis tombé dessus, hier, à la Bodleian (c'est la fameuse bibliothèque d'Oxford), je te raconterai. Je suis tombé en arrêt, avec le sentiment de l'hallucination (il est fou ou quoi? il s'est trompe de noms!), et d'une révélation apocalyptique: Socrate écrivant, écrivant devant Platon, je l'avais toujours su, c'était resté comme le négatif d'une photographie à développer depuis vingt-cinq siècles --en moi bien sûr... Le révélateur est là, à moins que je ne sache encore rien déchiffrer de cette image, et c'est en effet le plus probable. Socrate, celui qui écrit --assis, plié, scribe ou copiste docile, le secrétaire de Platon, quoi. Il est devant Platon, non, Platon est <u>derrière</u> lui, plus petit (pourquoi plus petit?) mais debout. Du doigt tendu il a l'air d'indiquer, de désigner, de montrer la voie ou de donner un ordre ou de dicter, autoritaire, magistral, impérieux. Méchant presque, tu ne trouves pas, et volontairement. J'en ai acheté tout un stock (CP, 13-14).

There are two issues to be considered here: first, the interpretation of the post card, its significance; and second, Derrida's relation to that interpretation.

What is most striking in the scene depicted by Paris is that Socrates, the philosopher who <u>did not write</u>, whose spoken words, therefore, were to have retained their proximity to him, is shown writing, and writing under Plato's direction, recording the dictation of the student who was supposed to have recorded his words. It thus depicts what Derrida calls the "catastrophe," an originary reversal of speech and writing, father and son, predecessor and successor, testator and heir. Derrida writes that

> tout est construit sur la charte protocolaire d'un axiome.... C'est simple, élémentaire, brève, stéréotypie apeurée... : Socrate vient avant Platon, il y a entre eux --et en général-- un ordre de génération, une irréversible séquence d'héritage (CP, 25).

186

This fundamental axiom, which organizes the archives of knowledge and the very notion of history and genealogy, is undermined by the post card from Oxford.

The post card, in fact, represents the relation between Plato and Socrates that Derrida had described a number of years earlier in the section of "La Pharmacie de Platon" called "L'Héritage du Pharmakon: La Scène de Famille." Tracing Plato's use of the father/son relationship as a figure for the rapport between a speaker or writer and his words, Derrida links Plato's comments on writing to the role he plays in relation to Socrates, his position as successor, son, and the philosopher who writes down Socrates' spoken words.

For Plato, the distinction between speech and writing is the difference between a good, honorable, legitimate son and an orphan or bastard. Writing is the son who has become separated from his father, who can no longer find his father, and who, in his absence, simply repeats the same thing over and over, unable to answer any questions that are posed of him:

> Courant les rues, il ne sait même pas qui il est, quelle est son identité, s'il en a une, et un nom, celui de son père. Il répète la même chose lorsqu'on l'interroge à tous les coins de rue, mais il ne sait plus répéter son origine (DIS, 165).

But this poor, forsaken orphan can always become a murderer and a usurper; he has it in his power to annihilate his father:

> Qu'est-ce que le père?.... Le père est. Le père est (le fils perdu). L'écriture, le fils perdu, ne répond pas à cette question, elle (s')écrit: (que) le père n'est pas, c'est-à-dire n'est pas présent. Quand elle n'est plus une parole déchue du père, elle suspend la question... 'qu'est-ce que le père?' et la réponse 'le père est ce qui est.' Alors se produit une avancée qui ne se laisse plus penser dans l'opposition courante du père et du fils, de la parole et de l'écriture (DIS, 169).

Since writing can function even in the absence of its father, it can always announce the father's death (his absence) and usurp his place. It is now the father who is lost, a lost son; and the son has become the father of the father. Represented and replaced by his murderous son, the father is (present) no more. In the next paragraph, Derrida writes that

> le moment est venu de rappeler que Socrate joue dans les dialogues le rôle du père, représente le père... il est le porte-parole du père. Et Platon écrit à partir de sa mort. Toute l'écriture platonicienne --et nous ne parlons pas ici de ce qu'elle veut dire, de son contenu

187

> signifié: la réparation du père au besoin contre la
> graphè qui décida de sa mort-- est donc, lue à partir de
> la mort de Socrate, dans la situation de l'écriture
> accusée dans le Phèdre (DIS, 169-70).

As the one who writes down Socrates' spoken words, Plato is the bad son (writing) who usurps his father's place; his comments on writing refer to his own position as Socrates'scribe.

But if Plato is able to usurp tbe place of the father, it is only because a certain lack allows for the usurpation to take place: Socrates' death and his "sterility," the mortality of his words that would otherwise die with him.

> Lorsque nous disons que Platon écrit à partir de la mort
> du père, nous ne pensons pas seulement à tel événement
> intitulé 'la mort de Socrate'... mais d'abord à la
> sterilité de la semence socratique abandonnée à elle
> seule.... Pour en réparer la mort, Platon a transgressé
> la loi. Il a répété la mort du père.... La
> transgression de la loi est d'avance soumise à une loi
> de la transgression (DIS, 177).

Socrates' death and sterility call for the transgression that Plato commits: if Socrates' name is to live on, his words must be written down. But this writing is a usurpation of the name of Socrates: in filling the absence caused by Socrates' death, Plato also signs Socrates' death warrant.

We begin to understand why a post card depicting Plato compelling Socrates to write should have such an effect on Derrida. In fact, Derrida suggests that what Socrates is writing under duress is his own death warrant or a testament that makes Plato his sole heir. He even goes so far as to suggest that Plato is performing an anal copulation on Socrates, compelling Socrates to bear his child, but a child conceived "dans le dos," in reverse as it were. Thus, Derrida views the post card as the representation of the genealogical reversal that he had traced in "La Pharmacie de Platon." The question is then: what is Derrida's role or position in this genealogy? What is his relation to the scene of heritage he interprets?

We recall that Derrida writes that the sight of Socrates writing in front of Plato "était resté comme le négatif d'une photographie à développer depuis vingt-cinq siècles --en moi bien sûr" (CP, 14, emphasis mine). This image of the photograph waiting for centuries to be developed blurs the distinction between an active, "subjective" interpretation that imposes a meaning, and a passive perception of an object. The impression existed as a negative for centuries, but certain historical circumstances and, no doubt, certain contingent factors in Derrida's life, were necessary for the image to be "developed." The scene becomes part of Derrida's autobiography, but it is the scene that imposes itself upon him. In some sense, Plato and Socrates are dictating to Derrida his autobiography.

At another point, this curious relationship between Derrida and his predecessors is described in the following terms: "Quand sauront-ils que Socrate aura écrit sous ma dictée le testament qui l'institue comme mon légataire universel parmi d'autres" (CP, 102). The first part of the sentence repeats the situation that Derrida traces between Plato and Socrates: it is the son who compels the father to write his will. But in this case, the will declares the father heir to the son, and sole heir among others. Socrates writes a will that names himself as heir to Derrida; Derrida compels his father to write a will that makes him (Derrida) the father's father. The order of generations is constantly reversing itself and it is impossible to say whether Derrida has imposed "his" interpretation on the post card depicting a scene of heritage or whether the post card, sent from Socrates, dictates to Derrida.

Women and Derrida

One of the things that Derrida likes about post cards is that

on ne sait pas ce qui est devant ou ce qui est derrière, ici ou là, près ou loin, le Platon ou le Socrate, recto ou verso. Ni ce qui importe le plus, l'image ou le texte, et dans le texte, le message ou la légende, ou l'adresse... ; la réversibilité se déchaîne, elle devient folle (CP, 17-18).

This is not only another instance of the reversals (of generations, of roles) that interest Derrida; it also raises the question of the relation between what one writes and to whom, and what one writes on, what supports one's writing. In the case of the famous post card, what Derrida writes on is a scene depicting two major figures of Western metaphysics; what he writes are private letters to a (presumably female) lover.[1] Thus, both the post card (a private message that circulates openly) and the postal service (a public institution charged with the transmission of private correspondence) are figures for the inseparability of the public and the private, the institutional and the individual, the metaphysical and the everyday. Nowhere is this relationship more strikingly depicted than in Derrida's relation to women.

As might be expected, this relation repeats a number of the motifs or patterns that Derrida discusses in regard to Freud and women. We have seen that Freud's position on women, and the existence of female psychoanalysts, form a detour or fold in what ought to have been a direct line of descent from father to son. Derrida also suggests that this detour has been repressed by a certain idealization of women. This is represented in the events following Sophie's death. Noting Freud's remark that Ernst does not mourn his mother's death, Derrida writes:

Cette chute donnerait à penser qu'on garde mieux une morte: l'idéalisation intériorise l'objet hors d'atteinte pour le rival. Sophie, donc, là fille, ici mère, est morte, soustraite et rendue à toutes les 'possessions exclusives'(CP, 348).

And later, alluding to Lacan's claim to Freud's legacy and the complications posed by Bonaparte's prior claim, Derrida asks: "Qui n'entrera alors en 'possession exclusive,' comme on entre dans la danse ou en transe?" (CP, 355). Once Sophie is dead, once her "materiality" has been reduced to ashes, she can be idealized and claimed by all those who were formerly rivals for her attentions. In the same way, Lacan's insistence on the indivisibility of the letter (the signifier) allows him to claim "exclusive possession" of Freud's insights and to bracket the difficulties of reading and interpreting Freud's texts. In other words, his idealization of the materiality of language allows him to take his place as rightful heir.

When we turn to "Envois," we find the same idealization of woman, and of the language used to address her, that Derrida criticizes in "Spéculer" and "Le Facteur." Following a conference, Derrida is introduced to a young American student who gives her name as "Métaphysique." Addressing the lover, he writes:

J'ai compris que c'était toi. Tu as toujours été 'ma' métaphysique, la métaphysique de ma vie, le 'verso' de tout ce que j'écris (mon désir, la parole, la présence, la proximité, la loi, mon coeur et mon âme, tout ce que j'aime et que tu sais avant moi) (CP, 212).

Although Derrida's writings, from the very first, have sought to undermine the metaphysical privilege of voice and presence, the desire for them resurfaces here in an apostrophe to a woman who takes on all the features of the desired object. Like Ayesha for Freud, "Métaphysique" is the ideal, unchanging woman.

Derrida's theory of writing and of telecommunication asserts that a destination is always multiple and the letter always divided. Even so, when he writes to his lover, he calls her "mon unique destinée" (CP, 28) and underlines the paradox involved in this desire for the unique:

Ils n'auront de moi que des cartes postales, jamais la vraie lettre, qui t'est reservée uniquement, pas à ton nom... à toi.... Tu me diras que cette détestation apparamment méprisante... contredit mon culte des cartes postales, et ce que je déclare de l'impossibilité pour un destinataire unique de jamais s'identifier.... Et que cela ne s'accorde pas avec le fait qu'une lettre à l'instant même où elle a lieu... se divise, se met en morceaux, tombe en carte postale. Eh oui, c'est là notre lot tragique, mon doux amour, l'atroce loterie, mais je commence à t'aimer depuis cet impossible (CP, 90).

Even though he recognizes at a theoretical level that the "true" letter, the letter bearing truth, can never arrive intact at its destination, Derrida continues to desire such a model of communication that would exclude all others but the unique; in fact, the very impossibility of attaining what he desires augments the desire.

As we have seen, Derrida criticizes Lacan for passing over in silence his debt to Bonaparte and locates Sophie's silence as the condition for Freud's discourse. Of his own silencing of woman, his failure to publish his lover's letters as well as his own, Derrida writes:

> et si parce que je les aime trop je ne publie pas tes lettres (qui en droit m'appartiennent), on m'accusera de t'effacer, de te taire, de te passer sous silence. Si je les publie, ils m'accuseront de m'approprier, de voler, de violer, de garder l'initiative, d'exploiter le corps de la femme, toujours le mec, quoi (CP, 247).

Such accusations, of course, are not simply what some anonymous "they," some malicious other, will say: they follow from Derrida's own theory and, in fact, Derrida himself directs the same accusations at his rivals.

In "Spéculer--sur 'Freud,'" Derrida traces Freud's incapacity, following the death of his grandson, to form new ties and his general inability to establish a contract with his lineage or to assume the debt of his ancestry. Writing to his lover, Derrida alludes to the nature of their relationship in the same terms: "...depuis ce jour où il fut clair que jamais entre nous aucun contrat, aucune dette, aucune garde sous scellé, aucune mémoire même ne nous retiendrait--aucun enfant même". Thus, in his "private" correspondence and in his private affairs, Derrida symptomatically repeats the very attitudes and behaviors toward woman that he criticizes in Freud and Lacan.

All of these elements --the silencing of woman, the idealization of language, the refusal of a female lineage-- reappear in the context of Derrida's discussion of one of the female heirs to deconstruction, Barbara Johnson. As American translator of a number of Derrida's works, including <u>La Dissémi-nation</u>, Johnson, like Bonaparte, is a sort of foreign minister or representative. In her book, <u>The Critical Difference</u>, she names <u>both</u> Derrida and Lacan as her theoretical "frame of reference."[2] The last chapter of this book is devoted to a discussion of Derrida's "Le Facteur," Lacan's "Séminaire sur 'La Lettre Volée,'" and Poe's short story. Derrida responds to the essay in a letter to his lover. He quotes Johnson at length, but without ever revealing her name :

> Il faut pour que tout soit en ordre que 'ma' 'dis-sémination' s'érige elle-même, qu'elle l'ait déjà fait pour que le dernier mot soit le dernier mot.... Si j'avais insisté encore davantage pour dire qu'il n'y avait pas de maître mot ou de dernier mot ou de premier

> mot, si j'avais insisté davantage (était-ce possible?) pour dire que 'dissémination' était l'un des mots, parmi tant d'autres, pour entraîner au-delà de tout 'last word,' on m'aurait reproché d'avoir, précisément par mon insistance, reconstitué un maître mot, n'importe lequel.... Tout en disant de façon 'apparemment non équivoque' que 'ce que veut dire' 'la lettre volée,' voire 'en souffrance,' c'est qu'une lettre arrive toujours à destination, Lacan voulait dire en vérité ce que j'ai dit, ce que j'aurai dit, sous le nom de dissémination. Fallait le faire! Quant à moi, tout en parlant en apparence de dissémination, j'aurais reconstitué ce mot en dernier mot et donc en destination (CP, 163–64).

This impatience approaching exasperation is thus directed at Johnson's efforts to reverse the respective positions of Derrida and Lacan. Derrida recognizes that Johnson's thesis has a certain bearing on his notion of the reversibility of genealogies; he instructs his lover to "illustrate" the post card of Socrates and Plato with a statement from Johnson's article that exchanges the positions of Derrida and Lacan.

In passages from Johnson's article that Derrida does not quote, however, the reasons for his negative reaction become evident. For Johnson situates Derrida within the family romance of psychoanalysis and shows his interested position in relation to Lacan. We have seen that Derrida accuses Lacan of not loving the mother Bonaparte enough, of sending her <u>fort</u> in an act of revenge. This, of course, identifies Lacan with the older brother Ernst. Derrida, defender of Bonaparte, becomes, then, the mother's son, the younger (but so much more clever) brother Heinerle. In fact, there are a number of indications in "Spéculer" that Heinerle is not only, like Sophie, the death drive of psychoanalysis, but also its rightful heir. Heinerle is a

> légataire universel et porteur du nom selon l'affect (filiation de la communauté assurée par la femme, ici par la fille 'préférée'; et le second petit-fils doit porter, dans certaines communautés juives, le prénom du grand-père maternel; tout pourrait être réglé par une loi judaïque) (CP, 355).

Thus, in taking the side of the mother Bonaparte, Derrida identifies himself with the favorite son, the brighter child and the one martyred by the vengeful older brother.

But Johnson points out that Derrida's position is not quite so innocent, nor so unassailable, as his identification with Heinerle would make it out to be. For Poe's "The Purloined Letter" is <u>also</u> about the rivalry of two brothers for the mother and Derrida's place in that story is anything but innocent. In Poe's short story, the inspector Dupin admits that he undertakes the mission in part to settle an account with the minister, who had earlier done him an evil turn. Thus, to seal his act of revenge, Dupin signs the facsimile of the purloined letter that he leaves in the minister's apartment with a quotation from Crébillon: "--Un dessein si funeste/ S'il n'est digne d'Atrée, est digne de Thyeste." Johnson glosses:

> Atreus, whose wife had long ago been seduced by Thyestes, is about to make Thyestes eat (literally) the fruit of that illicit union, his son Plisthenes. The avenger's plot may not be worthy of him, says Atreus, but his brother Thyestes deserves it. What the addressee of the violence gets is his own message backwards.[3]

In signing his deed with a quotation, Dupin takes on the role of vengeful brother and it is his vengefulness that makes him "partie prenante" in the scene of interpretation.

Johnson goes on to show that Derrida, like Dupin, undertakes his mission to undermine his rival, in a vengeful act to settle an old score with Lacan.

> The existence of the same kind of prior aggression on Lacan's part is posited by Derrida in a long footnote in his book Positions, in which he outlines what will later develop into Le Facteur de la Vérité: 'In the texts I have published up to now, the absence of reference to Lacan is indeed almost total. That is justified, not only by the acts of aggression in the form of, or with the intention of, reappropriation which, ever since De la grammatologie appeared in Critique (1965) (and even earlier, I am told) Lacan has multiplied...'[4]

Thus, in the sort of reversal that Derrida objects to in "Envois," Johnson shows that Derrida is the vengeful brother who wants to get back at Lacan.

In the rivalry between Atreus and Thyestes, it is once more a woman (the wife/sister-in-law this time) who is the object and, furthermore, what is involved is the legitimacy of the lineage: Thyestes' illegitimate son has a shared parentage with both brothers. As a result, Johnson's argument not only reverses Derrida's position as the younger, innocent brother Heinerle to that of a vengeful, murderous rival, it also inscribes her position in the family romance. For she, like Thyestes' illegitimate son, is the heir who shares a double parentage (Derrida and Lacan) and, like him, she becomes victim to the wrong(ed) father's act of revenge. When, in "Envois," Derrida vents his anger at Johnson, he is once more repeating the story of the purloined letter.

When Dupin quotes the passage from Crébillon, the two brothers, husbands and fathers in the original story, become sons: the quotation refers to Dupin and the minister, and their rivalry for the mother's (the Queen's) attentions. The quotation marks displace the rivalry and the generations are once more reversed. Just as easily, Johnson, the daughter of deconstruction can become

Derrida's mother (just as Plato becomes Socrates' father). In writing on him, she reinvents him, and she places the lineage, the order of generations, in danger. For, in siding with Lacan against Derrida and Bonaparte, she undermines Derrida's claim to represent the female lineage of psychoanalysis. Derrida, who wishes to stand among the female heirs, finds himself under assault by his own daughter. His defense is to claim that she has misrepresented him, fabricated a "Derrida" who bears no likeness to the original: "Est-il question de Derrida ou de 's 'Derrida'?" (CP, 163). In fact, this objection to Johnson extends to all of his heirs:

> Que faire? Je suis aimé mais ils ne me supportent pas, ils ne supportent pas que je dise quoi que ce soit qu'ils ne puissent 'reverser' d'avance chaque fois que la situation l'exige (naturellement, ma 'position,' ma 'place,' mes places, réponses ou non-réponses, etc., font partie, partie seulement de ladite situation et de 'what is at stake here'(CP, 164).

But, as in the case of his decision not to publish the lover's letters, Derrida once more projects onto "them" objections that in fact follow from his own theories. For he devotes a great deal of <u>La Carte Postale</u> to exploring Freud's position in the structures he describes, insisting on the inevitable reversibility of gene-alogies, assessing the "stake" involved. In fact everything Derrida has written on the question of influence and the problem-atics of reading suggests that there is always only "'s 'Derrida.'"

Positions

It could be argued that, since "Envois" is a literary rather than a philosophical text, an at least partially fictionalized account and a parody of certain literary conventions, one should not take the narrator's "confessions" seriously, nor confuse this narrator with the author and philosopher Jacques Derrida. In other words, "Envois" would be staging rather than expressing the desire for presence; it parodies a certain symptomatic relation to women rather than participating in it; and the apparent contradiction involved in Derrida's repetition of the very ills that he analyzes with acuity with regard to Freud and Lacan can be resolved by positing an ironic distance between Derrida and the I-narrator of "Envois."

This argument is not altogether false, but it assumes, for one thing, that the "author" Derrida manipulates all the strings without being manipulated in his turn. It overlooks, that is, the compulsion for autobiography that we were led to posit, and the undecidable limit between repetition as compulsion and repetition as mastery. It assumes the fullness of Derrida's intentions and his ultimate control over what he writes.[5]

It is more in keeping with Derrida's theoretical framework to recognize that, as he writes of Nietzsche's self-contradictory attitudes toward women,

> si on ne peut assimiler --entre eux d'abord-- les aphorismes sur la femme et le reste --c'est aussi que Nietzsche n'y voyait pas très clair... et que tel aveuglement régulier, rythmé, avec lequel on n'en finira jamais, a lieu dans le texte (EP, 82).

The fictionalized, parodic play of "Envois" does not indicate Derrida's "maîtrise infinie" (EP, 81); rather, "la parodie suppose toujours quelque part une naïveté, adossée à un inconscient, et le vertige d'une non-maîtrise, une perte de connaissance" (EP, 81). It is in part Lacan's naïveté on this point that Derrida criticizes in "Le Facteur de la vérité": Lacan assumes too easily that the textual effects of Poe's short story can be accounted for by the author's intentions. Even while reading "The Purloined Letter" as a powerful critique of interpretive assumptions, especially those held by the psychoanalytic institution, Derrida argues that Poe's intentions do not organize that critique; rather, Poe himself occupies an interested position in the scene depicted by "The Purloined Letter." Such a reading may elucidate the function that "Envois" performs within the context of Derrida's critique of psychoanalysis and the role that it assigns him. For both "The Purloined Letter" and "Envois" are literary texts that explore the role of the subject within the structure he interprets.

At the beginning of "Le Facteur," Derrida asks:

> Que se passe-t-il dans le déchiffrement psychanalytique d'un texte quand celui-ci, le déchiffré, s'explique déjà lui-même? Quand il en dit plus long que le déchiffrant.... Et surtout quand il inscrit <u>de surcroît</u> en lui la scène du déchiffrement? (CP, 442)

"The Purloined Letter," a story about resolving an enigma, discovering the location of a letter, uncovering a hidden truth, is, for that reason, a story about interpretation. It includes as part of its story its own scene of interpretation, and it is that scene that Lacan has excluded or misread in his own interpretation, in order to make claims for the privileged position of psychoanalytic truth.

Lacan divides Poe's story into two triangles, the second being a repetition of the first or primal scene. Each triangle is made up of three persons with different access to knowledge or truth. Lacan characterizes this difference as three kinds of gazes (<u>regards</u>):

> Le premier est d'un regard qui ne voit rien: c'est le Roi et c'est la police.
> Le second d'un regard qui voit que le premier ne voit rien et se leurre d'en voir couvert ce qu'il cache: c'est

la Reine, puis c'est le ministre.

Le troisième qui de ces deux regards voit qu'ils laissent ce qui est à cacher à decouvert pour qui voudra s'en emparer: c'est le ministre, et c'est Dupin enfin (quoted in CP, 464).

In the first scene, the queen tries to hide a compromising letter from the king who has entered her chambers unexpectedly. She does in fact conceal it from him (thus he <u>sees nothing</u>) but her efforts attract the attention of the minister. Before her eyes, he exchanges the letter for another and confiscates the compromising one. Fearful of being discovered by the king, the queen can do nothing but look on in silence.

The minister uses the letter to blackmail the queen: it thus becomes imperative to get the letter back from him. But after many months of searching his premises, the police are still unable to locate the letter: like the king in the first scene, they see nothing. The inspector Dupin, however, visits the minister and concludes that the letter in question is hanging in a letter-holder from the mantelpiece. In a second visit, he exchanges the letter for a facsimile he has fashioned, and confiscates the original for himself. Since the minister, in the privileged position of "seeing all" in the first scene, becomes Dupin's dupe in the second (thus occupying the queen's original position) it is clear that only Dupin succeeds in seeing all from a privileged, unchallenged position.

Derrida argues that Lacan maintains the privilege of Dupin's position in order to identify with him; or rather, Lacan splits Dupin into a "good" and a "bad" psychoanalyst and then identifies himself with the former while placing his colleagues in the position of the "bad" Dupin. Lacan writes that Dupin

est donc bien partie prenante dans la triade inter-subjective, et comme tel dans la position médiane qu'ont occupée précédemment la Reine et le Ministre. Va-t-il en s'y montrant supérieur, nous révéler en même temps les intentions de l'auteur? (quoted in CP, 481).

As Derrida points out, the allusion to the author's intentions implies that Poe is in the position of a "maîtrise générale, sa supériorité au regard des triangles mis en scène... étant représentable par la supériorité d'un acteur, à savoir Dupin" (CP, 481). By positing the ultimate mastery of the author, Lacan can also take his place: "Nous, c'est désormais Freud, Poe, un des deux Dupin et moi," (CP, 478) Lacan would be saying. In this way he achieves a "double bénéfice": first, he "sait voir ce que personne n'a vu" (CP, 479-80), like the omniscient Dupin; and second, he can "dénoncer la naïveté de la communauté analytique," saying "vous-psychanalystes, vous vous leurrez au moment précis où, comme Dupin, vous vous croyez les maîtres" (CP, 480). Lacan's strategy, however, not only makes it necessary to suspend the question of Dupin's superiority and to split him into a good and bad psychoanalyst; it also means reductively limiting Poe's short story to the two triangles and ignoring its "frame." For the three subjects of Lacan's triangles are supplemented by a fourth, the narrator who tells the tale. "A manquer la position du narrateur, son engagement dans le contenu de ce qu'il semble raconter, on omet tout ce qui de la scène d'écriture déborde les deux triangles" (CP, 511). In this intermediate position between the author and his characters, the narrator interprets and interpolates for the reader. Derrida traces this narrator's _interest_ in what he narrates, his identification with Dupin, his desire to _possess the same rare book_, and his financial debt to the inspector and his family. He concludes:

> dans [cette] économie... dès lors que le narrateur est mis en scène par une fonction qui est bien celle... du capital et du désir, aucune neutralisation n'est possible.... Ce n'est pas seulement Dupin, mais le narrateur qui est 'partie prenante'(CP, 517).

Even the narrator who, in appearance, sees the triangle from the outside, has an interested position in the scene. The interpreter is part of the scene he interprets. To characterize the "complexe intersubjectif" of the two triangular scenes, Lacan uses the analogy of three ostriches "dont le second se croirait revêtu d'invisibilité, du fait que le premier aurait sa tête enfoncée dans le sable, cependant qu'il laisserait un troisième lui plumer tranquillement le derrière" (quoted in CP, 464). Derrida adds that

> il n'y a que des autruches, personne n'évite de se laisser plumer, et plus on est le maître, plus on présente son derrière. Ce sera donc le cas de quiconque s'identifie à Dupin (CP, 481).

A few pages later, Derrida hints that the prospect of presenting one's behind to be plucked may involve an erotic element:

> Dupin, le lucide, n'a pu l'être qu'à entrer dans le circuit jusqu'à y occuper successivement toutes les places, y compris, sans le savoir, celles du Roi et de la Police.... Et 'se montrer supérieur' pour lui... c'était répéter le manège sans pouvoir regarder derrière. Ce qui ne le privait pas forcément de plaisir au moment où un autre garde alors la plume en main (CP, 483).

The _plume_, of course, is the pen that another holds, either the pen that interprets one's writings or simply, the force of writing that one's own hand can never control. But a _plume_ is also a feather, an ostrich's tailfeather that another grasps in order to pluck out. This suggests that the revealing of what one cannot see, always part of entering the circuit of writing and interpretation, may produce a yield of pleasure. Surrendering one's privileged position serves the desire to exhibit.

Derrida's reading of "The Purloined Letter," then, demonstrates that interpretation always proceeds from an interested position within a structure that the interpreter cannot master completely. He insists that the author Poe does not direct this tale from the outside, but must himself enter into the circuit that he describes. That is why, despite Derrida's hesitation in accepting the assumptions, if not the methods, of psychobiographical readings, he finds Marie Bonaparte's analysis of Poe's unconscious closer to his own interests than Lacan's reading, which ultimately centers the meaning of the story in Poe's conscious intentions.[6] The author too must enter the circuit of writing.

The image of the ostrich offering his behind to be plucked, which functions as a figure for the position of the interpreter in the structure he interprets, brings to mind once more the post card of Socrates and Plato and all that Derrida writes regarding Plato's position behind Socrates. In fact, the motif of the behind or the back, the derrière or the dos, recurs persistently throughout "Envois"; Derrida even suggests that it is the only thing that counts in his preface. Discussing the possibility of a secret or coded language hidden in published texts, he writes:

> Suppose qu'à la fin d'une lecture, une des voix du livre te murmure quelque chose du genre... : tout est connoté en do, il n'y a que les dos qui comptent, revoyez toute la scansion (pas les da comme dans fort/da ou derrida, mais aussi les do les plus traînants, comme derrière les rideaux), alors il faut tout reprendre... c'est un livre de plus (CP, 86-87).

We saw in our discussion of Glas that "derrière les rideaux" is an anagram for Derrida's signature, or rather, for his father's proper name. This anagram, like the various signatures that Genet disperses throughout his texts, both undermines the convention of the signature with its assumption of the author's mastery over what he writes, and attempts to reappropriate that mastery, to sign the text an infinite number of times. At this point in "Envois," Derrida links this autobiographics to the question of the dos and the derrière, that is, to the vulnerable position that the interpreter, like the ostrich, occupies in a structure. He thus suggests that his autobiographics in "Envois" is an effort to reveal his position.

The allusion to the anagram "do" takes the form of a "suppose que...": a hundred pages later, this "what if" is confirmed. Having decided to publish the private letters that he has been writing to his lover as the preface to his book on Freud, he tries to reassure her that he will be revealing nothing, that she will not even recognize herself in what he publishes. He writes that "avant tout il s'agit de tourner le dos. De leur tourner le dos en feignant de leur adresser la parole et de les prendre à temoin" (CP, 192); "bref il n'y aura que du dos" (CP, 202). At first glance, turning one's back seems to be a way of excluding the reader; by writing a text that appears literary, that plays with the conventions of fiction and autobiography, that makes contradictory statements about its referentiality and that undermines the whole notion of authenticity, Derrida would reveal nothing, would simply trick or confuse his readers. Thus, turning his back would be the equivalent of another method he employs to exclude the reader, and to keep his secrets to himself: "Je peux toujours dire 'ce n'est pas moi'" (CP, 255).

Given the context of <u>La Carte Postale</u>, and especially, given his comments on Lacan's ostriches, the passage takes on another meaning: in turning his back, Derrida reveals his behind. The gesture is both political and erotic: it is important to remember that Derrida emphasizes the pleasure involved in having one's behind plucked. No doubt Derrida's autobiographics undermines his privileged position by revealing his rivalry with Lacan, his contradictory attitudes toward women, his place in an institutional structure and in a genealogy (as both heir and testator). At the same time, however, these revelations serve the desire to exhibit, the desire for autobiography. That is why "ce livre serait d'une perversité polymorphe" (CP, 202) and why he does not hesitate to remind us that turning his back to his readers is a "position très amoureuse, n'oublie pas" (CP, 192).

199

CONCLUSION

I began this study by bracketing the problem of defining autobiography, proposing instead to explore the relation between "what we recognize as autobiography" and Freud's notions of screen memory, _Trauerarbeit_, and so forth. That strategy goes against a major current of autobiography criticism which is, in fact, concerned with identifying the specificity of the genre and distinguishing it from the other genres that it resembles. I have assumed that we share a certain notion of autobiography even as I have sought to problematize that notion. Such a strategy calls for some explanation.

Philippe Lejeune has formalized the modern reader's conception of autobiography, which he adopts as his working definition:

> Récit rétrospectif en prose qu'une personne réelle fait de sa propre existence, lorsqu'elle met l'accent sur sa vie individuelle, en particulier sur l'histoire de sa personnalité.[1]

Lejeune goes on to discuss such issues as the relation between author, narrator, and main character, the question of the signature, and the definition of "personne réelle." It is clear that these elements are also those that I have taken as pertinent to autobiography. But, whereas Lejeune chooses texts within the literary canon and attempts to demonstrate how they conform to that definition, I have chosen texts outside the canon and have shown how they call it into question. We recall that Derrida defines literature as "la transformation... de son nom propre, _rebus_, en choses, en nom de choses." This suggests that Lejeune and those like him who are concerned with defining the genre misunderstand the peculiar relationship between the subject "autobiography" and its predicates. In the case of a literary genre, then, the terms used to describe it are simply the elements that the genre takes as its subject matter, works through and transforms. Thus, autobiography would be that literary genre whose subject is the self, the relation of life to writing and to narrative, of the signature to the author, and so on. This means that no particular text would conform to the definition of autobiography, but that each text would take it as its object of inquiry. This suggests, of course, that literature contains, or rather enacts, its own theory. That raises a further issue: if, in fact, every autobiography involves the undermining of autobiography as a genre,

200

if every autobiographical text enacts its own theory, why choose theoretical texts that lie outside the literary canon in order to demonstrate that thesis?

It should be clear by now that the literary canon does not cover the entire field of "literature," and that literature, far from being a realm apart, is a part of every realm. What is most striking about Derrida's writings is not only that he locates the aesthetic in an activity as fundamental as a child's game, but that in his critique of the institutional power of psychoanalysis, he directs his attention to two aspects of language generally associated with literature: the primacy of form and the question of aesthetic effect. If the <u>reste inanalysé d'un inconscient</u> is to become readable, it is through the careful examination of the text's formal features, which Derrida views as symptomatic of a disturbance or a desire. What links Freud's autobiographics to the theoretical content of <u>Beyond the Pleasure Principle</u>, is the <u>fort/da</u> of his text that mimics his grandson's game. It is in the form of Freud's texts that he reveals his place in the structures he describes and it is in the form of Derrida's texts that he too reveals his position. It follows that formalism, so often viewed as opposed to sociological or ideology criticism, is in fact a powerful example of it.

The other face of form as symptom or compulsion is the notion of aesthetics as mastery. The desire to make sense of one's life is a drive to master and to produce order, to repeat in a controlled way. The relation between this effort at mastery and the effect produced on the reader is far from clear: Derrida writes that the mimetic form of the <u>fort/da</u> episode in <u>Beyond</u> "a dû jouer un rôle" in the fascination it exercises on the reader, but he does not say what that role is. In both <u>Glas</u> and "Envois," the models are seduction and trickery, which suggest deception but also a certain compliance on the part of the reader. In any case, by way of a detour through psychoanalytic and philosophical texts, the literary and the autobiographical emerge as central to the institutional discourses of power.

NOTES

Introduction

1. Avrom Fleishman, <u>Figures of Autobiography</u> (Berkeley, Los Angeles, London: Univ. of California Press, 1983), pp. 24-25.

2. Derrida has analyzed this persistent but ultimately unsuccessful attempt to distinguish between a good and a bad repetition in a number of places. See, for example, <u>La Voix et le Phénomène</u>, pp. 53-66 and <u>La Dissémination</u>, pp. 153-63 and passim.

3. Ernest Jones, <u>The Life and Works of Sigmund Freud</u>, 3 vols. (New York: Basic Books, 1953-57).

4. Marie Balmary, <u>L'Homme aux Statues</u> (Paris: Bernard Grasset, 1979).

5. See especially Luce Irigaray, <u>Speculum de l'Auture Femme</u> (Paris: Minuit, 1974) and Sarah Kofman, <u>L'Enigme de la Femme</u> (Paris: Galilée, 1980).

6. "Most autobiographies are inspired by a creative, and therefore fictional, impulse to select only those events and experiences in the writer's life that go to build up an integrated pattern." Northrop Frye, <u>The Anatomy of Criticism</u> (Princeton: Princeton Univ. Press, 1957), p. 307. The best discussion of the literary qualities of <u>The Interpretation of Dreams</u> is still Stanley Edgar Hyman, <u>The Tangled Bank</u> (New York: Atheneum, 1962). Hyman, however, does not raise the question of the relation between the literary and the scientific project.

7. Michael Ryan, <u>Marxism and Deconstruction</u> (Baltimore and London: The Johns Hopkins Univ. Press, 1982), p. 34.

Part One

1. Throughout the text, references to Sigmund Freud, <u>The Standard Edition of the Complete Psychological Works</u>, trans. and ed. James Strachey (London: The Hogarth Press, 1953-74), 24 vol.,

will be designated by volume number (in Roman numerals) followed by page number. Where the German is given, the reference is to the <u>Gesammelte Werke</u>, ed. Anna Freud, 18 vol. (Frankfurt am Main: S. Fischer Verlag, 1961-68) unless otherwise noted.

2. Two recent texts have exploited the aesthetic aspects of Freud's case histories by transforming them into literary texts: Hélène Cixous' <u>Portrait de Dora</u> (Paris: Des Femmes, 1976) stages the dialogue between Freud and his hysterical patient as a play; Nicolas Abraham and Maria Torok's <u>Cryptonymie: Le Verbier de l'Homme aux Loups</u> (Paris: Aubier-Flammarion, 1976) takes the elements of the Wolfman case history and constructs a fiction that illustrates the authors' psychoanalytic theories of mourning and incorporation. For a discussion of the role of narrative in treating patients, see Roy Schafer, "Narration in the Psychoanalytic Dialogue," <u>Critical Inquiry</u>, 7, no. 1 (Autumn 1980), 29-53. A more extensive, but ultimately disappointing study of the subject is Donald P. Spence's <u>Narrative Truth and Historical Truth: Meaning and Interpretation in Psychoanalysis</u> (New York and London: W. W. Norton and Co., 1982).

3. Jacques Derrida, <u>La Carte Postale de Socrate à Freud et Au-delà</u> (Paris: Aubier-Flammarion, 1980), 324 and passim. I will discuss Derrida's use of this notion in reference to Freud's <u>Beyond the Pleasure Principle</u> in a later chapter.

Chapter I

1. For narrative as the revelation of a secret, see John Frank Kermode, <u>The Genesis of Secrecy: On the Interpretation of Narrative</u> (Cambridge, Mass.: Harvard Univ. Press, 1979); for narrative as contract, see Roland Barthes, <u>S/Z</u> (Paris: Editions du Seuil, 1970), 95-97 and passim.

2. Sigmund Freud, <u>Three Case Histories</u>, ed. and intro. Philip Rieff (New York: Collier Books, c. 1963), 69n.

3. For a discussion of the relation between Derrida's notion of writing <u>sous rature</u> and Freud's theory of memory and perception, see Derrida, "Freud et la Scène de l'Ecriture," <u>L'Ecriture et la Différence</u> (Paris: Editions du Seuil, 1967).

4. This crucial concept of transference and its relation to the work of analysis will be discussed in the following section.

5. "Raten" means "installments" and this bridge leads the patient to associate rats with money and to coin "a regular rat currency" (X, 213). "Spielratte," literally "play-rat," is colloquial German for "gambler" and thus alludes to his father's gambling debt.

203

Chapter II

1. Although Freud habitually uses the masculine pronoun to refer to "the hysteric" and grants the existence of male hysterics, every published case of hysteria concerns a female patient. Furthermore, Dora's gender is not inconsequential to the outcome of the analysis. I have retained Freud's usage in the quotations but have substituted the more accurate "she" in my own text.

2. In the "Original Record" of the Rat Man case, Freud makes it clear that his theory of repression extends to the forgetting of the details of an analysis. Noting that he cannot recall one bit of information that the Rat Man had given him, and is uncertain about another, Freud comments, "My uncertainty and forgetfulness... seem to be intimately connected... (They were forgotten owing to complexes of my own.)" (X, 263-64).

3. Toril Moi's excellent essay, "Representation of Patriarchy: Sexuality and Epistemology in Freud's Dora," _Feminist Review_, 9 (October 1981), pp. 80-93, discusses the fragmented form of Freud's text and its relation to his countertransference in a rather different context. See also Jacques Lacan, "Intervention sur le Transfert" in _Ecrits_ (Paris: Editions du Seuil, 1966), 215-26; Jane Gallop, "Keys to Dora" in _The Daughter's Seduction: Feminism and Psychoanalysis_ (Ithaca, York: Cornell Univ. Press, 1982), 156-64; and the special issue of _Diacritics_, 13, no. 1 (Spring 1983) devoted to Freud's Dora. This issue also contains a bibliography of works on Dora.

Part Two

Chapter III

1. Ernest Jones, _The Life and Works of Sigmund Freud_, I, p. 324.

2. Jones, I, p. 351.

3. Jones, I, p. 320.

4. "Dream-work," "work of mourning," "revision" or "reworking" and "working through," respectively.

5. For a discussion along similar lines of Freud's use of the term _Entstellung_ (literally "de-presentation"), see Samuel Weber, _The Legend of Freud_ (Minneapolis: Univ. of Minnesota Press, 1982), p. 32 and passim.

Chapter IV

1. Freud, _The Origins of Psycho-Analysis_ (London: Imago Publishing Co., 1954), p. 313.

2. The quotation from Virgil appears on the title page of Montaigne's copy of the 1588 edition of _Les Essais_.

3. This, of course, is not the way to interpret dreams according to Freud's method of interpretation. A dream may be quoted (or "redreamt"), however, and its original meaning altered in the process. See, for example, V, 509.

4. I shall consider Derrida's discussion of the death knell (_glas_) and its relation to citationality in a later chapter.

5. Freud never questions the fundamental assumption that normal mourning involves no manic phase (a term he uses interchangeably with "phase of triumph") even though he speaks of reality "gaining the day" (_den Sieg behält_) i.e., triumphing. For a fine recent study of mourning, see Nicolas Abraham and Maria Torok, _L'Ecorce et le Noyau_ (Paris: Aubier-Flammarion, 1978) as well as _Cryptonymie: Le Verbier de l'Homme aux Loups_, and Derrida's "Fors," which serves as an introduction to both works.

6. Freud, _Origins_, p. 207.

7. Freud, _Origins_, p. 213.

8. For further discussion of the motif of micturition in _The Interpretation of Dreams_, see Hyman, _The Tangled Bank_, pp. 327-28 and David Willbern, "Freud and the Inter-penetration of Dreams," _Diacritics_, 9, No. 1 (1979), pp. 98-110.

9. See also Kofman's discussion of this dream in _L'Enigme de la Femme_, pp. 23-27.

10. "To our surprise, we find the child and the child's impulse still living on in the dream" (IV, 191).

11. The syllable "ab" is a signifying element in German, a separable prefix indicating "motion away from." The point that the unity "ab" is meaningful while its individual elements are not is lost in translation.

12. H. Rider Haggard, _She_ (London: Octopus Books, 1979), p. 252.

13. Haggard, p. 382.

14. Haggard, p. 362.

15. Jones, III, p. 21. 324

Part Three

Chapter V

1. All references to Derrida will be cited in the text. A list of abbreviations used to indicate individual works appears at the beginning of this work.

2. At another point in his critique of Husserl, Derrida shows that the material component of the sign is inseparable from its identity and in fact constitutes its ideality. Thus, in the later essay, "Signature Evénement Contexte," he uses the term "iterability" to suggest that the repetition of the sign involves both identity <u>and</u> difference. For more detailed discussion of a number of the issues raised in this chapter, see the second chapter of Jonathan Culler, <u>On Deconstruction</u> (Ithaca: Cornell Univ. Press, 1983).

3. Philippe Lejeune, <u>Le Pacte Autobiographique</u> (Paris: Seuil, 1975), p. 15.

4. Lejeune, pp. 25-26.

5. Lejeune, p. 23.

6. Lejeune, p. 23.

7. Lejeune, p. 26.

8. Lejeune, p. 22.

9. Lejeune, pp. 20-21.

10. Lejeune, p. 34.

11. Lejeune, p. 34.

12. J. L. Austin, <u>How to Do Things with Words</u> (Cambridge: Harvard Univ. Press, 1962-75), pp. 5-6.

13. Austin, p. 101.

14. In her "Translator's Introduction" to Derrida's <u>Dissemination</u>, Barbara Johnson rightly points out that "what Rousseau's text tells us is that our very relation to 'reality' already functions like a text. Rousseau's account of his life is not only itself a text, but it is a text that speaks only about the textuality of life." (Chicago: Univ. of Chicago Press, p. xiv).

Part Four

1. For Derrida's appraisal of the relation between <u>Glas</u> and his earlier texts, see EC, 102-03. The first pages of <u>Glas</u>, (left-hand column) examine the assumptions behind positing an "early" and a "late" period in a writer's career. See GL, 11-12-L; and 66-67-L.

2. For a discussion of the "generalized fetishism" of <u>Glas</u>, see Sarah Kofman, "Ça cloche" in <u>Les Fins de l'Homme</u>, ed. Philippe Lacoue-Labarthe and Jean-Luc Nancy (Paris: Galilée, 1981), pp. 89-116. See also below, 190-200. Kofman's essay has influenced my thinking on several points.

3. On the question of the intertext in <u>Glas</u>, see Michael Riffaterre, "La Trace de l'Intertexte," <u>La Pensée</u>, 215 (1980), pp. 5-9 and especially, Paul de Man's critique of same in "Hypogram and Inscription: Michael Riffaterre's Poetics of Reading," <u>Diacritics</u>, 11, No. 4 (1981), pp. 27-29.

Chapter VI

1. I have placed a slash mark in quotations from <u>Glas</u> to indicate the intervention of a <u>judas</u> that is not quoted.

2. See Derrida's "La Mythologie Blanche," MP, 247-324.

3. In fact, according to Freud, girls as well as boys believe that women have been castrated (XIX, 252-53). Derrida grafts Nietzsche's comments on women's scepticism onto Freud's theory of female sexuality in order to provide himself an escape route from phallogocentrism (i.e., that of becoming woman) not provided by Freud alone.

4. Jean Genet, <u>Journal du Voleur</u> (Paris: Gallimard, 1949), pp. 54-56.

5. In "Ça Cloche," Kofman argues that Derrida has failed to recognize that the fetish substitutes not for the man's penis but for the fantasmal woman's phallus and is thus less grounded in phallocentrism than Derrida leads us to believe. See "Ça Cloche," pp. 101-03 and Derrida' s reply to this criticism, p. 113.

Chapter VII

1. See Michel Foucault, <u>L'Archéologie du Savoir</u> (Paris: Gallimard, 1969), p. 138 and passim.

2. Genet, _Journal_, p. 10.

3. For an early Derridean analysis of the relation between the proper name and the law, see also GR, 157-73.

4. See Jean-Paul Sartre, _Saint Genet_, Vol. I of Genet's _Oeuvres Complètes_ (Paris: Gallimard, 1952-68), pp. 16-17.

5. Genet, _Journal_, pp. 46-47.

6. Genet, _Journal_, p. 29.

7. Genet, _Journal_, p. 29.

8. Genet, _Journal_, p. 30.

9. Genet, _Oeuvres Complètes_, IV, pp. 22-23.

10. Genet, _Oeuvres Complètes_, III. p. 14 and p. 57.

11. Nevertheless, for two recent studies that underline aspects of Montaigne's _Essais_ (and of the self-portrait as genre) similar to those I have been discussing in _Glas_, see Michel Beaujour, _Miroirs d'Encre_ (Paris: Seuil, 1980) and Antoine Compagnon, _La Seconde Main_ (Paris: Seuil, 1979).

Part Five

Chapter VIII

1. For the notion of the "exorbitant" reading and its necessity, see GR, pp. 226-34.

2. Derrida fails to note that the child utters the word "da" and not simply "a-a-a-a." This leads him to problematize Freud's interpretation of the child's utterance more than Freud's text would seem to warrant.

3. The "analyst" in "Screen Memories" alludes to his "patient's" earlier contact with psychoanalysis and his success in overcoming a train phobia by that means (III, 309-10).

4. See once more Kofman and Irigaray.

5. For an interesting discussion of the relation of the sounds "fort-da" to "Freud," see Patrick Mahony, _Freud as a Writer_ (New York: International Univ. Press, 1983), p. 53.

6. In _Marxism and Deconstruction_, published two years after _La Carte Postale_, Michael Ryan insists that "marxism and deconstruction can be articulated, but in one fundamental way they

cannot be related. Deconstruction is a philosophical interrogation of some of the major concepts of philosophy. Marxism, in contrast, is not a philosophy" (p. 1).

Chapter IX

1. There is a certain amount of evidence, however, that the lover is male and that Derrida is female. It is probably best to view this as the acting out of all possible sexual "positions".

2. Barbara Johnson, _The Critical Difference_ (Baltimore and London: The Johns Hopkins Univ. Press, 1980), p. 146.

3. Johnson, p. 117.

4. Johnson, p. 118, her emphasis.

5. This may be taken as a response to Barbara Johnson's claim concerning Derrida's "misreading" of Lacan that "the pattern is too interesting not to be deliberate" (Paul de Man, quoted in Johnson, p. 125). Freud recognized that the most "interesting" patterns are those that stem from the unconscious.

6. See, for example, CP, 475-76 and 483-84.

Conclusion

1. Lejeune, p. 14.

BIBLIOGRAPHY

Abraham, Nicolas and Maria Torok. *Cryptonymie: Le Verbier de l'Homme aux Loups*. Introd. Jacques Derrida. Paris: Aubier-Flammarion, 1976.

----------. *L'Ecorce et le Noyau*. Paris: Aubier-Flammarion, 1978.

Austin, J. L. *How to Do Things with Words*. Ed. J. O. Urmson and Marina Spisà. 2nd ed. Cambridge: Harvard Univ. Press, 1962-75.

Balmary, Marie. *L'Homme aux Statues: Freud et la Faute Cachée du Père*. Paris: Bernard Grasset, 1979.

Barthes, Roland. *S/Z*. Paris: Seuil, 1970.

Beaujour, Michel. *Miroirs d'Encre: Rhétorique de l'Auto-Portrait*. Paris: Seuil, 1980.

Berezdivin, Ruben. "Gloves: Inside-Out." *Research in Phenomenology*, 8 (1978), pp. 111-26. Special issue devoted to Derrida. Includes bibliography.

Bloom, Harold. *The Anxiety of Influence: A Theory of Poetry*. London, Oxford, New York: Oxford Univ. Press, 1973.

----------, et al. *Deconstruction and Criticism*. New York: The Seabury Press, 1979.

Bruss, Elizabeth. *Autobiographical Acts: The Changing Situation of a Literary Genre*. Baltimore and London: The Johns Hopkins Univ. Press, 1976.

Cixous, Hélène and Catherine Clément. *La Jeune Née*. Paris: Union Générale, 1975.

Cixous, Hélène. _Portrait de Dora_. Paris: Des Femmes, 1976.

Compagnon, Antoine. _La Seconde Main ou le Travail de la Citation_. Paris: Seuil, 1979.

Crawford, Claudia. "She." _Sub-stance_, 29 (1981), pp. 83-96.

Cuddihy, John Marray. _The Ordeal of Civility: Freud, Marx, Lévi-Strauss and the Jewish Struggle with Modernity_. New York: Basic Books, 1974.

Culler, Jonathan. _On Deconstruction: Theory and Criticism after Structuralism_. Ithaca: Cornell Univ. Press, 1982.

de Man, Paul. _Allegories of Reading: Figural Language in Rousseau, Nietzsche, Rilke, and Proust_. New Haven and London: Yale Univ. Press, 1979.

----------. "Autobiography as De-facement." _MLN_, 94 (1979), pp. 919-30.

----------. _Blindness and Insight: Essays in the Rhetoric of Contemporary Criticism_. New York: Oxford Univ. Press, 1971.

----------. "Hypogram and Inscription: Michael Riffaterre's Poetics of Reading." _Diacritics_, 11, No. 4 (1981), pp. 17-35.

Derrida, Jacques. _La Carte Postale de Socrate à Freud et Au-Delà_. Paris: Aubier-Flammarion, 1980.

----------. _La Dissémination_. Paris: Seuil, 1972.

----------. _L'Ecriture et la Différence_. Paris: Seuil, 1967.

----------. "Entre Crochets." _Digraphe_, 8 (1976), pp. 97-114.

----------. _Eperons: Les Styles de Nietzsche_. Introd. Stefano Agosti. Paris: Flammarion, 1978.

----------. "Fors: Les Mots Anglés de Nicolas Abraham et Maria Torok." In _Cryptonymie: Le Verbier de l'Homme aux Loups_. By Nicolas Abraham and Maria Torok. Paris : Aubier-Flammarion, 1976, pp. 7-73.

----------. _Glas_. Paris: Galilée, 1974.

----------. _De la Grammatologie_. Paris: Minuit, 1967.

----------. "Ja, ou le faux-bond." _Digraphe_, 11 (1977), pp. 83-121.

----------. "Limited Inc a b c..." _Glyph_, 2 (supplement) (1977), pp. 1-81.

----------. "La Loi du Genre." _Glyph_, 7 (1980), pp. 176-201.

----------. _Marges de la Philosophie_. Paris: Minuit, 1972.

----------. "Me--Psychoanalysis : An Introduction to 'The Shell and the Kernel' by Nicolas Abraham." _Diacritics_, 9, No. 1 (1979), pp. 4-12. Special issue devoted to Freud.

----------. "Pas I." _Gramma_, 3-4 (1976), pp. 111-125.

----------. _Positions: Entretiens avec Henri Ronse, Julia Kristeva, Jean-Louis Houdebine, Guy Scarpetta_. Paris: Minuit, 1972.

----------. "Signéponge." _Digraphe_, 8 (1976), pp. 17-39.

----------. "Signéponge." In _Ponge Inventeur et Classique, Colloque de Cerisy_. Paris: Union Générale, 1977, pp. 115-51.

----------. _La Vérité en Peinture_. Paris: Flammarion, 1978.

----------. _La Voix et le Phénomène: Introduction au Problème du Signe dans la Phénoménologie de Husserl_. Paris: Presses Universitaires de France, 1967.

Felman, Shoshana, ed. _Literature and Psychoanalysis--The Question of Reading: Otherwise_. Baltimore and London: The Johns Hopkins Univ. Press, 1977-80.

Finas, Lucette et al. _Ecarts: Quatre Essais à propos de Jacques Derrida_. Paris: Fayard, 1973.

Fleishman, Avrom. _Figures of Autobiography: The Language of Self-Writing in Victorian and Modern England_. Berkeley, Los Angeles, London: Univ. of California Press, 1983.

Foucault, Michel. _L'Archéologie du Savoir_. Paris: Gallimard, 1969.

----------, ed. _Moi, Pierre Rivière, Ayant Egorgé ma Mère, ma Soeur et mon Frère...: Un Cas de Parricide au XIXe Siècle_. Paris: Gallimard/Julliard, 1973.

----------. _La Volonté de Savoir_. Vol. I of _Histoire de la Sexualité_. Paris: Gallimard, 1976.

Freud, Sigmund. _Aus den Anfängen der Psychoanalyse: Briefe an Wilhelm Fliess, Abhandlungen und Notizen aus den Jahren 1887-1902_. Ed. Marie Bonaparte, Anna Freud, Ernst Kris. London: Imago Publishing Co. 1954.

----------. _Gesammelte Werke_. Ed. Anna Freud. 18 vols. Frankfurt am Main: S. Fischer Verlag, 1961-68.

----------. _The Origins of Psycho-Analysis: Letters to Wilhelm Fliess, Drafts and Notes 1887-1902_. Ed. Marie Bonaparte, Anna Freud, Ernst Kris. Trans. Eric Mosbacher and James Strachey. London: Imago Publishing Co., 1954.

----------. _The Standard Edition of the Complete Psychological Works of Sigmund Freud_. Trans. James Strachey. 24 vols. London: Hogarth Press, 1966-74.

----------. _Three Case Histories_. Ed. and introd. Philip Rieff. New York: Collier Books, 1963.

Frye, Northrop. _The Anatomy of Criticism: Four Essays_. Princeton: Princeton Univ. Press, 1957.

Gallop, Jane. _The Daughter's Seduction: Feminism and Psychoanalysis_. Ithaca: Cornell Univ. Press, 1982.

Genet, Jean. _Journal du Voleur_. Paris: Gallimard, 1949.

----------. _Oeuvres Complètes_. 5 vols. Paris: Gallimard, 1952-68.

Haggard, H. Rider. _She_. 1887; rpt. in _King Solomon's Mines/She/Allan Quatermain_. London: Octopus Books, 1979.

Harari, Josué V., ed. _Textual Strategies: Perspectives in Post-Structuralist Criticism_. New York: Cornell Univ. Press, 1976.

Hartman, Geoffrey R., ed. _Psychoanalysis and the Question of the Text_. Baltimore and London: The Johns Hopkins Univ. Press, 1978.

----------. _Saving the Text : Literature/Derrida/Philosophy_. Baltimore and London: The Johns Hopkins Univ. Press, 1981.

Hegel, G. W. F. _Phänomenologie des Geistes_. 1807; rpt. vol. V of _Gesammelte Werke_. Ed. Wolfgang Bonsiepen and Reinhard Heede. Hamburg: Mainer, 1980.

----------. _Phenomenology of Spirit_. Trans. A. V. Miller. Oxford, New York, Toronto, Melbourne: Oxford Univ. Press, 1977.

Hertz, Neil. "Dora's Secrets, Freud's Techniques." *Diacritics*, 13, No. 1 (1983), pp. 65-76. Special issue devoted to Freud's Dora. Includes bibliography.

Holland, Norman. "Unity Identity Text Self." *PMLA*, 90 (1975), pp. 813-22.

Hyman, Stanley Edgar. *The Tangled Bank: Darwin, Marx, Frazer, and Freud as Imaginative Writers*. New York: Atheneum, 1962.

Irigaray, Luce. *Speculum de l'Autre Femme*. Paris: Minuit, 1974.

Johnson, Barbara. *The Critical Difference: Essays in the Contemporary Rhetoric of Reading*. Baltimore and London: The Johns Hopkins Univ. Press, 1980.

----------. "Translator's Introduction." *Dissemination*. By Jacques Derrida. Chicago: Univ. of Chicago Press, 1982.

Jones, Ernest. *The Life and Works of Sigmund Freud*. 3 vols., New York: Basic Books, 1953-57.

Kermode, John Frank. *The Genesis of Secrecy: On the Interpretation of Narrative*. Cambridge: Harvard Univ. Press, 1979.

Kofman, Sarah. *L'Enfance de l'Art: Une Interprétation de L'Esthétique Freudienne*. Paris: Payot, 1970.

----------. *L'Enigme de la Femme: La Femme dans les Textes de Freud*. Paris: Galilée, 1980.

----------. *Quatre Romans Analytiques*. Paris: Galilée, 1973.

Lacan, Jacques. *Ecrits*. Paris: Seuil, 1966.

Lacoue-Labarthe, Philippe and Jean-Luc Nancy, eds. *Les Fins de l'Homme: A Partir du Travail de Jacques Derrida*. Paris: Galilée, 1981.

Lang, Candace. "Autobiography in the Aftermath of Romanticism." *Diacritics*, 12, No. 4 (1982), pp. 2-16.

Laplanche, Jean. *Vie et Mort en Psychanalyse*. Paris: Flammarion, 1970.

----------- and J.-B. Pontalis. *Vocabulaire de la Psychanalyse*. Paris: Presses Universitaires de France, 1968.

Lejeune, Philippe. *Le Pacte Autobiographique*. Paris: Seuil, 1975.

Lemaire, Anika. *Jacques Lacan*. Bruxelles: Pierre Mardaga, 1977.

Lentricchia, Frank. _After the New Criticism_. Chicago and London:Univ. of Chicago Press, 1980.

Levesque, Claude and Christie V. McDonald, eds. _L'Oreille de l'Autre--Otobiographies, Transferts, Traductions: Textes et Débats avec Jacques Derrida_. Montréal: VLB Editeur, 1982.

Lévi-Strauss, Claude. _Tristes Tropiques_. Paris: Libraire Plon, 1955.

Loselle, Andrea. "Freud/Derrida as _Fort/Da_ and the Repetitive Eponym." _MLN_, 97 (1982), pp. 1180-85.

Macksey, Richard and Eugenio Donato, eds. _The Structuralist Controversy: The Languages of Criticism and the Sciences of Man_. Baltimore and London: The Johns Hopkins Univ. Press, 1970-72.

Mahony, Patrick. _Freud as a Writer_. New York: International Univ. Press, 1982.

Mehlman, Jeffrey. _A Structural Study of Autobiography: Proust, Leiris, Sartre, Lévi-Strauss_. Ithaca and London: Cornell Univ. Press, 1974.

Moi, Toril. "Representation of Patriarchy: Sexuality and Epistemology in Freud's Dora." _Feminist Review_, 9 (1981), pp. 80-93.

Norris, Christopher. _Deconstruction: Theory and Practice_. London and New York: Metheun and Co., 1982.

Olney, James, ed. _Autobiography: Essays Theoretical and Critical_. Princeton: Princeton Univ. Press, 1980.

Parker, Andrew. "Taking Sides (On History) : Derrida Re-Marx." _Diacritics_, 11, No. 3 (1981), pp. 57-73.

Pascal, Roy. _Design and Truth in Autobiography_. Cambridge: Harvard Univ. Press, 1960.

Poe, Edgar Allan. "The Purloined Letter." _In The Annotated Tales of Edgar Allan Poe_. Ed. and introd. Stephen Peithman. Garden City, New York: Doubleday and Co., 1981, pp. 299-313.

Riffaterre, Michael. "La Trace de l'Intertexte." _La Pensée_, 215 (1980), pp. 4-18.

Rousseau, Jean-Jacques. _Les Confessions_. 1782; rpt. Ed. J. Voisine. Paris: Garnier Frères, 1964.

----------. _Emile ou de l'Education_. 1762; rpt. Introd. Michel

Launay. Paris: Garnier-Flammarion, 1966.

----------. *Essai sur l'Origine des Langues*. 1755; rpt. Aubin: Bibliothèque de Graphe, 1969.

Ryan, Michael. *Marxism and Deconstruction: A Critical Articulation*. Baltimore and London: The Johns Hopkins Univ. Press, 1982.

Schafer, Roy. "Narration in the Psychoanalytic Dialogue." *Critical Inquiry*, 7, No. 1 (1980), pp. 29-53.

Searle, John R. "The Logical Status of Fictional Discourse." *NLH*, 6 (1975), pp. 319-32.

----------. "Reiterating the Differences: A Reply to Derrida." *Glyph*, 1 (1976), pp. 198-208.

Shapiro, Stephen A. "The Dark Continent of Literature: Autobiography." *Comparative Literature Studies*, 5, No. 4 (1968), pp. 421-54.

Smith, Barbara Herrnstein. *On the Margins of Discourse: The Relation of Literature to Language*. Chicago: Univ. of Chicago Press, 1979.

Spence, Donald P. *Narrative Truth and Historical Truth: Meaning and Interpretation in Psychoanalysis*. New York and London: W. W. Norton and Co., 1982.

Spivak, Gayatri. "*Glas*-Piece: A Compte-Rendu." *Diacritics*, 7, No. 3 (1977), pp. 22-43.

----------. "Translator's Preface." In *Of Grammatology*. By Jacques Derrida. Baltimore: The Johns Hopkins Univ. Press, 1976, pp. i-xc.

Starobinski, Jean. *Les Mots sous les Mots: Les Anagrammes de Ferdinand de Saussure*. Paris: Gallimard, 1971.

Sturrock, John, ed. *Structuralism and Since: From Lévi-Strauss to Derrida*. London: Oxford Univ. Press, 1979.

Ulmer, Gregory. "The Post-Age." *Diacritics*, 11, No. 3 (1981), pp. 39-56.

Weber, Samuel. *The Legend of Freud*. Minneapolis: Univ. of Minnesota Press, 1982.

White, Hayden. *Metahistory: The Historical Imagination in Nineteenth-Century Europe*. Baltimore and London: The Johns Hopkins Univ. Press, 1973.

Willbern, David. "Freud and the Inter-penetration of Dreams."
    Diacritics, 9, No. 1 (1979), pp. 98-110.